Gilboy's Spell It Fast

Robert C. Gilboy
with his sons
Robert Michael, William Stephen,
and
Andrew Carrington Gilboy

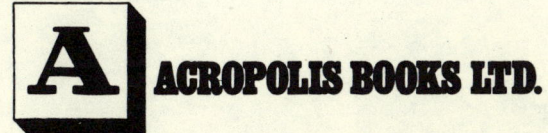
ACROPOLIS BOOKS LTD.

©Copyright 1981 by Robert C. Gilboy

All rights reserved.
Except for the inclusion of brief quotations in a review, no part of this book may be reproduced or utilized in any form or by any means, electronic or mechanical, including photocopying, recording or by any information storage and retrieval system, without permission in writing from the publisher.

ACROPOLIS BOOKS LTD.
Colortone Building, 2400 17th St., N.W.,
Washington, D.C. 20009

Printed in the United States of America by
COLORTONE PRESS Creative Graphics, Inc.
Washington, D.C. 20009

```
Gilboy, Robert C., 1903-
    Spell it fast.

    1. Spellers.  I. Title.
PE1145.2.G5        428.1      81-1146
ISBN 0-87491-071-4 (pbk.)     AACR2
```

Foreword

A new and different approach to spelling.

Most of us who have a spelling problem already know a word's meaning. We simply need to write it correctly. Unlike every other spelling aid, *SPELL IT FAST* groups commonly misspelled words into subject categories where a word can be easily located even if only the first letter is known.

SPELL IT FAST takes care of the question so often asked: "Why am I wading through this dictionary looking for a word I cannot spell?" We have done the wading, and people can now return their dictionaries to their proper job—to provide definitions, pronunciations, and etymological explanations.

Beyond serving as an essential at-hand spelling reference, *SPELL IT FAST* offers 60 fascinating categories ranging from Psychology and Psychiatry to Trees and Shrubs. These lists lend themselves to other imaginative uses—by speech writers, for example, or as a resource for crossword-puzzle buffs. So do the homonym (sound-alike) and demon (spelling toughies) lists. *SPELL IT FAST* will even help you find that word "on the tip of your tongue."

We have resisted the occasional urge to clutter this book with spelling rules, pronunciation symbols, definitions, or sub-subcategories. The homonym section includes some clues to meanings. We have held to straight alphabetical lists because they are quicker to use.

We are aware that reputable dictionaries and other reference books do not always agree as to whether a word is capitalized, hyphenated, or appears as one word or two words. We have tried to be consistent in our choices.

We hope our book will be useful to students, elementary and secondary teachers, self-employed persons, word buffs, executives, secretaries, and foreign students grappling with English as a second or third language. If readers can quickly turn to their problem words and enjoy the search, then we have done what we set out to do—helped them *SPELL IT FAST!*

Robert C. Gilboy
Hendersonville, North Carolina

To Our Readers

We hope you have fun with this book—as much as we had preparing it. New and old words are forever popping up begging to be included in this or that list. If you think of a useful hard-to-spell word that we have overlooked, please send it to: SPELL IT FAST, Acropolis Books Ltd., 2400-17th St., N.W., Washington, D.C. 20009. We await your suggestion with *antissipashun*.

Beeing sum of the world's wurst spelers, we hoape that this littel volum will be greatfuly recieved by others afflicted with the same maladie!

The Authors

The Story Behind The Book

THE IDEA for this book came from William Swinton's *Word-Book of English Spelling,* published in 1872 by Ivison, Blakeman, Taylor and Company. It was the speller my father used during the latter part of the 19th century and one of the last efforts to teach spelling by grouping words thematically.

Swinton's book encouraged students to spell correctly by arranging everyday words into familiar classifications. He included such categories as Objects in the School Room, Names of Boys and Girls, Farm Life, Human Body, Clothing and Dress, Common Abbreviations, Flowers, Colors, Birds, Food, and Occupations.

After exhaustive research in the Library of Congress, we were unable to turn up even one such spelling book printed after 1900. *SPELL IT FAST* is the first modern attempt to use Swinton's approach to help people spell correctly.

We have adapted and enlarged this system for today's user in response to the current widespread uncertainty about correct spelling and the recurring difficulties we all have with certain words. In the process we surprised ourselves by compiling some challenging word lists whose interest reaches far beyond spelling! In fact, the quest for better spelling became an invitation to learn the meanings and origins of many words. We soon realized that all the lists broadened our knowledge. Perhaps this is why Noah Webster's blue-backed speller, published in 1783, outsold his famous dictionary.

As Swinton wrote:
> Spelling is the leading idea; but at the same time a foundation is laid for the subsequent study of words and of language. Correct spelling is rightly regarded as a sign of culture, and bad spelling as indicating a lack of it.

R.C.G.

To Dorothy

Acknowledgments

While this has been essentially a family project for the last several years, we have benefitted from the assistance of professionals in the preparation of many lists, especially those in music, medicine, economics, psychology, religion, history, and geography.

We are particularly grateful to Richard L. Forstall whose thoughtful overview kept us on the track. Many thanks also to Liz Butler, William Floersch, Margot Goldberg, Jon Hedrich, Evelyne Hepburn, Carolyn Hinkle, Michael Houlahan, David Johnson, Margaret Mason, Victor Mategrano, Elizabeth F. Noon, Oliver Powell, Jerome Schwarz and members of our family, Deborah Kieffer, Dorothy, Joan, William. And R.C.G. is especially grateful to his sons and co-authors Michael, Stephen, and Andrew.

Contents

	Page
How To Use This Book .... Inside Front Cover	

Foreword...5
To Our Readers..6
The Story Behind The Book..............................7
Acknowledgments..8

60 Lists of Easily Misspelled Words
    Arranged by Alphabet................................10-11
    Arranged by Subject.................................12-13

The Sixty Lists
    From Aeronautics to Weather........................15-242

Spelling Demons
    4500 Commonly Misspelled Words..................243-281

Sound-Alike Words
    With Clues To Meanings............................283-286

60 Lists Of Easily Misspelled

Turn to the Proper Category to Spell the Word You Want

Aeronautics 15
Animals — *Birds* 19
Animals — *Fishes and Other Aquatic Creatures* 21
Animals — *Insects and Other Arthropods* 23
Animals — *Mammals and Reptiles* 25
Architecture 29
Astronomy 33
Authors 37
Automotive Terms 45
Building Materials and Construction Terms 49
Business and Economics 55
Chemical Elements 61
Cities and Historic Places of Foreign Countries 63
Cities and Towns of the United States 71
Clothing and Fabrics 77
Colors and Pigments 81
Countries and Dependencies of The World 83
Diseases and Physical Disorders 87
Drugs and Remedies 91
Earth and Landforms 97
Flowers 99
Food 103
Foreign Words and Phrases 109
Games Of Chance and Skill 113
Human Body 117
Instruments for Measuring, Recording, and Viewing 121
Islands 125
Languages 129
Law 133
Military and Naval Leaders 137

Words In Alphabetical Order

Minerals, Gems, and Rocks 141
Mountains and Ranges 143
Music — *Composers* 145
Music — *Operas* 149
Musical Terms 153
Mythology 157
Names — *Boys* 163
Names — *Girls* 167
Occupations 171
Oceans, Seas, Gulfs, and Lakes 177
Painters, Sculptors, and Architects 179
Philosophers, Theologians, and Other Famous Thinkers 183
Politics and Government 187
Presidents, their wives, and Vice-Presidents 191
Psychology and Psychiatry 193
Races, Tribes, and Peoples 195
Religion — *Biblical Names and Places* 199
Religions, Faiths, Groups, and Isms 203
Religious Terms 205
Rivers 209
Sciences 213
Scientists and Explorers 215
Sports 221
States, their Abbreviations and Capitals 223
Statesmen, Diplomats, and Other Political Leaders 225
Transportation — *Land* 229
Transportation — *Water* 231
Trees and Shrubs 233
Violence 237
Weather 241

60 Lists of Easily Misspelled

Turn to the Proper Category to Spell the Word You Want

ANIMALS AND PLANTS
   Animals—*Birds*..19
   Animals—*Fishes and Other Aquatic Creatures*..................21
   Animals—*Insects and Other Arthropods*.......................23
   Animals—*Mammals and Reptiles*...............................25
   Flowers...99
   Trees and Shrubs.....................................233

ARTS AND HUMANITIES
   Architecture..29
   Authors...37
   Languages..129
   Music—*Composers*....................................145
   Music—*Operas*.......................................149
   Musical Terms..153
   Mythology..157
   Painters, Sculptors, and Architects..................179
   Philosophers, Theologians, and Other Famous Thinkers......183

FAMILY AND PERSONAL LIFE
   Automotive Terms......................................45
   Clothing and Fabrics..................................77
   Colors and Pigments...................................81
   Drugs and Remedies....................................91
   Food...103
   Games of Chance and Skill............................113
   Names—*Boys*...163
   Names—*Girls*..167
   Sports...221
   Weather..241

GEOGRAPHY AND LANGUAGES
   Cities and Historic Places of Foreign Countries.......63
   Cities and Towns of the United States.................71
   Countries and Dependencies of the World...............83
   Earth and Landforms...................................97
   Foreign Words and Phrases............................109
   Islands..125
   Languages..129
   Mountains and Ranges.................................143
   Oceans, Seas, Gulfs, and Lakes.......................177
   Races, Tribes, and Peoples...........................195
   Religion—*Biblical Names and Places*.................199
   Rivers...209
   States, Their Abbreviations and Capitals.............223

Words Arranged By Subject

MEDICINE
- Diseases and Physical Disorders 87
- Drugs and Remedies 91
- Human Body 117
- Psychology and Psychiatry.................................193
- Scientists and Explorers..................................215
- Violence 237

PEOPLE
- Authors..37
- Military and Naval Leaders................................137
- Music — *Composers* 145
- Painters, Sculptors, and Architects 179
- Philosophers, Theologians, and Other Famous Thinkers......183
- Presidents, their wives, and Vice-Presidents 191
- Religion — *Biblical Names and Places*.....................199
- Scientists and Explorers..................................215
- Statesmen, Diplomats, and Other Political Leaders 225

PROFESSIONS AND OCCUPATIONS
(See also Arts and Humanities, and Science and Technology)
- Architecture...29
- Business and Economics 55
- Law...133
- Occupations 171
- Psychology and Psychiatry.................................193

RELIGION AND PHILOSOPHY
- Mythology...157
- Philosophers, Theologians, and Other Famous Thinkers......183
- Religion — *Biblical Names and Places*.....................199
- Religions, Faiths, Groups, and Isms 203
- Religious Terms 205

SCIENCE AND TECHNOLOGY
(See also Medicine, and Professions and Occupations)
- Aeronautics 15
- Astronomy 33
- Automotive Terms 45
- Building Materials and Construction Terms 49
- Chemical Elements 61
- Colors and Pigments 81
- Earth and Landforms 97
- Instruments for Measuring, Recording and Viewing 121
- Minerals, Gems, and Rocks.................................141
- Psychology and Psychiatry.................................193
- Sciences..213
- Scientists and Explorers..................................215
- Transportation — *Land*....................................229
- Transportation — *Water*...................................231
- Weather 241

13

AERONAUTICS

ablation
abort
acceleration
accelerometer
acoustic vibration
aeroballistic
aerodynamic
aeropause
aerospace
aerothermodynamic
afterburner
agravic
aileron
air compressor
airflow
airfoil
airplane
altimeter
altitude
ambient
amphibian
anacoustic
anemometer
angstrom
anomalistic
anoxia
antenna
antiaircraft rocket
antimissile rocket
aphelion
apogee
Apollo
apolune
artificial satellite
ascent
asteroid
astrionics
astrobiology
astrocompass
astrometer
astronaut
astronautical
astronomy
astrophysics

Atlas
atmosphere
attitude
Aurora
autopilot
axis
azimuth

ballistic
balloon
batteries
Bernoulli's law
bioastronautic
biosatellite
biosphere
biplane
bipropellant
blimp
booster
braking ellipses
bulkheads
burble
burnout

camber
canards
Cape Canaveral
capillary action
capsule
cargo
catapult
cavitation
ceiling
celestial
Centaur
centrifugal force
centrifuge
checkout
chord
chromosphere
cislunar
cockpit
combustion chamber
comet
communications satellite

compass
COMSAT
condensation trail
contamination
contingency
contour seat
controls
copilot
Coriolis force
corona
cosmic rays
cosmonauts
cosmos
countdown
craters
cryogenic
curvature

damping
deboost
debug
deceleration
decompression
de-icing
density
depressurization
descent
Diamant
dirigible
Discoverer
Doppler effect
dosimeter
drag
drogue parachute
drone
duplexer

eccentric orbit
ecliptic
ecological system
egress
ejection
electromagnetic
elevator

15

AERONAUTICS

elevon
ellipse
empennage
ESSA
exobiology
exosphere
Explorer
extravehicular

fallout
fission
flaps
flash point
free fall
fuselage
fusion

galaxy
Gemini
G force
geocorona
geodesy
geophysical
geosynchronous
gimbal
glider
gravipause
gravitation
gravity
guidance
gyro
gyroscope

hangar
helicopter
heliocentric
helium
horizontal stabilizer
hydrogen
hypergolic
hypersonic
hypoxia

igniter

inclination
inclinometer
inertial guidance
infrared
injection
integral
interplanetary
interstellar
intravehicular
ionization
ionized plasma sheath
ionosphere

jetavator
Jet Propulsion Laboratory
jettison
Jupiter

knot
Kosmos

landing gear
laser
launching vehicle
launch platform
lift-off
light-year
liquid propellant
longitudinal
luminance
lunar module
Lunar Orbiter

Mach number
magnetic compass
maneuver
manned
mare
Mariner
megacycle
Mercury
mesosphere
meteor
meteoroid

methane
microwaves
Midas
Minuteman
missile
mock-up
module
monitor
monocoque
monoplane
monopropellant
moon
multistage
multiwing

nacelle
needle and ball
Newton
nitrogen
nuclear reaction

observatory
occultation
omnidirectional
omnirange
orbit
orbital velocity
oxidizer
ozone
ozonosphere

parachute
paraglider
parameter
pararescuemen
payload
perigee
perihelion
perilune
perturbation
phenomena
photon
photosphere
pilot
Pioneer

16

AERONAUTICS

piston engine
pitch
planet
planetoid
plasma sheath
pods
Polaris
posigrade rocket
pressurized
probe
propellant
propeller
pulsars
pulsejet

quasar
quantum theory

radar
radiation
ramjet
reactor
recovery
redundancy
re-entry
regenerative cooling
rendezvous
retrograde
retro-rocket
revolutions
rill
rocket
rotation
rudder

Samos
satellite
satelloid
Saturn

Scout
seaplane
sensor
shuttle
sidereal
slats
slipstream
slots
solar cell
sonic barrier
Soyuz
spacecraft
space station
spacesuit
space vehicle
spars
spatial
spectrometer
Sputnik
stabilizer
stewardess
stratosphere
stringers
subsonic
sunspots
supernova
supersonic
surveillance
Surveyor
sustainer
synchronous
Syncom

tachometer
tail grab
takeoff
telemeter
telemetry
Telstar

terrestrial
theodolite
thermal
thermodynamics
thermosphere
Thor
thrust
Tiros
Titan
touchdown
tracking
trajectory
translunar
transonic
turbojet
turboprop

ultrasonic
ultraviolet
umbilical cord

vacuum
Van Allen belt
Vanguard
vector
velocity
vernier
vertigo
Viking
visibility
Vostok

weightlessness
wind tunnel

yaw

zero gravity
zenith

ANIMALS—Birds

albatross
anhinga
ani
auk
avocet

bald eagle
banana quit
bay duck
bittern
blackbird
black brant
black scoter
black vulture
bluebird
blue-winged teal
bobolink
bobwhite
booby
brant
budgerigar
bufflehead
bulbul
bunting
bush tit
buteo
buzzard

cahow
California condor
Canada goose
canary
canvasback
caracara
cardinal
chachalaca
chewink
chickadee
chimney swift
chukar
cinnamon teal
cockatoo
condor
Cooper's hawk

coot
cormorant
cowbird
creeper
crossbill
cuckoo
curlew

dickcissel
dipper
dotterel
dovekie
dowitcher
dunlin

egret
eider duck
emperor goose
emu

falcon
finch
flamingo
flicker
flycatcher

gadwall
gannet
gnatcatcher
goatsucker
godwit
goldeneye
goldfinch
goose
goshawk
grackle
green-winged teal
greylag
guillemot
gull
great horned owl
grebe
grosbeak
grouse

guan
guinea fowl

harlequin duck
harrier
hawk
heron
honey creeper
hummingbird

ibis

jacana
junco

killdeer
kingbird
kingfisher
kinglet
kittiwake

lapwing
limpkin
longspur
loon
lyrebird

macaw
magpie
mallard
marsh hawk
meadowlark
merganser
Mexican duck
Mississippi kite
mockingbird
motmot
murre
mute swan
myna

nighthawk
nightingale
nightjar

19

ANIMALS—Birds

nutcracker
nuthatch

old squaw
oriole
osprey
ostrich
owl
oystercatcher

parakeet
parrot
partridge
peacock
pelican
penguin
peregrine falcon
petrel
pewee
phainopepla
phalarope
pheasant
phoebe
pigeon
pileated woodpecker
pintail
pipit
plover
prairie chicken
ptarmigan
puffin
purple martin
pyrrhuloxia

quail
quetzal

rail
raven
razor-billed duck
redhead
redpoll
redshank
redstart
Rhode Island Red
ring-necked pheasant
roadrunner
robin
ruffed grouse

sanderling
sandpiper
sapsucker
scaup
scoter
sea duck
sharp-shinned hawk
shearwater
shoveler
shrike
siskin
skimmer
skua
skylark
sparrow
sparrow hawk
spoonbill
starling
stifftail
stilt
surfbird
swallow
swan

tanager
tattler
teal
tern
thrasher
thrush
titmouse
toucan
towhee
tree duck
trogon
tropic bird
trumpeter swan
turkey
turnstone

vireo
Virginia rail
vulture

wagtail
warbler
water turkey
waxwing
whippoorwill
whistling swan
whooping crane
widgeon
willet
woodcock
wood duck
woodpecker
wren
wren-tit

yellowlegs

20

ANIMALS—Fishes and Other Aquatic Creatures

Alaska cod
albacore
alewife
alligatorfish
alligator gar
amberjack
anabas
anchovy
angelfish
angler
arctic flounder

barbel
barnacle
barracuda
bass
batfish
blenny
blindfish
blue crab
bluefish
bocaccio
bonefish
bonito
bony fish
bowfin
bullhead
butterfish
butterfly fish

caribe
carp
catfish
cavefish
channel catfish
characin
chinook salmon
chub
cisco
clam
climbing fish
cobia
cod
coho
crappie

crayfish
croaker
cutlass fish
cuttlefish

dace
damselfish
darter
doctorfish
dogfish
dolphin
dorado
dory

eel
electric eel

flier
flounder
fluke
flying fish
flying gurnard

gambusia
gar
globefish
goatfish
goldfish
goosefish
grayling
grouper
grunt
guppy

haddock
hagfish
hake
halibut
herring
horseshoe crab

jellyfish
jewfish

killifish
king crab
kingfish

ladyfish
lamprey
langouste
lingcod
livebearer
loach
lobster
lungfish

mackerel
madtom
mahimahi
mahseer
maigre
manta ray
marlin
menhaden
minnow
moray
mosquito fish
mossbunker
mullet
muskellunge
mussel

needlefish

octopus
opah
oyster

palometa
perch
permit
pickerel
pike
pikeperch
pilchard
piranha
plaice
plankton
pollock
pompano
porcupine fish

21

ANIMALS—Fishes and Other Aquatic Creatures

prawn	shiner	surf fish
pumpkinseed	shrimp	swordfish
	skate	
quinnat salmon	skipjack	tarpon
	smelt	toadfish
ray	snail	tomcod
razor clam	snapper	tomtate
red snapper	snook	tope
rock bass	sockeye	trout
rockfish	soft-shell crab	trunkfish
	sole	tuna
salmon	spiny dogfish	turbot
sardine	spiny lobster	
sargassum fish	squawfish	
sauger	squid	wahoo
scallop	squirrelfish	walleye
scorpionfish	stickleback	warmouth
scrod	stingray	weakfish
sculpin	striped bass	whitefish
shad	sturgeon	whiting
shark	sucker	
sheepshead	sunfish	yellowtail

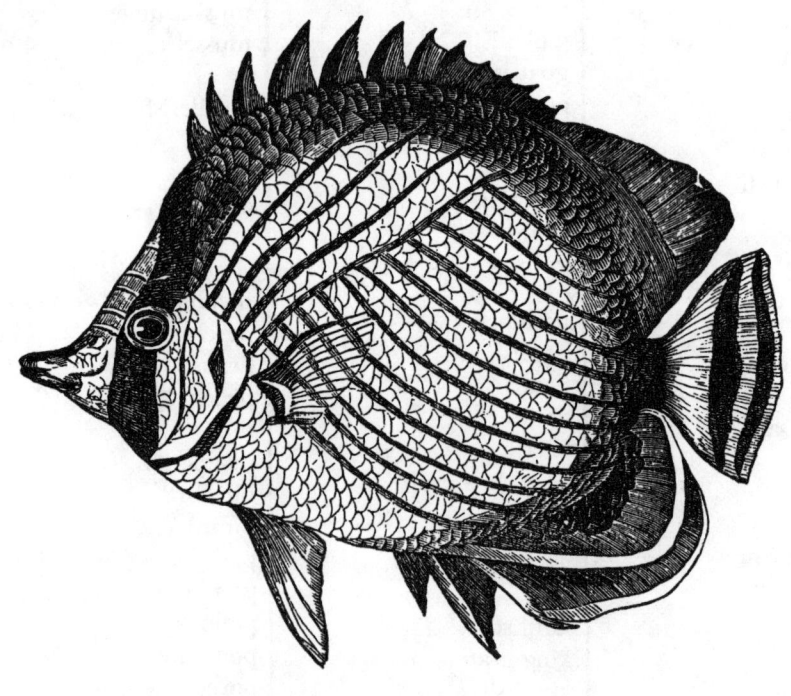

22

ANIMALS—Insects and Other Arthropods

alder fly
antlion
aphid
arachnid
armyworm
arthropod
assassin bug

bagworm
bean beetle
beetle
billbug
biting midge
black fly
black widow
blowfly
bluebottle fly
body louse
boll weevil
bollworm
bombardier beetle
book louse
borer
botfly
box-elder bug
bristletail
buffalo gnat
bumblebee
buprestid
butterfly

caddisfly
cadelle
calicoback
cankerworm
carpenter ant
carpet beetle
caseworm
caterpillar
Cecropia moth
centipede
cereal leaf beetle
chalcid fly
chigger

chigoe
chinch bug
cicada
clothes moth
cockroach
codling moth
conenose
corn borer
corn earworm
cotton stainer
cowpea weevil
crab louse
crane fly
cricket
cuckoo spit
cucumber beetle
curculio
cutworm

daddy-longlegs
damselfly
darkling beetle
darning needle
deer fly
digger wasp
diving beetle
dobsonfly
dragonfly

earwig
European corn borer

face fly
figeater
firebrat
firefly
flea
froghopper
fruit fly

gelechiid
gnat
goldsmith beetle

grasshopper
ground beetle
grub
gypsy moth

harvestman
hawk moth
head louse
hellgrammite
Hessian fly
honeybee
hornet
horntail
hornworm
horsefly
horseleech
housefly

ichneumon fly
inchworm
itch mite

Japanese beetle
June bug

katydid
kissing bug

lacewing fly
ladybug
lantern fly
leafhopper
lightning bug
locust
long-horned grasshopper
louse

maggot
mantis
maple borer
mayfly
mealworm
mealybug
meloid beetle
Mexican bean beetle

23

ANIMALS—Insects and Other Arthropods

midge
mite
mosquito
mud dauber

noctuid

paper wasp
Pharaoh ant
pigeon horntail
pink bollworm
potato beetle
praying mantis
punkie
pyralid

robber fly
rose beetle

sawfly
scorpion fly

seventeen-year locust
short-horned grasshopper
silkworm
silverfish
skipper
snapping beetle
snout beetle
snow flea
sow bug
sphinx moth
spider
spittle fly
squash bug
springtail
stag beetle
stink bug
stonefly
strawworm
syrphid fly

tabanid

tachina fly
termite
thrips
tick
tiger beetle
tobacco hornworm
tomato hornworm
tortoise beetle
tsetse fly
tumblebug

velvet ant

walking stick
wasp
water boatman
whipworm
white ant
white-faced hornet

yellow-fever mosquito
yellowjacket

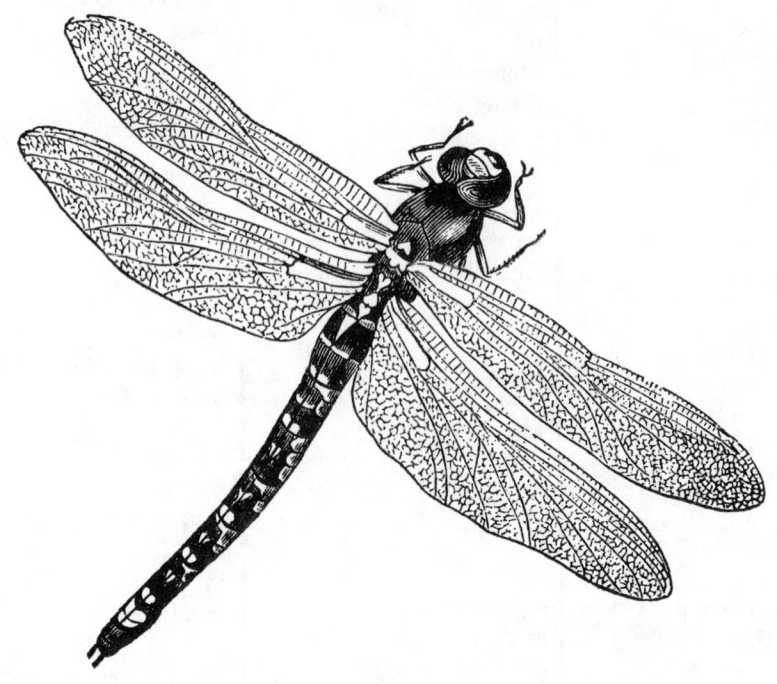

24

ANIMALS—Mammals and Reptiles

aardvark
aardwolf
Aberdeen Angus
Abyssinian cat
addax
adder
Afghan hound
Airedale
Alderney
alligator
alpaca
anaconda
Angora cat
ankylosaur
ant bear
anteater
antelope
aoudad
ape
Arabian horse
armadillo
asp
aye-aye
Ayrshire

babirusa
baboon
badger
banteng
barb
basilisk
basset
beagle
bear
beaver
Belgian draft horse
Belgian sheepdog
bison
blacksnake
boa constrictor
borzoi
Boston terrier
boxer
Brahma

briard
brontosaur
Brown Swiss
buffalo
bull terrier
Burmese cat
bushmaster

cacomistle
caiman
cairn terrier
camel
capybara
caribou
catamount
chameleon
chamois
cheetah
Chihuahua
chimpanzee
chinchilla
chipmunk
chousingha
chow chow
chuckwalla
civet
Clydesdale
coati
cob
cobra
cocker spaniel
collie
Colobus
colocola
coonhound
copperhead
coral snake
cottonmouth
cougar
crocodile

dachshund
Dandie Dinmont terrier

deer
deerhound
dinosaur
Doberman pinscher
dolphin
donkey
dormouse
dromedary
dugong

echidna
eohippus
eland
elephant
elk
ermine
Eskimo dog

fennec
fer-de-lance
ferret
fisher
fox terrier

Galloway
garter snake
gaur
gayal
gazelle
gecko
genet
gerbil
German shepherd
gibbon
Gila monster
giraffe
gnu
goat
gopher
gorilla
grampus
Great Dane
Great Pyrenees
greyhound

25

ANIMALS—Mammals and Reptiles

grivet
grizzly bear
guanaco
guereza
Guernsey
guinea pig

Hambletonian
hamster
hare
hartebeest
hedgehog
heifer
Hereford
hippopotamus
hog
Holstein
horned toad
horse
husky
hyena

ibex
ichneumon
iguana
impala
Irish setter
Irish terrier
Irish water spaniel
Irish wolfhound

jackal
jackass
jaguar
jenny
jerboa
Jersey cow

Kaffir cat
kangaroo
karakul
keeshond
Kerry blue terrier
king snake

kinkajou
koala
kookaburra
krait
kudu

Labrador retriever
langur
lemming
lemur
leopard
Lhasa apso
lion
Lippizaner
lizard
llama
lynx

macaque
Maltese
mamba
mammoth
manatee
mandrill
Manx cat
mare
margay
marmoset
marmot
marten
mastiff
mastodon
merino
milk snake
mink
moccasin
mole
moloch
mongoose
monitor
monkey
moose
Morgan horse
mouse

mule
musk deer
musk ox
muskrat

narwhal
Newfoundland
nilgai
Norwegian elkhound

ocelot
okapi
olingo
onager
opossum
orangutan
ornithopod
otter
oxen

paca
pack rat
palomino
panda
pangolin
panther
papillon
peccary
Pekingese
Percheron
Persian cat
phalanger
pig
pinto
pit viper
platypus
pointer
polar bear
polecat
Pomeranian
porcupine
porpoise
prairie dog
pronghorn

ANIMALS—Mammals and Reptiles

pterodactyl
pug
puma
python

quarter horse

rabbit
raccoon
rattlesnake
reindeer
rhesus
rhinoceros
ringtail
Rocky Mountain goat
Russian wolfhound

saber-toothed tiger
sable
Saint Bernard
saki
Saluki
Samoyed
sauropod
Schipperke
schnauzer
Scottish deerhound
Scottish terrier
seal

Sealyham terrier
serval
sheep
Shetland pony
Shetland sheepdog
shorthorn
shrew
Siamese cat
skink
skunk
sloth
sow
spitz
springbok
squirrel
springer spaniel
stallion
standardbred
stegosaur
stoat
swine

tabby cat
tamarin
tanuki
tapir
terrapin
Texas longhorn
tiger

tortoise
triceratops
tuatara
turtle
two-toed sloth
tyrannosaur

vicuña
viper

walrus
wapiti
water buffalo
weasel
Welsh corgi
whale
whippet
whiptail lizard
wildebeest
wolf
wolverine
wombat
woodchuck

yak
Yorkshire swine

zebra
zebu

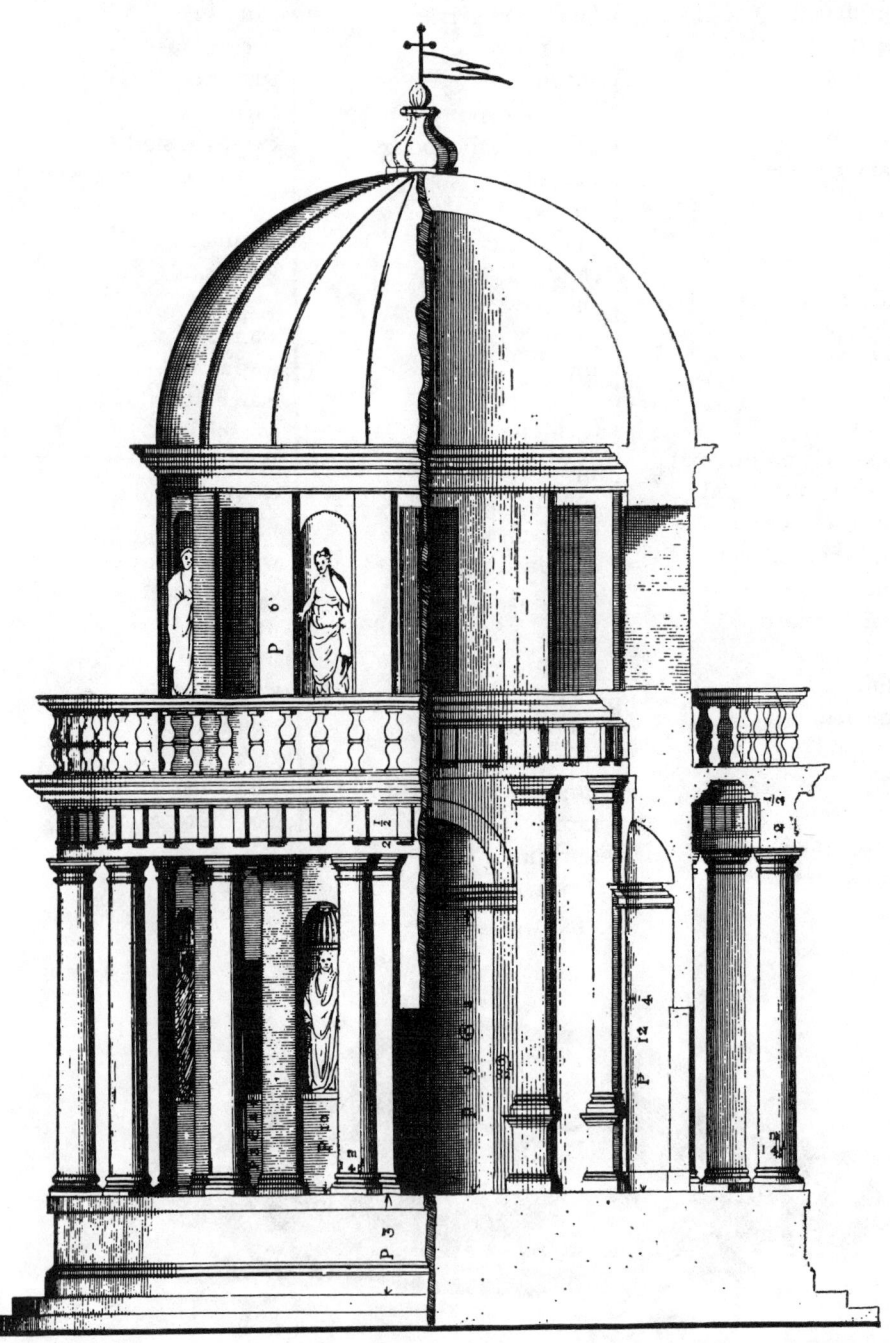

ARCHITECTURE

Aaron's rod
abacus
abate
acanthus
acropolis
acroterium
adobe
adytum
A-frame
agora
aisle
alette
ambo
ambulatory
amphiprostyle
amphitheater
anaglyph
anta
antefix
anthemion
apophyge
apse
apteral
aqueduct
arabesque
arcade
arch
architrave
arcuate
arena
arris
astylar
atrium

balcony
baldachin
baluster
balustrade
bargeboard
baroque
barrel vault
basement
basilica

bastion
beakhead
belfry
bilevel
billet
bungalow
buttress

calathus
campanile
canephora
capital
cartouche
caryatid
castle
cathedral
cella
cellar
chancel
cheneau
choir
ciborium
circus
citadel
classical
clerestory
cloister
Colonial
colonnade
column
condominium
console
corbeled arch
Corinthian
cornice
corona
coving
crocket
crossing
crypt
cupola
cusp
cyma
cymatium

dado
dais
dentil
diastyle
dipteral
dogtooth
dome
Doric
dowel

ecclesiastical
echea
echinus
egg and dart
embrasure
entablature
entasis
epistyle
exedra

facade
fan vault
fascia
fenestration
festoon
fillet
finial
flamboyant
flute
flying buttress
foliation
forum
foyer
fresco
fret
frieze
frontispiece
fusarole

gable
gablet
gallery
gambrel roof
garage
gargoyle

ARCHITECTURE

garland
gazebo
geison
Georgian
glyph
Gothic
graffito
Greco-Roman
griffe
grille
groin
grotesque
grotto
guilloche
gutta
gymnasium
gynaeceum

hagioscope
halftimbered
herma
hexastyle
hippodrome
hypaethros
hypostyle

imbrex
inglenook
intaglio
intarsia
intercolumniation
interlacing arcades
intrados
Ionic

jerkinhead
joggle piece

keystone
kiosk

lancet
lantern
lewis
linenfold

lintel
loggia
lozenge molding

maisonette
mansard roof
marble
marquee
martyrium
mausoleum
Mayan
megalith
metope
mezzanine
minaret
modillion
module
molding
monastery
mosaic
mosque
mullioned windows
mutule
Mycenaean

naos
narthex
nave
nebule
necking
niche
Norman
null

obelisk
octastyle
oculus
odeum
ogee curve
opisthodome
orb
orchestra
order
ordonnance
oriel
orthostyle

ovolo

pagoda
palaestra
Palladian
palmate
palmette
panel
panopticon
pantheon
pantile
parapet
patera
patio
pavilion
pendant
pendentive
pedestal
pediment
pentastyle
pergola
peristyle
perpendicular
perron
piazza
pier
pilaster
pillar
pinnacle
podium
poppyhead
porch
portal
portico
prefecture
propylaeum
proscenium
prostyle
pteroma
pulpit
pylon

quadrifrons
quadripartite
Queen Anne

30

ARCHITECTURE

quoin
Quonset hut

rabbet
rafter
raking cornice
ranch
regula
relief
Renaissance
ribbed vault
rococo
romanesque
roof comb
rosette
rotunda
roundel
rudenture

saddle
sanctuary
sarcophagus
scamillus
sconce
scotia
scroll
segmental arch
semiarch

sexpartite
shaft
skirting
slype
socle
soffit
spandrel
spire
squinch
stadium
staircase
steeple
stele
stoa
striation
stylobate
systyle

tabernacle
talon
terrace
terra-cotta
tessara
tester
tetrastyle
thrust
tie rod

torso
torus
tower
trabeated
tracery
transept
transom
transverse
trefoil
trellis
triglyph
trilithon
Tudor
turret
Tuscan
tympanum

vault
veneer
Venetian blind
veranda
Victorian
villa
vitrail
volute
voussoir
ziggurat
ziyada

ASTRONOMY

aberration
ablator
abort
Acamar
Achernar
Acrux
Adhara
aeon
aeronomy
albedo effect
Aldebaran
Alkaid
Almagest
almanac
Alpha Centauri
Alpha Crucis
Alphecca
Altair
altitude
Aludra
Amalthaea
Anasazi
Andromeda Nebula
annular eclipse
annularity
Antares
Antlia
aphelion
apogee
Apollo
apparent magnitude
appulse
Apus
Aquarius
Aquila
Ara
Archimedes
Arcturus
Argo Navis
Argus
Aries
aspect and node
asteroid
astrobiology

astrology
astrometry
astrophysics
Auriga
aurora australis
aurora borealis
azimuth

Barnard's star
barorecepter
Beta Crucis
Betelgeuse
Big Bang theory
Big Dipper
binary star
black hole
Boötes
Borrelly's comet

Caelum
calendar
Calisto
Cambrian explosion
Camelopard
Cancer
Canes Venatici
Canicula
Canis Major
Canis Minor
Canopus
Capella
Capricornus
Carina
Cassiopeia
Castor
celestial longitude
celestial sphere
Centaurus
Cepheid
Cephus
Ceres
Cetus
Chamaeleon
Chandler's wobble

Chara
Charon
Circinus
circumsolar
circumstellar
cislunar
Columba
Coma Berenices
comet
conjunction
constant
constellation
Copernicus
Corona Australis
Corona Borealis
Corvus
cosmic
cosmogony
cosmology
cosmos
crab nebula
Crater
crux
Cujam
culmination
cusp
Cygnus

declination
Deimos
Delphinus
Deneb
Doppler effect
Dorado
Draco
Duhr

Earth
eclipse
ecliptic
electromagnetic spectrum
elongation
ephemeris
epoch

ASTRONOMY

equinox
Equuleus Pictoris
Eratosthenes
Eridanus

Faraday rotation
Fomalhaut
Fornax
Fraunhofer

galactic
galaxy
Galileo
gamma ray
Ganymede
Gemini
gravity
Greenwich time
Grus

Halley's comet
halo
Hare
Harmonic Law
heliocentric
helium
Hercules
Herschel
Hilbert space
Hipparchus
Horologium
horoscope
Hubble's constant
Humason comet
Hyades
Hydra
hydrogen
Hydrus

Ikeya-Seki comet
Indus
infrared
interstellar

Io
irradiation
Izar

Julian Day
Juno
Jupiter

Kearns-Kwee comet
Kepler's Laws
Kirchhoff
Kitalpha

Lacerta
Lalande
Leo
Leo Minor
Lepus
Lesath
Libra
light-year
limb
Little Dipper
luminosity
lunar
Lupus
Luyten
Lynx
Lyra

Magellanic cloud
magnetosphere
magnitude
Malus
Mariner
Mars
Martian Year
Mensa
Mercury
meridian
meteor
meteorite
meteoroid
Microscopium

Milky Way
millennium
Mizar
Monoceros
moon
Murzim
Musca Borealis

nadir
nebula
Neptune
Newton's Law
norma
Nova
Nunki

observatory
occultation
Octans
Ophiuchus
opposition
orbit
Orion

Pallas
parallax
Pavo
Pegasus
penumbra
perigee
perihelion
Perseus
perturbation
Phobos
Phoenix
photometry
Pioneer
Pisces
Piscis Australis
Piscis Volans
planet
planetary nebulae
planetesimal hypothesis
Pleiades

34

ASTRONOMY

Pluto	seasons	Titan
Polaris	Seginus	transit
pole star	Serpens	Triangulum Australe
Pollux	Sextans	Tucana
Procyon	Shapley	
Propus	Shaula	Unicorn
pulsar	shooting stars	universe
pulsating stars	sidereal	Uranus
Puppis	Sirius	Ursa Major
	solar system	Ursa Minor
quark	solar wind	
quasar	solstice	Van Allen belt
	Southern Cross	variable stars
radar	spectroscope	Vega
reflector	spectrum	Vela
refractor	sphere	Venus
Regulus	Spica	vernal equinox
Reticulum	spiral galaxies	vertex
Rigel	star cluster	Vesta
right ascension	stellar	Virgo
Roemer	Sun	Vulpecula
	sunspot	
Sabik	supernova	white dwarf star
Sagitta	Swift-Tuttle comet	Wolf
Sagittarius		
satellite	Talitha	Yildun
Saturn	Taurus	
Schedar	telescope	
scintillation	Telescopium	zenith
Scorpio, Scorpius	terraforming	zodiac
Sculptor	terrestrial	Zosma
Scutum	tides	

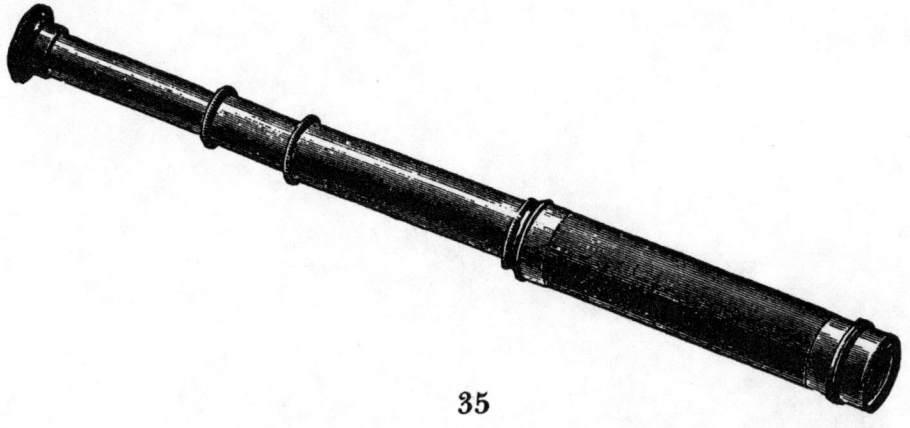

35

AUTHORS

Abelard, Peter
Abrahams, Peter
Achebe, Chinua
Adams, Henry
Addison, Joseph
Ade, George
Aeschylus
Aesop
Agathias
Agee, James
Aiken, Conrad
Akhmatova, Anna
Aksakov, Sergei
Albee, Edward
Alcaeus
Alcott, Louisa May
Aldington, Richard
Aldrich, Thomas Bailey
Alfieri, Vittorio
Alger, Horatio
Allen, Hervey
Amis, Kingsley
Anacreon
Andersen, Hans Christian
Anderson, Maxwell
Anderson, Sherwood
Andreyev, Leonid
Apollinaire, Guillaume
Apollonius, Rhodius
Apuleius, Lucius
Aquinas, Thomas
Ariosto, Ludovico
Aristophanes
Aristotle
Arlen, Michael
Arnold, Matthew
Artsibashev, Mikhail
Asimov, Isaac
Atherton, Gertrude
Auchincloss, Louis
Auden, Wystan Hugh
Augustine, Saint
Auslander, Joseph
Ausonius

Austen, Jane
Austin, Alfred
Awoonor, Kofi
Aytoun, William

Bacon, Francis
Bailey, Philip
Baillie, Joanna
Bakunin, Mikhail
Baldwin, James
Balzac, Honoré de
Baraka, Amiri
Barbour, John
Baroja, Pío
Barrie, James M.
Barry, Philip
Barth, John
Baudelaire, Charles
Beard, Charles A. and Mary
Beaumarchais, Pierre de
Beaumont, Francis
Beckett, Samuel
Bede, Saint
Beebe, William
Beerbohm, Max
Behan, Brendan
Bellamy, Edward
Bellman, Karl
Belloc, Hilaire
Bellow, Saul
Benét, Stephen Vincent
Benét, William Rose
Bennett, Arnold
Béranger, Pierre Jean de
Bergerac, Cyrano de
Bernardin de Saint-Pierre, Jacques Henri
Berryman, John
Betjeman, John
Bierce, Ambrose
Bishop, Elizabeth
Björnson, Björnstjerne

Blackwood, Algernon
Blake, William
Blasco Ibáñez, Vicente
Blok, Aleksandr
Boccaccio, Giovanni
Bodenheim, Maxwell
Bontemps, Arna
Borges, Jorge Luis
Boswell, James
Bowen, Elizabeth
Bradbury, Ray
Brecht, Bertolt
Bridges, Robert
Bromfield, Louis
Brontë, Charlotte, Emily, and Anne
Brooke, Rupert
Brooks, Gwendolyn
Brown, Sterling
Brownell, William
Browning, Elizabeth Barrett
Browning, Robert
Bryant, William Cullen
Buck, Pearl
Buckley, William F.
Bulgakov, Mikhail
Bullins, Ed
Bulwer-Lytton, Edward R.
Bunin, Ivan
Bunyan, John
Burgess, Frank
Burnett, Frances Hodgson
Burns, Robert
Burroughs, Edgar Rice
Burroughs, William
Burton, Richard F.
Burton, Robert
Butler, Samuel
Byron, George Gordon (Lord)

Cabell, James Branch

AUTHORS

Cable, George W.
Caedmon
Cain, James M.
Caine, Hall
Calderón de la Barca, Pedro
Caldwell, Erskine
Callimachus
Calverley, Charles
Camara, Laye
Camoëns, Luis de
Campbell, Thomas
Camus, Albert
Canfield (Fisher), Dorothy
Capote, Truman
Carducci, Giosuè
Carlyle, Thomas
Carman, Bliss
Carroll, Lewis (Charles L. Dodgson)
Cary, Joyce
Casanova de Seingalt, Giovanni
Cassiodorus, Flavius
Castiglione, Baldassare
Cather, Willa
Catton, Bruce
Catullus, Gaius Valerius
Cavendish, George
Cervantes, Miguel de
Chamisso, Adelbert von
Chapman, George
Chateaubriand, François René de
Chatterton, Thomas
Chaucer, Geoffrey
Cheever, John
Chekhov, Anton
Cheney, John
Chesterfield, Lord (Philip Stanhope)
Chesterton, Gilbert K.
Chrétien de Troyes

Christie, Agatha
Churchill, Winston
Cicero, Marcus Tullius
Clark, Walter van Tilburg
Clarke, James
Claudius, Matthias
Cobb, Irvin S.
Cocteau, Jean
Cohan, George M.
Coleridge, Samuel Taylor
Collier, John
Colonna, Vittoria
Commager, Henry Steele
Congreve, William
Connelly, Marc
Conrad, Joseph
Cooper, James Fenimore
Corneille, Pierre
Costello, Louise
Coward, Noel
Cowper, William
Cozzens, James Gould
Crabbe, George
Craik, Dinah Maria
Crane, Hart
Crane, Stephen
Creasy, E.S.
Crémazie, Octave
Cullen, Countee
Cummings, Edward Estlin (e.e. cummings)

Damas, Léon-Gentran
Dana, Richard Henry
D'Annunzio, Gabriele
Dante Alighieri
Darwin, Charles
Daudet, Alphonse
Davies, William Henry
Davis, Richard Harding
Defoe, Daniel
Dekker, Thomas

de la Mare, Walter
Deledda, Grazia
De Quincey, Thomas
Derzhavin, Gavril
Dickens, Charles
Dickey, James
Dickinson, Emily
Diop, Birago
Disraeli, Benjamin
Dixon, Thomas
Donleavy, J.P.
Donne, John
Dos Passos, John
Dostoevsky, Feodor
Douglas, Norman
Dowson, Ernest C.
Doyle, Arthur Conan
Drayton, Michael
Dreiser, Theodore
Drinkwater, John
Drummond, W.H.
Dryden, John
Du Bois, W.E.B.
Dumas, Alexandre
Du Maurier, Daphne
Dunbar, Paul Laurence
Dunne, Finley Peter (Mr. Dooley)
Durant, Will
Durrell, Lawrence

Eliot, George (Mary Ann Evans)
Eliot, Thomas Stearns
Ellis, Havelock
Ellison, Ralph
Emerson, Ralph Waldo
Ennius, Quintus
Erskine, John
Ertz, Susan
Euripides
Eusebius

Fanon, Frantz

AUTHORS

Farquhar, George
Farrell, James T.
Faulkner, William
Ferber, Edna
Ferlinghetti, Lawrence
Ferreira, Antonio
Feuchtwanger, Lion
Field, Eugene
Fielding, Henry
Fitzgerald, Edward
Fitzgerald, F. Scott
Flaubert, Gustave
Fleming, Ian
Fletcher, John
Ford, Ford Madox
Forester, Cecil S.
Forster, Edward Morgan
Foster, Stephen
Fowles, John
France, Anatole (Jacques Anatole Thibault)
Franklin, Benjamin
Franzén, Frans Michael
Freneau, Philip
Freytag, Gustav
Froissart, Jean
Frost, Robert
Fry, Christopher

Galbraith, John K.
Gale, Zona
Gallico, Paul
Galsworthy, John
Garcia Lorca, Federico
Gardiner, Samuel R.
Gardner, Erle Stanley
Gautier, Théophile
Gay, John
Gibbon, Edward
Gibran, Kahlil
Gide, André
Gilbert, William S.
Gilder, Richard
Gilroy, Frank

Ginsberg, Allen
Giraudoux, Jean
Goethe, Johann Wolfgang von
Gogol, Nikolai
Golding, William
Goldoni, Carlo
Goldsmith, Oliver
Goncourt, Edmond de
Gordimer, Nadine
Gordon, C.W. (Ralph Connor)
Gorky, Maxim
Gosse, Edmund
Gozzi, Carlo
Grass, Günter
Graves, Robert
Gray, Thomas
Green, Julian
Greene, Graham
Grey, Zane
Grimm, Jakob and Wilhelm
Grote, George
Grotius, Hugo
Guest, Edgar
Guicciardini, Francesco
Guizot, Francois

Hackett, Francis
Hafiz
Hale, Edward Everett
Halleck, Fitz-Greene
Hammerstein, Oscar
Hammett, Dashiell
Hamsun, Knut
Hansberry, Lorraine
Hardy, Thomas
Harris, Joel Chandler
Hart, Moss
Harte, Bret
Hauptmann, Gerhart
Hawkes, John
Hawthorne, Nathaniel

Hazlitt, William
Hebbell, Friedrich
Hecht, Ben
Heine, Heinrich
Heller, Joseph
Hellman, Lillian
Hemans, Felicia
Hemingway, Ernest
Henley, William Ernest
Henry, O. (William Sydney Porter)
Herder, Johann
Heredia, José Maria de
Hergesheimer, Joseph
Herodotus
Herrick, Robert
Hersey, John
Hesiod
Hesse, Hermann
Heyward, DuBose
Hilton, James
Hobbes, John Oliver
Hodgson, Ralph
Hofmannsthal, Hugo von
Holberg, Ludvig
Holmes, Oliver Wendell
Homer
Hope (Hawkins), Anthony
Horace (Quintus Horatius Flaccus)
Houghton, Richard
Housman, Alfred Edward
Housman, Laurence
Hovey, Richard
Howe, Julia Ward
Howells, William Dean
Hughes, Langston
Hughes, Rupert
Hugo, Victor
Hume, David

AUTHORS

Hunt, Leigh
Hurst, Fannie
Huxley, Aldous
Huxley, Julian

Ibsen, Henrik
Inge, William R.
Ionesco, Eugene
Irving, Washington

Jackson, Helen Hunt
James, Henry
Jarrell, Randall
Jewett, Sarah Orne
Jiménez, Juan Ramón
Johnson, James Weldon
Johnson, Samuel
Jókai, Mór
Jones, James
Jong, Erica
Jonson, Ben
Josephus, Flavius
Joyce, James

Kafka, Franz
Kant, Immanuel
Kaufman, George S.
Kazan, Elia
Kazantzakis, Nikos
Keats, John
Keble, John
Kerouac, Jack
Key, Francis Scott
Kilmer, Joyce
Kingsley, Charles
Kipling, Rudyard
Klopstock, Friedrich
Koestler, Arthur
Körner, Karl
Kunitz, Stanley

La Fontaine, Jean de
Lagerlöf, Selma
Laing, Dilys Bennett

Lamartine, Alphonse de
Lamb, Charles and Mary
Lampedusa, Giuseppe di
Landor, Walter Savage
Langland, William
Lanier, Sidney
Lardner, Ring
La Rochefoucauld, François de
Lawrence, D.H.
Layamon
Lazarus, Emma
Leacock, Stephen
Lear, Edward
Leconte de Lisle, Charles Marie
LeGallienne, Richard
Le Guin, Ursula K.
Leopardi, Giacomo
Lermontov, Mikhail
Le Roux, H.R.
Lessing, Gotthold
Lewis, Cecil Day
Lewis, Clive Staples
Lewis, Matthew
Lewis, Sinclair
Leyden, John
Lindsay, Vachel
Lippmann, Walter
Livy (Titus Livius)
Llewellyn, Richard
Locke, William J.
London, Jack
Longfellow, Henry Wadsworth
Longus
Loos, Anita
Loti, Pierre (Julien Viaud)
Lovelace, Richard
Lowell, James Russell
Lowell, Robert
Lowry, Malcolm

Lucian
Lucretius Carus, Titus
Ludwig, Emil
Luther, Martin
Lyly, John

Macaulay, Thomas B.
Machen, Arthur
Machiavelli, Niccolò
MacLeish, Archibald
McCarthy, Mary
McCrae, John
McCullers, Carson
McCutcheon, G.B.
McKay, Claude
Maeterlinck, Maurice
Mailer, Norman
Malory, Thomas
Malraux, André
Mann, Thomas
Mansfield, Katherine
Manzoni, Alessandro
Marcus Aurelius
Markham, Edwin
Marlowe, Christopher
Marquand, John P.
Marquis, Don
Martial (Marcus Valerius Martialis)
Martin du Gard, Roger
Martínez Sierra, Gregorio
Masefield, John
Mason, T. van Wyck
Masters, Edgar Lee
Mather, Cotton
Maugham, W. Somerset
Maupassant, Guy de
Mauriac, François
Maurois, André
Melville, Herman
Menander
Mencken, Henry Louis
Meredith, George

AUTHORS

Mérimée, Prosper
Metastasio, Pietro
Michelangelo
   Buonarroti
Michener, James
Middleton, Thomas
Mill, John Stuart
Millay, Edna St.
   Vincent
Miller, Arthur
Miller, Henry
Mills, C. Wright
Milne, Alan Alexander
Milton, John
Mistral, Gabriela
Mitchell, Margaret
Molière, Jean-Baptiste
   Poquelin
Montaigne, Michel de
Montgomery, James
Moore, Clement C.
Morand, Paul
More, Hannah
More, Thomas
Morison, Samuel Eliot
Morley, Christopher
Motley, John
Mphahlele, Ezekiel
Muir, John
Mumford, Lewis
Murasaki, Shikibu

Nabokov, Vladimir
Nash, Ogden
Nathan, Robert
Neihardt, John
Nemerov, Howard
Neruda, Pablo
Norris, Frank
Norris, Kathleen
Noyes, Alfred

O'Casey, Sean
O'Connor, Flannery

Odets, Clifford
O'Hara, John
O'Keeffe, John
Omar Khayyám
O'Neill, Eugene
Oppenheim, E. Phillips
Ortega y Gasset, José
Orwell, George
Osborne, John
O'Shaughnessy,
   Arthur W.
Ostrovsky, Alexander
Ovid (Publius Ovidius
   Naso)
Owen, Wilfred

Paine, Thomas
Palgrave, Francis Turner
Palladius
Park, Mungo
Parker, Dorothy
Parker, Gilbert
Parkinson, Cyril N.
Parkman, Francis
Pascal, Blaise
Pasternak, Boris
Patmore, Coventry
Paton, Alan
Pausaniàs
Payne, John
Peacock, Thomas Love
Pepys, Samuel
Perelman, S.J.
Pérez Galdós, Benito
Perrault, Charles
Petrarch
Petronius, Gaius
Philostratus
Pindar
Pinero, Arthur
Pinter, Harold
Pirandello, Luigi
Plath, Sylvia
Plato

Plautus, Titus
Plutarch
Poe, Edgar Allen
Polo, Marco
Polybius
Pope, Alexander
Porter, Jane
Porter, Katherine Anne
Pound, Ezra
Powys, Llewelyn
Priestley, John Boynton
Pringle, Thomas
Pritchett, V.S.
Procter, Adelaide
Propertius, Sextus
Proust, Marcel
Pulci, Luigi
Purdy, James
Pushkin, Alexander
P'u Sung-ling

Queen, Ellery (Frederick
   Dannay)

Rabelais, François
Racine, Jean
Raleigh, Walter
Ramuz, Charles
   Ferdinand
Rawlings, Marjorie
   Kinnan
Reed, Ishmael
Reese, Lizette
Remarque, Erich Maria
Richter, Conrad
Richter, Johann Paul
   (Jean Paul)
Riley, James Whitcomb
Rilke, Rainer Maria
Rimbaud, Arthur
Rinehart, Mary Roberts
Roberts, Elizabeth
   Madox
Robinson, Edwin
   Arlington

AUTHORS

Rolland, Romain
Rölvaag, Ole Edvart
Ronsard, Pierre de
Rossetti, Dante Gabriel
Rostand, Edmond
Roth, Philip
Rouget de Lisle, Claude
Rousseau, Jean-Jacques
Runyon, Damon
Ruskin, John
Russell, Bertrand

Sabatini, Rafael
Sachs, Hans
Sainte-Beuve, Charles
Saint-Exupéry, Antoine de
Saki (H.H. Munro)
Salinger, Jerome D.
Sand, George (Amandine Aurore Dupin)
Sandburg, Carl
Santayana, George
Sappho
Sardou, Victorien
Saroyan, William
Sartre, Jean-Paul
Sassoon, Siegfried
Sayers, Dorothy
Schiller, Friedrich
Schlesinger, Arthur M.
Schnitzler, Arthur
Schopenhauer, Arthur
Scott, Walter
Sembène, Ousmane
Senghor, Leopold Sédar
Service, Robert W.
Seuss, Dr. (Theodor Seuss Geisel)
Sexton, Anne
Shakespeare, William
Shaw, George Bernard
Shelley, Mary Godwin
Shelley, Percy Bysshe

Sheridan, Richard
Sherwood, Robert E.
Shevchenko, Taras
Shirer, William L.
Sholokhov, Mikhail
Sienkiewicz, Henryk
Sinclair, Upton
Singmaster, Elsie
Sitwell, Edith, Osbert, and Sacheverell
Skelton, John
Slaughter, Frank
Smits, Dirk
Smollett, Tobias
Snow, Charles Percy
Solzhenitsyn, Alexander
Sophocles
Sorley, C.H.
Southey, Robert
Southy, Caroline
Soyinka, Wole
Spender, Stephen
Spenser, Edmund
Spillane, Mickey
Staël, Germaine Necker de
Stanton, Frank
Stedman, Edmund
Steele, Richard
Steffens, Lincoln
Stein, Gertrude
Steinbeck, John
Stendhal
Stephens, James
Sterne, Laurence
Stevens, Wallace
Stevenson, Robert Louis
Stockton, Frank
Stoddard, Richard
Stone, Irving
Stout, Rex
Stowe, Harriet Beecher
Strachey, G. Lytton
Strindberg, August

Styron, William
Suckling, John
Sudermann, Hermann
Sully-Prudhomme, René
Sumner, William Graham
Surtees, Robert Smith
Swift, Jonathan
Swinburne, Algernon
Swinnerton, Frank
Symonds, John Addington
Synge, John Millington

Tacitus, Cornelius
Tagore, Rabindranath
Taliesin
Tanizaki, Junichiro
Tarbell, Ida M.
Tarkington, Booth
Tasso, Torquato
Teasdale, Sara
Teilhard de Chardin, Pierre
Tennyson, Alfred (Lord)
Terence (Publius Terentius Afer)
Terhune, Albert Payson
Tersteegen, Gerhard
Tey, Josephine
Thackeray, William M.
Thaxter, Celia
Theocritus
Thespis
Thomas, Dylan
Thomas à Kempis
Thompson, Francis
Thomson, James
Thoreau, Henry David
Thucydides
Thurber, James
Tocqueville, Alexis Charles de
Tolkien, J.R.R.

AUTHORS

Tolstoy, Leo
Toynbee, Arnold
Trevelyan, George M.
Trollope, Anthony
Tsao Hsueh-chin
Tuchman, Barbara
Turgenev, Ivan
Turner, Frederick Jackson
Twain, Mark (Samuel Clemens)

Undset, Sigrid
Untermeyer, Louis
Updike, John
Uris, Leon
Utrich, Anton

Valéry, Paul
Vance, Jack
Van Dine, S.S. (Willard H. Wright)
Van Doren, Carl
van Dyke, Henry
Van Loon, Hendrik
Vasari, Giorgio
Vaughan, Henry
Vega, Lope de
Verga, Giovanni
Vergil (Publius Vergilius Maro)

Verhaeren, Emile
Verlaine, Paul
Verne, Jules
Viaud, Louis Marie
Vidal, Gore
Vigny, Alfred de
Villon, Francois
Voltaire, François Marie Arouet de
Vonnegut, Kurt

Wallace, Irving
Wallace, Lewis
Walpole, Horace
Walpole, Hugh
Warren, Robert Penn
Watts, Isaac
Waugh, Evelyn
Wedgwood, Cicely Veronica
Wells, Herbert George
Welty, Eudora
Werfel, Franz
Wesley, Charles
Wharton, Edith
White, Elwyn Brooks
White, Terence Hanbury
Whitman, Walt
Whittier, John Greenleaf
Wickham, Anna

Wiggin, Kate Douglas
Wilbur, Richard
Wilde, Oscar
Wilder, Thornton
Williams, Tennessee
Wilson, Edmund
Wister, Owen
Wodehouse, Pelham Grenville
Wolfe, Humbert
Wolfe, Thomas
Woolf, Virginia Stephen
Wordsworth, William
Wouk, Herman
Wright, Richard
Wu Ch'eng-en
Wycherley, William
Wylie, Elinor
Wyss, Johann Rudolf

Xenophon

Yeats, William Butler
Yerby, Frank

Zola, Émile
Zweig, Arnold
Zweig, Stefan

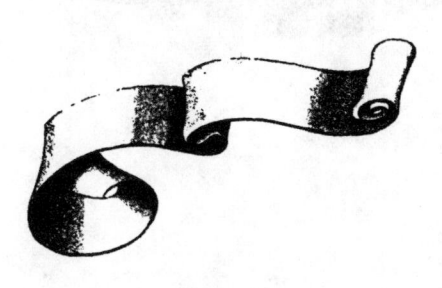

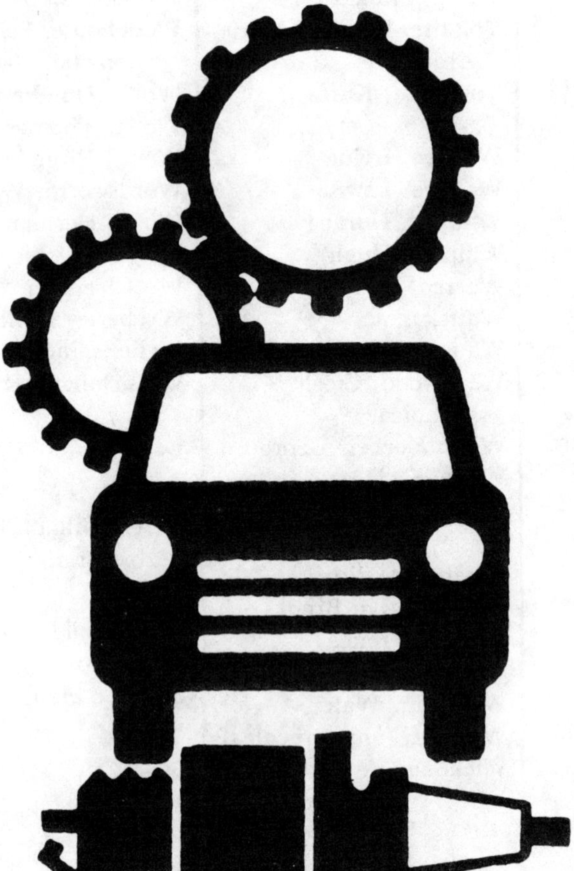

AUTOMOTIVE TERMS

abrasion
accelerator
accessories
accumulator
adaptor
additive
adiabatic
afterboil
afterburning
aftercooler
afterglow
air bag
air comparators
air compressor
air conditioner
air-cool
air filter
air-fuel mixture
alignment
Allen wrench
alternator
aluminizing
ammeter
aniline
antenna
anti-corrosion
antifreeze
antiknock
antisiphon circuit
antisway bar
apron
armature
atomization
autoignition
automatic choke
automatic transmission
auxiliary
axle yaw

babbitt
backfire
backlash
back-up light
baffle plate

baffling
ballast
ball bearing
battery
beaming
belly pan
belted-bias tires
benzene
bevel
blast gate
blow-by
blowdown
bonnet
booster
boot
bore
brake fluid
breathing
bucket seat
bull nose
bumper
bushing
bypass

cable
calibrate
caliper
cam
camber
camshaft
capacitor
carbon monoxide
carburetor
casing
caster
catalytic converter
cell tester
cetane
channeling
charger
chassis
choke
chopping
chrome

circuit
clearance
clunker
clutch
cockpit
coil
combustion
commutator
compression stroke
compression test
compressor
condensation
condenser
conductor
connecting rod
convector
convertible
coolant
cooling system
corrosion
cotter pin
coupe
coupling
cowl
crankcase
crankpin
crankshaft
cross bead piston
crossfire
current
cycle
cylinder

damper
de-arching
deceleration
deflection
defroster
demountable rim
dephaser
detergency
detonation
diaphragm
diesel

45

AUTOMOTIVE TERMS

differential
diodes
dipstick
directional signals
disc brake
displacement
distortion
distributor
doorlight
doorlock
dowel pin
downdraft
downshift
drag
drive shaft
dual

electrical system test
electric clock
emission control
engine
erosion
evaporator
exhaust system

fan
fan belt
feather
fender
F-head engine
filament
filter
firing order
fishtail
flashers
flat head
flex dam
float bowl
flutter
flywheel
fouling
four door
frame
freeze plug

frequency
fresh air vents
friction
fuel gauge
fuel injection
fuel pump
fuse

gallon
galvanize
gapping spark plug
gasket
gasoline
gearbox
gearshift
generator
glass
glaze
governor
grease
grid
grind
grommet
groove
ground

halogen light
hardtop
hatchback
headers
head gaskets
headlight dimmer
headrest
head restraints
heat riser
hemi-head
high gear
high-test
horn
horsepower
hose
housing
hubcap
hydraulic

hydro-boost
hydrocarbon
hydrodynamic

ignition
ignition switch
I-head engine
indicator
inducer
injector
in-line cylinder
instrument panel
insulator
intake manifold
intake stroke
intake valve
intercooler
interlock
ionization
isochronic
isomerization

jack
joint
journal
jump start
junker

kerosene
keyway
kick down switch
kick up
kingbolt
kingpin
knock
knockometer

lacquer
lakes pipe
lakester
landau
leaded
lead-free
leaf spring

46

AUTOMOTIVE TERMS

L-head engine
limousine
linkage
lock
lubricant
luggage compartment
lug wrench

MacPherson strut
magnetic
magneto
manifold
manual
manual transmission
master cylinder
mileage
mirror
misfire
modulator
modules
motor
mounting
mph
muffler
mushroom valve

needle bearing
needle valve
nozzle
nylon bushing

octane
odometer
oil additive
oil filter
oil pan
oil pump
output shaft
overboosting
overbore
overdrive
overhaul
overhead
overheat

packing
pancake engine
parking brake
parking light
percolation
performance
petcock
petroleum
pinion
piston
piston rod
pitch
plastigage
pneumatic tire
points
power break
power seat
power stroke
power window
precombustion chamber
propane
propeller shaft
pump

quad carburetor
quenching

radial engine
radial ply
radiator
rake
rear suspension
rearview mirror
reclining seats
rectifier
refrigerant
regenerator
regulator
relay
resistor
retractible hard-top
rheostat
rim head
rings

rivets
roadster
rocker arm
roll bar
roller bearing
rotary engine
rotor
rpm
rumble seat
runabout
running board
running light
rust inhibitor

safety glass
scatter shield
scavenging
seal
sealed-beam
seat belt
sedan
selfstarter
semiconductor
shaft
shear
shim
shimmy
shock absorber
shooting brake
sideswipe
sidewall
silencer
silica deposits
slave control
sludge
snow tires
socket
socket wrench
solenoid
solvent
spark plug
speedometer
spill valve
splash pan

AUTOMOTIVE TERMS

spoiler
sports car
spring
squish area
stabilizer
starter solenoid
starter switch
steering wheel
stick shift
stroboscope
stroke
stud
supercharger
suspension
swaged tube
sway
switch
synchro-mesh
synchronize

tachometer
taillight
tailshaft governor
tangential
tappet
temperature
template
tension
terminal
T-head engine
thermocouple
thermostat

throttle
throttle linkage
thrust bearing
timing
tire ply
toe change
toe-in
toe-out
tolerance
torque
torsion
torus
tracking
traction bar
trailing shoe
transaxle
transistor
transmission
tread shoulder
trunk piston
tube
tumbling
tune-up
turbine
turbocharger
turbulence
turning track

U-bolt
unbalance
undamped
undercoat

universal joint
unleaded
unsprung

vacuum
valve
vaporizer
vapor lock
vents
vibration
voltage regulator
volt meter
vortex
V-type engine

Wankel engine
warm-up
warning light
water hose
water pump
watt
wedge
wheel balance
wheel fight
windshield jet
wing
wiper
wobbler plate
wrecker

yoke

zigzag

48

BUILDING MATERIALS AND CONSTRUCTION TERMS

abat-jour
abrasive
absorption
abutment
acclivity
accolade
accordion doors
accumulator
acetone
acoustical
acroterium
acrylic
adaptor
addendum
adduct
adhesive
adiabatic
admixture
adobe
adsorbent
adz
aeration
aerography
aerosol
A-frame
aggregate
air-condition
air conditioning
alabaster
alcove
alignment
alkyd
aluminate
ambient
anchorage
ancon
annex
annunciator
aperture
appendage
apron
arcade
arch
architect

arc light
arris
asbestos
ashlar
asphalt
assize
asymptote
attic
auger
awl
ax

babbitt
baffle
ballast
baluster
balustrade
banister
baseboard
batten
bay window
bead
beam ceiling
beetle
bevel
bidet
billet
bituminous
blemish
blueprint
bluestone
bonding
brace
bracket
brander
breezeway
bricklayer
bridging
briquette
brisance
broach
buckling
bullnose
burr

buttress
butyl

cabinet
cable
caisson
calcimine
caliper
calk
camber
canopy
cantilever
capillary
capital
capstan
carbon steel
carpenter
casein
casement
cast iron
catalyst
catch basin
caul
caulking
cellular
cellulose
cement
cementation
ceramic
chalking
chamfer
chimney
chisel
circuit
clapboard
coal tar
cofferdam
column
compound
compressor
concha
concrete block
condenser
conduit
convector

49

BUILDING MATERIALS AND CONSTRUCTION TERMS

coping
corbel
cornice
corridor
corrosion
corrugate
countersink
coving
cradling
crawl space
cremone bolt
creosote
cubage
culvert
curing
cylindrical

dado
damper
darby
datum
dead bolt
decking
demarcation
dentil
derrick
detonator
diaphragm
diffraction grating
dike
disposal
diverter
dolly
dope
dormer window
dovetail
dowel
downspout
dry rot
drywall
duct
dynamite

easement
eaves

efflorescence
effluent
egg and dart
eggshelling
elasticity
electrician
elevator
emery
emulsion
enamel
encaustic
engineer
environmental
epoxy
equilibrium
escalator
escutcheon
estimate
excavator
expansion joint
extrusion

fabricator
facade
face brick
fagoting
faucet
ferrule
fettle
fiberboard
fictile
filter
finial
fireproof
fixtures
flagstone
flange
flashing
fleam
flexural
flitch
flue
foam insulation
footing

foreman
Formica
foundation
foyer
framing
fret saw
frieze
furnace
furring

gabion
gable
galvanize
gambrel roof
ganger
garderobe
garret
garth
gasket
gauge
girder
girth
glazing
gooseneck
gradation
grain
granite
Granolith
grapple
gravel
gravity
grille
grommet
grout
grub
gullet
gusset
gutter
gypsum board

haft
haha
hammer
hard-hat
hardpan

BUILDING MATERIALS AND CONSTRUCTION TERMS

hasp
hatchet
header
heat pump
herringbone
hinge
hoistway
hollow brick
honeycomb
honing
huckbolt
humidifier
hydrant
hydraulic
hypogeal

impedance
incrustation
inductance
inspector
installation
insulation
intertie
isotropic line

jacal
jalousie
jamb
jenny winch
jetting
jib
joint
joist
journeyman
jut

kerf
kevel
keystone
kibble
kiln
kilowatt hour
kiosk
kneeler
knot

laborer
lac
lacquer
laitance
laminate
latch
lath
lathe
lattice
limestone
linoleum
lintel
locksmith
longitudinal
louver
lucarne
lyceum

macadam
magnetic
maintenance
mallet
mansard
mantel
marble
masonry
mastic
matrix
medallion
melamine
meter
miter
modillion
modulation
molding
Molly
mortar
mortise
mosaic
muffle
mullion

nail
newel

niche
node
nomograph
nonferrous metal
notching
nozzle
nylon

oakum
oblique
obsolescence
ogee
oleoresin
opaque
orb
oriel
orifice
orlo
ovolo
oxychloride

paddock
panel
pantile
parallelogram
parget
parging
parquet
partition
patio
pattern
pedestal
peen
pendent
pergola
perlite
permeability
perron
photoelectric
pier
pigment
pilaster
pile driver
plaster

BUILDING MATERIALS AND CONSTRUCTION TERMS

plumb
plumber
plywood
polyurethane
porcelain
portal
pneumatic
precast
prefabricate
preservation
pumice
punner
purlin
putty

quarry
quicklime

rabbet
radial
radiator
rafter
ratchet
reflection
reinforce
relief
replum
resin
resistance
rheostat
riser
riveting
router
rustication

sapwood
saturation
sawhorse
scaffold
scagliola
sconcheon
screed
screwdriver
scriber

scutch
sealer
septic tank
settlement
shake
shale
shear
sheathing
sheeting
sheet rock
shellac
shingle
shiplapped
shoring
shrinkage
sieve
silicate
silicone
sill
skive
skylight
skyscraper
slake
sledgehammer
slurry
smokestop
soffit
softwood
solvent
spall
spandrel
spatterdish
specification
spigot
splice
split-level
sprinkler
sprocket
staircase
stave
stile
stilex
stirrup
stonemason

story
straightedge
strain
stress
stretcher
strike plate
structural glass
stucco
stud
subcontract
subsoil
sump pump
swage
symmetrical
synthetic

tangential
template
tensile
termites
terneplate
terrace
terra-cotta
terrazzo
thermoplastic
thermostat
thinner
threader
threshold
thumbscrew
toeing
toggle
tolerance
topsoil
torsion
traction
transom
tread
trowel
truss
tuck pointing
tufa
tumbler
turpentine

52

BUILDING MATERIALS AND CONSTRUCTION TERMS

underpinning	vermiculite	weather strip
urea	vestibule	weld
urethane	viaduct	wheelbarrow
	vibration	windowpane
vacuum	vinyl	windowsill
veneer	voltage	wire mesh
Venetian blind		wood siding
vent	waffle	wrench
ventilation	wainscot	wrought iron
ventilator	wallboard	

BUSINESS AND ECONOMICS

abandonment
abatement
absorb
abstract money
accelerated depreciation
accommodation
accountant
account executive
accounts payable
accounts receivable
accretion
accrue
accumulated depreciation
accumulation
accurate
acid-test ratio
acknowledgment
acquisition
acreage allotment
across-the-board
actuals
actuary
adjustment
administration
adulterate
advances
advertise
advertisement
affidavit
affiliated
after-tax
agate
agenda
agent
aggregate
agreement
allocation
allotment
allowance
amalgamation
amortization
analyze
analyst
annual report

annuity
antitrust
application
appraiser
apprentice
arbitrage
arrears
assembly plant
assessable stock
assessment
assets
assignation
assigned risk
assignment
attorney
auction
audit
auditor
automated data processing

backlog
balance sheet
bankruptcy
barter economy
bearish
beneficiary
bid and asked
bilateral monopoly
bill of exchange
bill of lading
bimetallism
blanket mortgage
blue chip
blue sky law
board of directors
bonanza
bondholder
bond premium
bonus
bookkeeping
borrow
bottom out
boycott
brokerage

budgeting
bullish
buoyant
bureaucrat
business cycle
bylaw
by-product

calculate
calendar
callable bond
call money
canceled check
capitalization
capitation tax
cargo
cartage
cartel
cashier
cashier's check
caveat emptor
certificate of deposit (C/D)
certified
chairperson
chartist
check protector
classified stock
clearinghouse
clientele
clique
collateral
collective bargaining
collusion
columnar journal
commercial paper
commissary
commission
commodity
common stock
commute
comparative advantage
compensation
competition
complementary goods

55

BUSINESS AND ECONOMICS

compound interest
comptroller
computer
concession
confidential
confirmation
conflagration hazard
conglomerate
consignment
consignee
consolidation
consumer
consumption schedule
contingent fund
contra account
controllable cost
controller
conversion ratio
convertible
cooperative
copyright
copywriter
corporation
correspondent
countercheck
countermand
countervailing power
coupon return
credentials
creditor
crossfoot
cumulative
curb exchange
currency
customer
customs
cycle
cyclical theory

datamation
day trader
debenture
debit balance
decimal

deduction
default
deferred
deficit
deflation
deflator
demurrage
depletion allowance
depositor
depreciation
depression
dereliction
descending tops
deteriorated goods
devaluation
differentials
diminishing returns
disbursement
disclosure
discount rate
discretionary
disposable income
dissipate
diversification
divestiture
dividend
document
Dow theory
down tick
draft
dragage
drawling account
due bill
dun
duty

earnings
economical
efficiency
elastic
embezzlement
enclosure
endorsement
enterprise
entrepreneurial ability

envelope
environment
equilibrium
equipment
equity
escrow
escalator clause
estimate
evaluation
exchange
excise
ex dividend
executive
exempt
expedite
expenditure
expiration date
ex-rights
external debt

fabricate
featherbedding
feedback
fiat money
fiduciary
financial
financier
fiscal
fluctuation
forecasting
foreclosure
forfeit
forgery
franchise
frank
fraudulent
freight
fundamental
futures

galley
galloping inflation
gilt-edged
glamour stock

56

BUSINESS AND ECONOMICS

graph
gratuity
Gresham's law
grievance
gross profit
guarantee

hedge
holding company
hyperinflation
hypothecated stock

imports
incidental costs
inclusive
income
incorporated
indenture
indicia
inelastic
inflation
infringement
inheritance
injunction
insolvent
installment
institutional investor
insurance
intangible assets
integrated
integrity
interim dividend
interlocking
interstate
intraday
intrastate
intrinsic value
inventory
inverted market
investment
investor
invoice
issue
itinerary

jettison
jobber
joint account
journal
journeyman

Keogh plan
Keynesian
kiting
kurtosis

laissez faire
ledger
legal tender
lend-lease
lessee
lessor
letterhead
letter of credit
leverage
liability
license
lien
liquidation
liquidity
loan
locked-in
long-term
lucrative

macroeconomics
maintenance
management
manifest
manifold
manipulation
manufacturer
marginal
margin call
margin of profit
markdown
marketable
markup

maturity
media
mediation
memorandum
mercantile
merchandise
merger
microeconomics
middleman
monetary policy
monopoly
mortgage
mortgagee
mortgagor
multiplier effect
municipal

near-term
negotiable securities
net
nominal price
nonassessable stock
noncallable securities
noncompeting groups
noncumulative
noncurrent
nonperformance
nonprice
nonrecourse
nonrecurring
nonunion stock
no-par
notary public
novation

obsolescence
occupation
odd-lot
oligopoly
omnibus
operand
opportunity costs
option
organization

57

BUSINESS AND ECONOMICS

overage
overdraw
over-the-counter

parity
partnership
par value
passbook
patent
paternalism
patronage
pawnbroker
payee
pegged price
percentage
perpetual inventory
pivotal stock
portfolio
postdated
power of attorney
predepreciation
preemptive
preferential hiring
preferred
premium
price-earnings ratio
prime rate
principal
principle
proceeds
productivity
profit
promissory
propensity
proprietorship
prospectus
proxy
pyramiding

qualitative
quality
quantitative
quick-ratio test
quorum

quota
quotation

rebate
receipt
receivable
receivership
recession
reciprocal
reclamation
reconciliation
recoup
redeemable
redemption
rediscount rate
reference
refund factor
registered
registrar
regulation
reinvestment
reissuance
remittance
remuneration
replacement
reproduction
requisition
rescind
reserve
residual securities
restructure
résumé
retail
retained earnings
revenue
royalty

salability
salary
salutation
salvage value
sampling
saturation level
scalper

scarcity
script
secular
securities
seniority
serial bonds
severance
shareholder
short-term
shrinkage
sluggish
solvent
specialization
specie
speculator
spoilage
stabilizer
stagnation
stapler
stationery
statistics
stenographer
stockholder
stop payment
subsidiary
surety
surplus
syndicate

tangible assets
tariff
tax-exempt
technological
teller
ten-share-unit
ticker
till money
tracer
trademark
trader
transaction
transfer agent
traveler's check
treasury bond

58

BUSINESS AND ECONOMICS

trust	usury	waive
trustee	utility	warrant
turnover		waybill
two-dollar broker	valorization	wealth
	variable cost	weight
uncollectible account	vault	whipsawed
underwriter	vendee	wholesale
unemployment	vendor	withdrawal
unissued stock	verification	
unlisted security	volume discount	
unregistered stock	voucher	yield

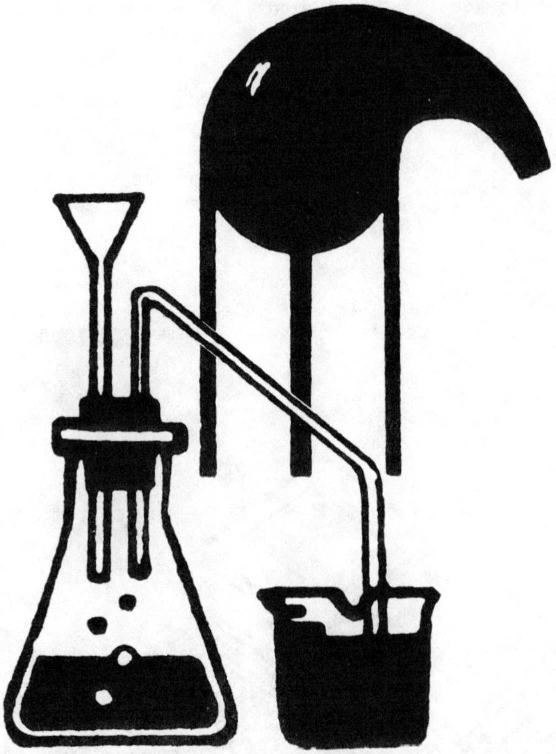

CHEMICAL ELEMENTS

actinium
aluminum
americium
antimony
argon
arsenic
astatine

barium
berkelium
beryllium
bismuth
boron
bromine

cadmium
calcium
californium
carbon
cerium
cesium
chlorine
chromium
cobalt
copper
curium

dysprosium

einsteinium
erbium
europium

fermium
fluorine
francium

gadolinium
gallium
germanium
gold

hafnium
hahnium
helium
holmium
hydrogen

indium
iodine
iridium
iron

krypton

lanthanum
lawrencium
lead
lithium
lutetium

magnesium
manganese
mendelevium
mercury
molybdenum

neodymium
neon
neptunium
nickel
niobium
nitrogen
nobelium

osmium
oxygen

palladium
phosphorus
platinum
plutonium
polonium
potassium

praseodymium
promethium
protactinium

radium
radon
rhenium
rhodium
rubidium
ruthenium
rutherfordium

samarium
scandium
selenium
silicon
silver
sodium
strontium
sulfur

tantalum
technetium
tellurium
terbium
thallium
thorium
thulium
tin
titanium
tungsten

uranium

vanadium

xenon

ytterbium
yttrium

zinc
zirconium

CITIES AND HISTORIC PLACES OF FOREIGN COUNTRIES

Aachen
Abadan
Aberdeen
Abidjan
Abu Dhabi (Abu Zaby)
Acapulco
Accra
Addis Ababa
Adelaide
Aden
Agana
Agra
Ahmedabad
Alborg
Aleppo (Halab)
Alexandria (Al-Iskandariya)
Algeciras
Algiers
Alicante
Allahabad
Alma-Ata
Amalfi
Amiens
Amman
Amoy (Xiamen)
Amritsar
Amsterdam
Andorra la Vella
Angers
Ankara
Anshan
Antananarivo (Tananarive)
Antibes
Antioch (Antakya)
Antwerp (Antwerpen)
Anzio
Apia
Arecibo
Arhus
Arkhangelsk (Archangel)
Arles
Armagh

Armentières
Arnhem
Asansol
Ashkhabad
Asmera (Asmara)
Asti
Astrakhan
Asunción
Aswan
Athens
Aubusson
Auckland
Augsburg
Avignon
Ávila

Baden-Baden
Baghdad
Baku
Bamako
Bandung
Bangalore
Bangkok (Krung Thep)
Bangui
Banjul (Bathurst)
Barcelona
Bari
Barranquilla
Basel
Basra (Al-Basrah)
Basse-Terre
Bayonne
Bayreuth
Be'er Sheva (Beersheba)
Beirut (Bayrut)
Belém (Pará)
Belfast
Belgrade (Beograd)
Belize City
Belmopan
Belo Horizonte
Benares (Varanasi)
Benghazi
Berchtesgaden

Bergamo
Bergen
Berlin
Bern (Berne)
Besançon
Bethlehem (Bayt Lahm)
Biarritz
Bilbao
Birmingham
Bissau
Bizerte (Banzart)
Bogotá
Bologna
Bolzano
Bombay
Bonn
Bordeaux
Boulogne
Bourges
Bournemouth
Bradford
Brandenburg
Brasília
Brasov
Bratislava
Braunschweig (Brunswick)
Brazzaville
Bremen
Bremerhaven
Brest
Bridgetown
Brighton
Brindisi
Brisbane
Bristol
Brno
Bruges (Brugge)
Brussels (Bruxelles)
Bucharest (Bucuresti)
Budapest
Buenos Aires
Bujumbura
Burgas

CITIES AND HISTORIC PLACES OF FOREIGN COUNTRIES

Burgos

Cádiz
Caen
Cagliari
Cairo (Al-Qahira)
Calais
Calcutta
Calgary
Cali
Calicut (Kozhikode)
Callao
Cambrai
Cambridge
Canberra
Cannes
Canterbury
Canton (Guangzhou)
Cape Town
Cap-Haïtien
Caracas
Carcassonne
Cardiff
Carlisle
Carrara
Cartagena
Casablanca (Dar-el-Beida)
Castries
Catania
Cayenne
Cebu
Ceuta
Chambéry
Changchun
Charleroi
Charlotte Amalie
Charlottetown
Chartres
Chatham
Cheltenham
Chelyabinsk
Chengtu (Chengdu)
Cherbourg

Chester
Chihuahua
Chittagong
Christchurch
Chungking (Chongqing)
Ciudad Juárez
Clermont-Ferrand
Cluj
Cochin
Cognac
Coimbra
Cologne (Koln)
Colombo
Colón
Como
Conakry
Concepción
Constance (Konstanz)
Copenhagen (Köbenhavn)
Córdoba (Cordova)
Corinth (Korinthos)
Cork
Cotonou
Coventry
Cremona
Cuernavaca
Curitiba
Cusco (Cuzco)

Dacca
Dairen (Lüda)
Dakar
Damascus (Dimashq)
Danang
Dar-es-Salaam
Darmstadt
Darwin
Debrecen
Delft
Delhi
Derby
Detmold
Dijon

Dili
Djibouti
Dnepropetrovsk
Doha (Ad-Dawhah)
Donetsk
Dortmund
Douala
Dover
Dresden
Dubai (Dubayy)
Dublin
Dubrovnik (Ragusa)
Duisburg
Dundee
Dunkerque (Dunkirk)
Durango
Durban
Dushanbe
Düsseldorf

Edinburgh
Edmonton
El Aaiun
El Alamein
Entebbe
Esfahan (Isfahan)
Essen
Évora
Exeter

Faisalabad (Lyallpur)
Falmouth
Ferrara
Fès (Fez)
Flensburg
Florence (Firenze)
Fontainebleau
Foochow (Fuzhou)
Fortaleza
Fort-de-France
Frankfurt am Main
Freetown
Freiburg
Frunze

CITIES AND HISTORIC PLACES OF FOREIGN COUNTRIES

Fukuoka
Funchal
Fushun

Gaborone (Gaberones)
Gallipoli (Gelibolu)
Galway
Garmisch-Partenkirchen
Gaza (Ghazzah)
Gdansk (Danzig)
Gdynia
Geneva (Genève)
Genoa (Genova)
Georgetown
Ghent (Gent)
Gibraltar (Gibilterra)
Giessen
Glasgow
Gloucester
Godthab (Nuuk)
Gorkiy
Göteborg (Gothenburg)
Gotha
Göttingen
Gouda
Granada
Graz
Grenoble
Guadalajara
Guanajuato
Guatemala
Guayaquil

Haarlem
Hague, The
  ('s-Gravenhage)
Haifa (Hefa)
Haiphong
Halifax
Halle
Hamburg
Hamilton
Hangchow (Hangzhou)
Hannover (Hanover)

Hanoi
Harbin (Haerbin)
Harwich
Havana (La Habana)
Heidelberg
Helsinki (Helsingfors)
Henley-on-Thames
Herat
Hiroshima
Hobart
Hong Kong (Victoria)
Honiara
Hue
Hull
Hyderabad

Ibadan
Inchon
Indore
Innsbruck
Interlaken
Inverness
Ipswich
Irkutsk
Islamabad
Ismailia (Al-Ismailiyah)
Istanbul
Izmir (Smyrna)

Jaipur
Jakarta (Djakarta)
Jena
Jerez de la Frontera
Jericho (Ariha)
Jerusalem
Jidda (Juddah)
Johannesburg

Kabul
Kaliningrad
  (Königsberg)
Kampala
Kananga (Luluabourg)
Kandahar

Kano
Kanpur (Cawnpore)
Kaohsiung
Kaolack
Karachi
Karl-Marx-Stadt
  (Chemnitz)
Karlovy Vary (Carlsbad)
Karlsruhe
Kassel
Kathmandu
Katowice
Kaunas
Kazan
Khabarovsk
Kharkov
Khartoum (Al-Khartum)
Khorramshahr
Kiel
Kiev
Kigali
Kilkenny
Killarney
Kimberley
Kingston
Kingstown
Kinshasa
Kishinev
Kitakyushu
Kitchener
Klaipeda (Memel)
Kobe
Koblenz
Kosice
Kowloon
Krakow
Krasnoyarsk
Kuala Lumpur
Kumamoto
Kumasi
Kunming
Kuwait (Al-Kuwayt)
Kuybyshev

Lagos

CITIES AND HISTORIC PLACES OF FOREIGN COUNTRIES

Lahore
Lanchow (Lanzhou)
La Paz
La Plata
La Rochelle
Las Palmas
Lausanne
Leeds
Le Havre
Leicester
Leiden
Leipzig
Le Mans
Leningrad
Lens
León
Lhasa (Lasa)
Libreville
Liège
Lille
Lilongwe
Lima
Limerick
Limoges
Linz
Lisbon (Lisboa)
Liverpool
Livorno (Leghorn)
Locarno
Lodz
Lomé
London
Londonderry (Derry)
Lourdes
Louvain (Leuven)
Luanda
Lubeck
Lubumbashi (Elisabethville)
Lucca
Lucknow
Lugano
Lusaka

Luxembourg (Luxemburg)
Luxor (Al-Uqsur)
Luzern (Lucerne)
Lvov
Lyon

Macao (Macau)
Madras
Madrid
Madurai
Magdeburg
Mainz
Malabo (Santa Isabel)
Malacca (Melaka)
Málaga
Male
Malmö
Managua
Manama
Manaus
Manchester
Mandalay
Manila
Mannheim
Mantova (Mantua)
Maputo (Lourenço Marques)
Maracaibo
Marathon
Marrakech
Marsala
Marseille
Maseru
Mashhad
Matamoros
Mayagüez
Mbabane
Mecca (Makkah)
Medan
Medellín
Medina (Al-Madinah)
Meissen
Melbourne

Mendoza
Mérida
Messina
Metz
Mexicali
Mexico City
Milan (Milano)
Minsk
Mocha (Al-Mukha)
Modena
Mogadishu (Muqdisho)
Mombasa
Monaco
Monrovia
Monterrey
Montevideo
Montpellier
Montréal
Moroni
Moscow (Moskva)
Mosul (Al-Mawsil)
Multan
Munich (München)
Murcia
Murmansk
Muscat (Masqat)

Nagasaki
Nagoya
Nagpur
Nairobi
Nancy
Nanking (Nanjing)
Nantes
Naples (Napoli)
Nassau
Nazareth (Nazerat)
Ndjamena (Fort Lamy)
Newcastle
New Delhi
Niagara Falls
Niamey
Nice
Nicosia (Levkosia)

CITIES AND HISTORIC PLACES OF FOREIGN COUNTRIES

Nîmes
Norwich
Nottingham
Nouakchott
Nouméa
Novgorod
Novosibirsk
Nuevo Laredo
Nukualofa
Nuremberg (Nürnberg)

Oberammergau
Odense
Odessa
Omsk
Oran
Orléans
Osaka
Oslo
Ostend (Oostende)
Ottawa
Ouagadougou
Oviedo
Oxford

Padova (Padua)
Pago Pago
Palembang
Palermo
Palma de Mallorca
Palmyra (Tudmur)
Pamplona
Panamá (Panama City)
Papeete
Paramaribo
Paris
Parma
Patna
Patras (Patrai)
Pavia
Pecs
Peking (Beijing)
Perm
Perpignan

Perth
Perugia
Peshawar
Petra (Batra)
Phnom Penh
Pilsen (Plzen)
Pinang (George Town)
Pisa
Pistoia
Plovdiv
Plymouth
Pompeii (Pompei)
Ponce
Poona (Pune)
Port-au-Prince
Port Elizabeth
Port Harcourt
Port Louis
Port Moresby
Porto (Oporto)
Pôrto Alegre
Port-of-Spain
Porto Novo
Port Said (Bur Said)
Portsmouth
Potsdam
Poznan (Posen)
Prague (Praha)
Praia
Pretoria
Pskov
Puebla
Puerto Barrios
Punta Arenas
Pusan
Pyongyang

Québec
Quetta
Quezon City
Quito

Rabat
Rangoon

Ravenna
Rawalpindi
Recife
Regensburg
Regina
Reims (Rheims)
Remagen
Rennes
Reykjavík
Riga
Rio de Janeiro
Riyadh (Ar-Riyad)
Road Town
Rochefort
Rome (Roma)
Ronda
Rosario
Roseau
Rosetta (Rashid)
Rostock
Rostov-na-Donu
Rotterdam
Rouen
Rugby

Saarbrücken
Saigon (Ho Chi Minh City)
Saint Catharines
Saint-Denis
Saint George's
Saint Helier
Saint John
Saint John's
Saint-Moritz (Sankt Moritz)
Saint-Pierre
Saint-Quentin
Salamanca
Salamis
Salerno
Salisbury
Salvador
Salzburg

CITIES AND HISTORIC PLACES OF FOREIGN COUNTRIES

Sana
San José
San Juan
San Marino
San Miguel de Allende
San Salvador
San Sebastián
Santa Cruz
Santander
Santiago
Santiago de Cuba
Santo Domingo
Santos
São Paulo
São Tomé
Sapporo
Sarajevo
Saratov
Saskatoon
Sault Ste. Marie
Sedan
Segovia
Semarang
Sendai
Seoul
Sevastopol
Seville (Sevilla)
Shanghai
Sheffield
Shenyang (Mukden)
Shizuoka
Sian (Xi'an)
Siena
Singapore
Siracusa (Syracuse)
Skopje
Sofia (Sofiya)
Soissons
Sorrento
Southampton
Spa
Sparta (Sparti)
Split
Srinagar

Stanley
Stavanger
Stockholm
Strasbourg
Stratford-on-Avon
Stuttgart
Sucre
Sudbury
Suez (As-Suways)
Surabaya
Surat
Suva
Sverdlovsk
Swansea
Swatow (Shantou)
Sydney
Szeged

Tabriz
Taegu
Taipei
Taiyüan
Tallinn
Tampico
Tanger (Tangier)
Tangshan
Taormina
Taranto
Tashkent
Tbilisi (Tiflis)
Tegucigalpa
Tehran
Tel Aviv (Tel Aviv-Yafo)
Thessaloniki (Salonika)
Thimbu
Thunder Bay
Tientsin (Tianjin)
Tijuana
Timbuktu (Tombouctou)
Tipperary
Tirane (Tirana)
Tobruk (Tubruq)
Tokyo
Toledo

Toronto
Tórshavn
Toulon
Toulouse
Tours
Trento (Trent)
Trier
Trieste
Tripoli (Tarabulus)
Trois-Rivières
Trondheim
Troyes
Tsinan (Jinan)
Tsingtao (Qingdao)
Tübingen
Tucumán
Tula
Tunis
Turin (Torino)
Tyre (Sur)

Ufa
Ulan Bator
Ulm
Uppsala
Urbino
Utrecht

Vaduz
Valencia
Valladolid
Valletta
Valparaíso
Vancouver
Varna
Venice (Venezia)
Veracruz
Verdun
Versailles
Vicenza
Vichy
Victoria
Vienna (Wien)
Vientiane (Viangchan)

CITIES AND HISTORIC PLACES OF FOREIGN COUNTRIES

Vila
Vilnius
Vladimir
Vladivostok
Volgograd (Stalingrad)

Warsaw (Warszawa)
Waterford
Weimar
Welland
Wellington

Wiesbaden
Wilhelmshaven
Willemstad
Winchester
Windhoek
Windsor
Winnipeg
Wittenberg
Wolfsburg
Wroclaw (Breslau)
Wuhan

Wuppertal
Wurzburg

Yaoundé
Yerevan
Yokohama
York

Zagreb
Zamboanga
Zaragoza (Saragossa)
Zurich (Zürich)

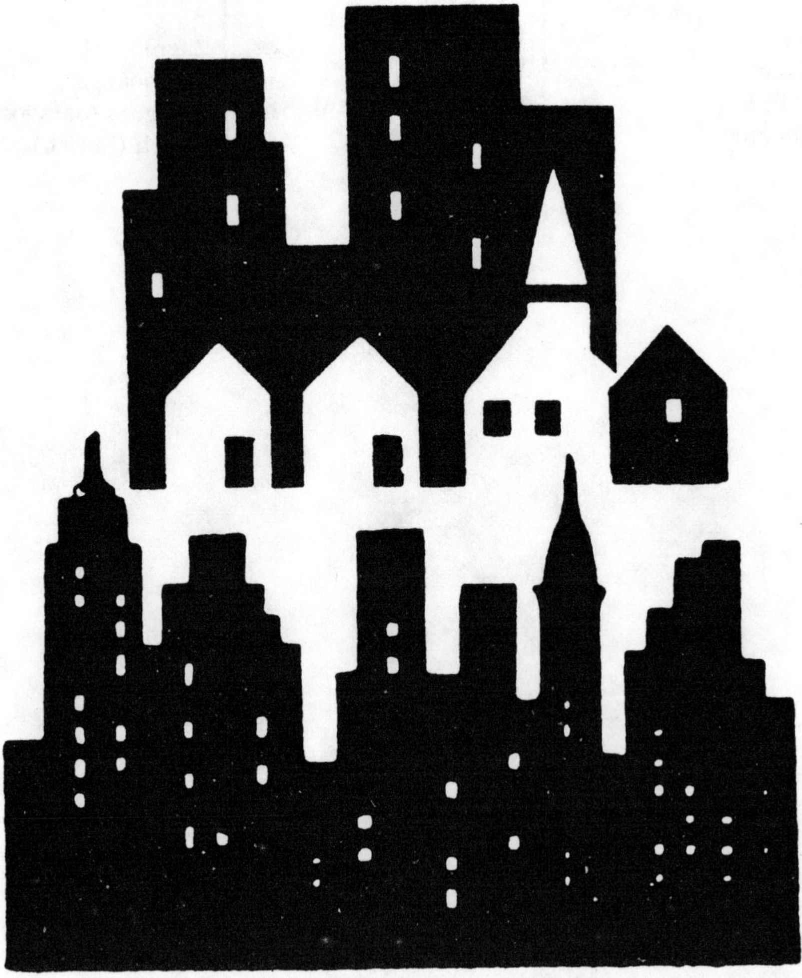

CITIES AND TOWNS OF THE UNITED STATES

Abilene
Aiken
Akron
Alameda
Alamogordo
Albany
Albert Lea
Albuquerque
Alexandria
Alhambra
Aliquippa
Allentown
Alliance
Alpena
Altadena
Alton
Altoona
Altus
Amarillo
Ames
Amherst
Anaconda
Anaheim
Anchorage
Anderson
Annapolis
Ann Arbor
Anniston
Antietam
Appleton
Arcadia
Arlington
Arvada
Asbury Park
Asheboro
Asheville
Ashtabula
Aspen
Astoria
Atchison
Atlanta
Atlantic City
Attleboro
Auburn

Augusta
Aurora
Austin

Babylon
Bakersfield
Baltimore
Bangor
Bar Harbor
Barre
Bartlesville
Batavia
Baton Rouge
Battle Creek
Bayonne
Beaufort
Beaumont
Bellefontaine
Belleville
Bellevue
Bellingham
Beloit
Bemidji
Bennington
Berea
Berkeley
Berwyn
Bessemer
Bethesda
Bethlehem
Bethpage
Beverly Hills
Biddeford
Billings
Biloxi
Binghamton
Birmingham
Bismarck
Bloomington
Boca Raton
Bogalusa
Boise
Bossier City
Boston

Boulder
Bowling Green
Bradenton
Braintree
Brattleboro
Bremerton
Bridgeport
Bristol
Brockton
Brookline
Brownsville
Brunswick
Bucyrus
Buena Park
Buffalo
Burbank
Burlingame
Burlington
Butte

Cairo
Cambridge
Camden
Canton
Cape Girardeau
Carlisle
Carmel
Carson City
Carteret
Casper
Catonsville
Cedar Rapids
Chalmette
Champaign
Charleston
Charlotte
Charlottesville
Chattanooga
Cheektowaga
Chehalis
Chelsea
Chesapeake
Chevy Chase
Cheyenne

71

CITIES AND TOWNS OF THE UNITED STATES

Chicago
Chickasha
Chicopee
Chillicothe
Chincoteague
Cicero
Cincinnati
Clearwater
Cleburne
Cleveland
Clinton
Cocoa
Cody
Coeur d'Alene
Coffeyville
Cohoes
Colorado Springs
Columbia
Columbus
Concord
Coos Bay
Coral Gables
Corning
Corpus Christi
Corvallis
Coshocton
Costa Mesa
Council Bluffs
Covina
Covington
Cripple Creek
Cucamonga
Cudahy
Cumberland
Cuyahoga Falls

Dallas
Daly City
Danvers
Danville
Darien
Davenport
Dayton
Daytona Beach

Dearborn
Decatur
Dedham
Defiance
De Kalb
De Land
Delray Beach
Del Rio
Denver
De Pere
Des Moines
Des Plaines
Detroit
Dodge City
Dothan
Dubuque
Duluth
Durham

East Liverpool
Eau Claire
Edina
El Cajon
El Dorado
Elgin
Elkhart
Elmhurst
Elmira
El Monte
El Paso
Elyria
Emporia
Enid
Erie
Escanaba
Escondido
Euclid
Eugene
Eureka
Evanston
Evansville
Everett

Fairbanks

Fall River
Fargo
Faribault
Fayetteville
Findlay
Fitchburg
Flint
Florence
Florissant
Fond du Lac
Fort Collins
Fort Lauderdale
Fort Myers
Fort Pierce
Fort Wayne
Fort Worth
Fostoria
Framingham
Frankfort
Fredericksburg
Fremont
Fresno
Fullerton

Gadsden
Gainesville
Gaithersburg
Galesburg
Gallup
Galveston
Gardena
Garden Grove
Gardner
Garland
Gary
Gastonia
Gettysburg
Glendale
Glens Falls
Gloucester
Gloversville
Grand Forks
Grand Junction
Grand Prairie

CITIES AND TOWNS OF THE UNITED STATES

Grand Rapids
Great Falls
Greece
Greeley
Green Bay
Greensboro
Greensburg
Greenwich
Grosse Pointe
Groton
Gulfport

Hackensack
Hagerstown
Hammond
Hampton
Hamtramck
Hannibal
Harlingen
Harrisburg
Hartford
Hattiesburg
Haverhill
Havre
Hays
Hazleton
Helena
Hempstead
Hialeah
Hibbing
Hickory
High Point
Hilo
Hoboken
Hollywood
Holyoke
Honolulu
Hornell
Houma
Houston
Huntington
Huntington Beach
Huntsville
Hutchinson

Hyannis
Hyattsville
Hyde Park

Independence
Indianapolis
Inglewood
Inkster
Irondequoit
Irvine
Islip
Ithaca

Jackson
Jacksonville
Jamestown
Janesville
Jeannette
Jefferson City
Jenkintown
Jersey City
Joliet
Joplin
Juneau

Kalamazoo
Kalispell
Kankakee
Kannapolis
Kansas City
Keene
Kennewick
Kenosha
Keokuk
Ketchikan
Kettering
Kewanee
Key West
Killeen
Kingsport
Kinston
Klamath Falls
Knoxville
Kokomo

Lackawanna
Laconia
La Crosse
Lafayette
La Grange
La Jolla
Lake Charles
Lakeland
Lake Placid
Lancaster
Lansdale
Lansing
La Porte
Laramie
Laredo
La Salle
Las Cruces
Las Vegas
Lawrence
Lead
Leavenworth
Lenoir
Leominster
Levittown
Lexington
Lima
Lincoln
Little Rock
Livermore
Livonia
Lodi
Lompoc
Long Beach
Longview
Lorain
Los Altos
Los Angeles
Los Gatos
Louisville
Lowell
Lubbock
Lufkin
Lynchburg
Lynn

CITIES AND TOWNS OF THE UNITED STATES

Mackinac Island	Moberly	New Ulm
Macon	Mobile	New York
Madison	Modesto	Niagara Falls
Mamaroneck	Moline	Nogales
Manassas	Monroe	Nome
Manchester	Monrovia	Norfolk
Mandan	Montclair	Northampton
Manitowoc	Monterey	North Platte
Mankato	Montgomery	Norwalk
Marblehead	Montpelier	Norwich
Marietta	Moorhead	
Marion	Muncie	Oakland
Marquette	Murfreesboro	Oak Park
Mason City	Muscatine	Ocala
Massapequa	Muskegon	Ocean City
Massena	Muskogee	Oceanside
Massillon	Myrtle Beach	Oconomowoc
Mattoon		Odessa
Maumee	Nacogdoches	Ogden
McAlester	Nantucket	Oklahoma City
McAllen	Napa	Olathe
McKeesport	Nashua	Olean
Melbourne	Nashville	Olympia
Memphis	Natchez	Omaha
Menasha	Natchitoches	Oneonta
Mentor	Natick	Ontario
Meriden	Naugatuck	Opelousas
Meridian	Nederland	Orange
Merritt Island	Neenah	Oriskany
Mesa	Newark	Orlando
Mesquite	New Bedford	Oshkosh
Metairie	New Bern	Oskaloosa
Methuen	New Brunswick	Ossining
Metuchen	Newburgh	Oswego
Miami	Newburyport	Ottumwa
Miami Beach	New Canaan	Owatonna
Milwaukee	New Castle	Owensboro
Mineola	New Haven	Owosso
Minneapolis	New Iberia	Oxnard
Minnetonka	New London	
Minot	New Orleans	Paducah
Mishawaka	Newport	Painesville
Missoula	Newport News	Palm Beach
Moab	New Rochelle	Palm Springs

74

CITIES AND TOWNS OF THE UNITED STATES

Palo Alto
Panama City
Paramus
Park Forest
Parma
Pasadena
Pascagoula
Pasco
Passaic
Patchogue
Paterson
Pawtucket
Peabody
Peekskill
Pekin
Pendleton
Pennsauken
Pensacola
Peoria
Perth Amboy
Petaluma
Petersburg
Petoskey
Phenix City
Philadelphia
Phoenix
Pico Rivera
Pierre
Piqua
Piscataway
Pittsburgh
Pittsfield
Plano
Plattsburgh
Plymouth
Pocatello
Pomona
Pompano Beach
Ponca City
Pontiac
Port Angeles
Port Arthur
Port Chester
Port Huron

Portland
Portsmouth
Pottstown
Pottsville
Poughkeepsie
Prichard
Princeton
Providence
Provincetown
Provo
Pueblo
Puyallup

Quincy

Racine
Rahway
Raleigh
Rantoul
Rapid City
Reading
Redding
Redlands
Redondo Beach
Red Wing
Reno
Revere
Richmond
Riverside
Roanoke
Rochester
Rockford
Rock Hill
Rock Island
Rolla

Sacramento
Saginaw
St. Augustine
St. Clair Shores
St. Cloud
St. Joseph
St. Louis
St. Paul

St. Petersburg
Salem
Salina
Salinas
Salisbury
Salt Lake City
San Angelo
San Antonio
San Bernardino
San Diego
Sandusky
San Fernando
San Francisco
San Jose
San Leandro
San Luis Obispo
San Mateo
San Rafael
Santa Ana
Santa Barbara
Santa Cruz
Santa Fe
Santa Monica
Santa Rosa
Saranac Lake
Sarasota
Saratoga Springs
Saugus
Sault Sainte Marie
Savannah
Scarsdale
Schaumburg
Schenectady
Scottsdale
Scranton
Seattle
Sedalia
Sewickley
Seymour
Shaker Heights
Shamokin
Sharon
Sheboygan
Shreveport

75

CITIES AND TOWNS OF THE UNITED STATES

Silver Spring
Simi Valley
Sioux City
Sioux Falls
Sitka
Skaneateles
Skokie
Somerville
Southampton
South Bend
Spartanburg
Spokane
Springfield
Stamford
State College
Staunton
Steubenville
Stockton
Stratford
Streator
Suffolk
Sumter
Sunnyvale
Superior
Syracuse

Tacoma
Tallahassee
Tampa
Taos
Taunton
Teaneck
Tempe
Terre Haute
Texarkana
Thibodaux
Titusville
Toledo
Tomahawk
Tombstone
Tonawanda
Tonopah
Topeka
Torrance

Towson
Traverse City
Trenton
Troy
Truth or Consequences
Tucson
Tucumcari
Tulsa
Tupelo
Tuscaloosa
Tyler

Urbana
Utica

Vail
Valdosta
Vallejo
Valparaiso
Vancouver
Van Nuys
Ventura (San Buena-
 ventura)
Vicksburg
Vincennes
Vineland
Virginia Beach
Virginia City
Visalia

Waco
Walla Walla
Waltham
Wantagh
Warner Robins
Warwick
Washington
Waterbury
Waterloo
Waukegan
Waukesha
Wausau
Wauwatosa
Weehawken

Weirton
Wellesley
Wenatchee
Weslaco
West Covina
Westminster
West Palm Beach
Westport
Wethersfield
Weymouth
Wheaton
Wheeling
White Plains
Whittier
Wichita
Wichita Falls
Wilkes-Barre
Williamsport
Willimantic
Willmar
Wilmette
Wilmington
Winnemucca
Winnetka
Winona
Winston-Salem
Woburn
Woonsocket
Wooster
Worcester
Wyandotte
Wyoming

Xenia

Yakima
Yemassee
Yonkers
Yorktown
Youngstown
Ypsilanti
Yuma

Zanesville

CLOTHING AND FABRICS

acetate
Acrilan
acrylic
à jour
Alençon lace
A line
aloe lace
alpaca
angora
appenzell
appliqué
apron
armure
ascot
astrakhan
Axminster

Bagheera
bainin
baize
bandana
bandeau
barathea
barrette
bathing suit
bathrobe
batiste
beaver
bed jacket
Belgian lace
belt
beret
Binche lace
blanket cloth
blazer
blouse
blouson
blucher
bobbinet
bodice
body shirt
bolo tie
bombazine
bonnet

Botany wool
bourdon lace
bowler
bow tie
braces
brassiere
breeches
Breton lace
broadcloth
brocade
brocatelle
brogan
brogue
buckram
bunting
burlap
burnoose

cable-stitch
caftan
cage
calico
cambric
camel's hair
camisole
camlet
Canton crepe
canvas
cape
Capri pants
caracul
car coat
cardigan
carpeting
cashmere
cassimere
Celanese
cerecloth
challis
chambray
chamois
Chantilly lace
chaps

chemise
chenille
cheongsam
chesterfield
cheviot
chevron
chiffon
chinchilla
chino
chintz
chiton
chukka boot
cloak
cordovan
corduroy
cotton
covert
cowhide
cowl
crash
cravat
crêpe de Chine
crepon
cretonne
crewel
crew neck
crinoline
crochet
cuff links and studs
culotte
cummerbund
cutaway

Dacron
damask
dashiki
delaine
denim
derby
dickey
dimity
dirndl
doeskin
Donegal

CLOTHING AND FABRICS

dotted swiss
double-breasted
double knit
drawers
dressing gown
dress shirt
drill
drugget
duster
duvetyn

écru
embroidery
epaulette
espadrille
Eton jacket
evening dress

faille
fatigues
fedora
felt
fichu
flannel
flannelette
fleece
foulard
frieze
fustian

gabardine
galatea
galloon
galosh
garter belt
gauntlet
gauze
genappe yarn
georgette
gimp
gingham
girdle
glove
gossamer

grenadine
grisaille
grosgrain
guimpe
gunny

habutai
halter
handkerchief
hard hat
Harris tweed
hemp
herringbone
Holland
homespun
hopsacking
hosiery
huckaback

interfacing
interlining

jabot
jacket
jacquard
jersey
jodhpur
jute

kersey
khaki
kilt
kimono
Koroseal

lambskin
Lastex
lasting
lawn
leatherette
leisure suit
leno
leotard
linen

lingerie
lisle
llama
loafer
longcloth
lounge wear

madras
mantilla
marmot
marquisette
maxi
meisen
melton
merino
midi
mink
mittens
moccasin
mohair
moleskin
monk's cloth
moreen
mousseline
mouton
muffler
muskrat
muslin

nainsook
nankeen
neckerchief
needlepoint
nightgown
ninon
Norfolk jacket
nutria
nylon

organdy
organzine
Orlon
overalls

CLOTHING AND FABRICS

overcoat
oxford

paisley
pajamas
palazzo pants
panama
panne
pannier
pantaloon
panty hose
peignoir
pelisse
penung
percale
Persian lamb
petticoat
picot
piqué
plaid
polonaise
polyester
poncho
pongee
poplin
puff
purse

rabbit
raccoon
raincoat
rayon
rebozo
reticule
rompers
rubbers
Russian blouse

sacking
safari jacket
sailcloth

sandal
saran
sarcenet
sari
sarong
sash
sateen
satin
satinet
scarf
sealskin
seersucker
selvage
serape
serge
shagreen
shalloon
shammy
shantung
sharkskin
shawl
sheath
Shetland
shift
shirting
shirtwaist
shorts
skirt
slip
smock
sombrero
spandex
spun silk
suede cloth
surah
suspender
swallow-tailed coat
sweater
sweatshirt
swimsuit

taffeta
tails

tammy
tapestry
tarlatan
tartan
tatting
terry cloth
thongs
tiffany
tinsel
toga
toile
toweling
trench coat
tricot
trousers
tulle
tunic
tuque
turtleneck
tussah
tutu
tuxedo
tweed

underwear
uniform

velvet
velveteen
vicuna
viscose
V neck
voile

warm-up suit
waistcoat
whipcord
wigan
wing tip shoe
woolen
worsted
wrap coat

zipper

COLORS AND PIGMENTS

acorn
Algerian
alizarin
amethyst
apple green
apricot
aquamarine
auburn
azurite blue

baby blue
baby pink
beige
blue
bottle green
brick red
brown
burnt sienna
burnt umber
buttercup yellow

cadmium
cadmium green
cadmium orange
cadmium purple
cadmium red
cadmium yellow
calamine blue
canary yellow
cardinal red
carmine
carnation red
celandine green
cerulean blue
chartreuse
cherry
chestnut
Chinese green
Chinese red
chrome green
chrome red
chrome yellow
chromium green
chrysolite green

citrine
claret red
cobalt blue
cobalt green
cobalt violet
cocoa
coral
corydalis green

dahlia
dark gray
Dresden blue

email

emerald

flesh
fuchsia

gamboge
geranium
golden yellow
green
gray

heliotrope
henna
hyacinth

indigo blue
ivory
ivory black
ivory yellow

jonquil yellow

khaki

lavender
lemon yellow
light gray
lilac

magenta

malachite green
mallow
mandarin orange
marigold yellow
maroon
mauve
mulberry
myrtle green

Naples yellow
navy
Nile green

ocher
olive
olive green
orange
orchid

pansy
peach
peacock blue
pink
plum
primrose
primrose green
primrose yellow
puce
purple
pyrethrum yellow

raw sienna
raw umber
red
rose
rose Caroline
royal purple
ruby

saffron yellow
safrano pink
salmon pink
sapphire blue
sepia
shamrock green
sienna brown
sky blue
slate gray

COLORS AND PIGMENTS

tan
tanbark
tea rose
terra cotta
terre-verte
titanium white
turquoise blue
turquoise green

ultramarine blue
ultramarine green
ultramarine yellow

Venetian red
Venice blue
vermilion
violet

viridian
viridine green
viridine yellow

wisteria blue

yellow
yellow ocher

COUNTRIES AND DEPENDENCIES OF THE WORLD
(Countries)

Afghanistan
Albania
Algeria
Andorra
Angola
Argentina
Australia
Austria

Bahamas, The
Bahrain
Bangladesh
Barbados
Belgium
Benin (Dahomey)
Bhutan
Bolivia
Botswana
Brazil
Bulgaria
Burma
Burundi

Cambodia (Kampuchea)
Cameroon
Canada
Cape Verde
Central African
  Republic
Chad
Chile
China, People's
  Republic of
China, Republic of
  (Taiwan)
Colombia
Comoros
Congo
Costa Rica
Cuba
Cyprus
Czechoslovakia

Denmark

Djibouti
Dominica
Dominican Republic

Ecuador
Egypt
El Salvador
Equatorial Guinea
Ethiopia

Fiji
Finland
France

Gabon
Gambia, The
German Democratic
  Republic (East
  Germany)
Germany, Federal
  Republic of (West
  Germany)
Ghana
Greece
Grenada
Guatemala
Guinea, People's
  Republic of
Guinea-Bissau
Guyana

Haiti
Honduras
Hungary

Iceland
India
Indonesia
Iran
Iraq
Ireland
Israel
Italy
Ivory Coast

Jamaica
Japan
Jordan

Kenya
Kiribati (Gilbert Islands)
Korea, Democratic
  People's Republic of
  (North Korea)
Korea, Republic of
  (South Korea)
Kuwait

Laos
Lebanon
Lesotho
Liberia
Libya
Liechtenstein
Luxembourg

Madagascar
Malawi
Malaysia
Maldives
Mali
Malta
Mauritania
Mauritius
Mexico
Monaco
Mongolia
Morocco
Mozambique

Nauru
Nepal
Netherlands
New Zealand
Nicaragua
Niger
Nigeria
Norway

Oman

COUNTRIES AND DEPENDENCIES OF THE WORLD

Pakistan
Panama
Papua New Guinea
Paraguay
Peru
Philippines
Poland
Portugal

Qatar

Romania
Rwanda

Saint Lucia
Saint Vincent and the Grenadines
San Marino
Sao Tome and Principe
Saudi Arabia
Senegal
Seychelles
Sierra Leone
Singapore
Solomon Islands

Somalia
South Africa
Spain
Sri Lanka (Ceylon)
Sudan
Suriname
Swaziland
Sweden
Switzerland
Syria

Tanzania
Thailand
Togo
Tonga
Trinidad and Tobago
Tunisia
Turkey
Tuvalu (Ellice Islands)

Uganda
Union of Soviet Socialist Republics (Soviet Union)
United Arab Emirates

United Kingdom of Great Britain and Northern Ireland
United States of America
Upper Volta
Uruguay

Vanuatu (New Hebrides)
Vatican City
Venezuela
Vietnam

Western Samoa

Yemen Arab Republic (North Yemen)
Yemen, People's Democratic Republic of (South Yemen)
Yugoslavia

Zaire
Zambia
Zimbabwe (Rhodesia)

(Dependencies and Parts of Countries)

Anguilla
Antigua
Aruba
Ascension Island
Azores

Balearic Islands
Barbuda
Belize
Bermuda
Bonaire
British Virgin Islands
Brunei

Canary Islands

Cayman Islands
Channel Islands
Christmas Island
Cocos (Keeling) Islands
Cook Islands
Corsica
Crete
Curacao

England
Estonia

Falkland Islands
Faroe Islands
French Guiana

French Polynesia

Gaza Strip
Gibraltar
Great Britain
Greenland
Guadeloupe
Guernsey

Hong Kong

Isle of Man

Jersey

COUNTRIES AND DEPENDENCIES OF THE WORLD

Latvia
Lithuania

Macao (Macau)
Madeira Islands
Martinique
Mayotte
Montserrat

Namibia (South-West Africa)
Netherlands Antilles
Nevis
New Caledonia
Niue
Norfolk Island
Northern Ireland

Okinawa

Pitcairn Islands

Reunion
Ryukyu Islands

Saba
St. Christopher—Nevis—Anguilla
St. Eustatius
St. Helena
St. Pierre and Miquelon
Sardinia
Scotland
Sicily
Svalbard (Spitsbergen)

Tokelau
Tristan da Cunha
Turks and Caicos Islands

Wallis and Futuna
Western Sahara

(U.S. Outlying Areas)

American Samoa
Guam
Midway Islands
Northern Mariana Islands
Puerto Rico
Trust Territory of the Pacific Islands
Virgin Islands of the U.S.
Wake Island

DISEASES AND PHYSICAL DISORDERS

abscess
Achilles tendonitis
acidosis
acne
Addison's disease
adenitis
adenoma
ague
alcoholism
allergy
amoebic dysentery
anemia
anesthesia
aneurysm
angina pectoris
anorexia
anoxia
anthrax
anuria
anxiety
aphasia
apnea
apoplexy
appendicitis
arbovirus
arteriosclerosis
arthritis
ascariasis
asphyxia
asphyxiation
asthenia
asthma
astigmatism
ataxia
athlete's foot
autointoxication

bacillary dysentery
barber's itch
bed-wetting
beriberi
biliary cirrhosis
black lung disease
blastomycosis

blennorrhea
boils
botulism
bronchitis
brucellosis
bubo
bubonic plague
bunion
bursitis

calculus
cancer
carbuncles
carcinoma
cardiac arrest
cardiomyopathy
carditis
catarrh
celiac disease
cellulitis
cerebral hemorrhage
cerebrospinal meningitis
cervicitis
cheilitis
chicken pox
chilblain
chlorosis
cholecystitis
cholera
chorea
cirrhosis
cold sore
colitis
Colorado tick fever
congenital malformation
conjunctivitis
consumption
convulsion
coronary thrombosis
Coxsackie virus
Creutzfeldt-Jakob disease
Crohn's disease
cryptorchidism
cyanosis

cyst
cystic fibrosis
cystitis
cytomegalovirus

dandruff
deficiency diet
delirium
delusions
dengue
dermatitis
dermatosis
dermoid cyst
diabetes
diarrhea
diphtheria
diverticulitis
diverticulosis
duodenal ulcer
duodenitis
dysentery
dyspepsia
dystrophy

echovirus
eczema
elephantiasis
embolism
emphysema
empyema
encephalitis
endocarditis
endocytosis
enteritis
epididymitis
epilepsy
erysipelas

fibrositis
food poisoning
fungal
furuncle

gangrene
gastric ulcer
gastritis

DISEASES AND PHYSICAL DISORDERS

gastroenteritis
German measles
gingivitis
glaucoma
glycemia
goiter
gonorrhea
gout
Guillain-Barre Syndrome

halitosis
hay fever
headache
heart disease
hemophilia
hemorrhage
hemorrhoid
hepatitis
hepatoma
hepatopathy
hernia
herpangina
herpes
hiatal hernia
hiccup
Hodgkin's disease
hydrophobia
hypertension
hyperthyroidism
hypertrophy
hypochondria
hysteria

impetigo
infertility
influenza
insomnia
itching

jaundice

keloid
ketosis
kidney stone
kwashiorkor

laryngitis
leprosy
leukemia
lockjaw
lymphadenitis

malaria
malignancy
manic-depressive
Marburg disease
mastitis
mastoiditis
measles
melancholia
melanoma
meningitis
mesothelioma
migraine
molluscum
moniliasis
mononucleosis
multiple sclerosis
mumps
muscular dystrophy
myelofibrosis
myocarditis
myopia

narcolepsy
nausea
nephritis
neuralgia
neuritis
Newcastle disease
nyctophobia

obesity
odontalgia
oophoritis
ophthalmia
osteoarthritis
osteomalacia
osteomyelitis

Paget's disease

palsy
paranoia
paratyphoid
paresthesia
Parkinson's disease
parrot fever
pellagra
peptic ulcer
peritonitis
pernicious anemia
pertussis
pestilence
pestular dermatitis
phlebitis
phlebotomus fever
plague
pleurisy
pleuropneumonia
pneumonia
poison ivy
polio
poliomyelitis
postnasal drip
prostatitis
psittacosis
psoriasis
psychosis
puerperal fever
pulmonary edema
pureapeal septis
pustule
pyelitis
pyelonephritis
pyemia
pyorrhea

quinsy

rabbit fever
rabies
Raynaud's disease
reovirus disease
respiratory infection
retinitis
Reye's syndrome

DISEASES AND PHYSICAL DISORDERS

rheumatic fever
rheumatism
rhinitis
rickets
ringworm
Rocky Mountain
  spotted fever
rubella
rubeola
rupture

sandfly fever
sarcoma
scabies
scarlatina
scarlet fever
schizophrenia
sciatica
scirrhous
sclerosis
scurvy
senility
septicemia
septic sore throat
shingles
sickle-cell anemia

sinusitis
smallpox
spasm
spinal meningitis
spur
sterility
stomachache
stomach ulcer
stomatitis
streptococcal
stress
Sudden Infant
  Death Syndrome
syphilis

tapeworm
Tay-Sachs' disease
tendinitis
tendonitis
tetanus
thrombosis
tick-borne encephalitis
tonsillitis
toxic shock syndrome
trachoma
trench mouth

trichinosis
trichosis
tuberculosis
tularemia
tumescent
tumor
typhoid fever
typhus

ulcer
undulant fever
uremia
urinary calculus
urticaria

vaginal discharge
venereal disease
vertigo
vesicular stomatitis
Vincent's angina
viremia
vomiting

wart
whooping cough

yaws
yellow fever

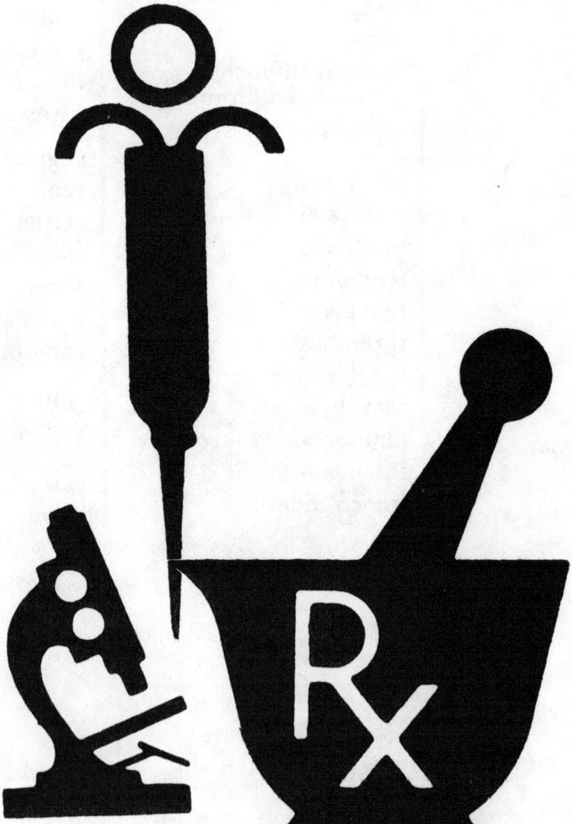
Rx

DRUGS AND REMEDIES
(Brand names are capitalized)

A and D Ointment
Absorbine
acetaminophen
acetone
Achromycin
Actifed
Actifed-C
Adrenalin
adrenocorticotropic hormone
Afrin
alcohol
Aldactazide
Aldactone
Aldomet
Aldoril
Alka-Seltzer
allergenic extracts
allopurinol
Ambenyl
Amcill
Amicar
amino acid
aminophylline
Amipaque
amobarbital
Amoxil
amphetamine
Amphojel
amphotericin B
ampicillin
Amyl Nitrate
Amytal
anagesic
Anahist
androgens
anodine
Antabuse
antacid
antihemophilic
Antivert
Anusol
aperient
Apresoline

Aquamephyton
Aramine
Arfonad
Aristocort
Artane
ascorbic acid
Aspergum
aspirin
Atarax
Atromid-S
atropine
Auralgan Otic
AVC Cream
Azo
Azulfidine

bacitracin
Bactine
Bactrim
Banalg
barbiturate
barium
Bayer
belladonna
Benadryl
Bendectin
Benemid
Ben-Gay
Bentyl
Benylin
Benzedrine
benzocaine
benzoin
Betadine
bicarbonate
Biphetamine
bismuth
Bisodol
bleomycin
Blistex
bone meal
boric acid
Breacol
bromide

Bromo-Seltzer
Bronkaid
Bufferin
busulfan
Butazolidin
Butazolidin Alka
Butisol Sodium

Cafamine
Cafergot
caffeine
Caladryl
calamine
Calciferol
calcitonin
calcium
caldesene
camphor
cannabis
carbenicillin
carbon dioxide
Carbrital
cascara sagrada
caster oil
Catapres
Cēpacol
chloral hydrate
chloramphenicol
Chloraseptic
chlordiazepoxide
chloroform
chlorophyll
chloroquine
chlorothiazide
chlorpromazine
Chlor-Trimeton
cholestyramine
chorionic gonadotropin
chymotrypsin
cimetidine
Clearasil
Cleocin
coal tar
cocaine
codeine

DRUGS AND REMEDIES

cod-liver oil
Colace
colchicine
collodion
Coly-Mycin S Otic
Combid
Compazine
Compoz
Comtrex
Congrespirin
copper sulfate
Cordran
Coricidin
Cortisporin Otic
CoTylenol
Coumadin
Cruex
Cyanocobalamin
cyclophosphamide
Cyclospasmol
Cytomel
cytosine arabinoside
Cytoxan

Dalmane
Darvocet-N
Darvon
Darvon-N
DBI-TD
Decadron
Declomycin
Deltasone
Deltra
Demerol
Demulen
Dermacort
Desenex
Desitin
Desoxyn
dexamethasone
Dexamyl
Dexatrim
dextran-40
dextroamphetamine
dextrose

Diabinese
Diamox
Diaparene
diatrizoate
diazepam
diazoxide
dicumarol
diethylstilbestrol
Di-Gel
digitalis
digitoxin
digoxin
dihydrotachysterol
Dilantin
dimercaprol
Dimetane
Dimetapp
dimethyl sulfoxide
 (DMSO)
diphenhydramine
diphenoxylate
diphtheria antitoxin
disulfiram
Diuril
Donnagel
Donnatal
Doriden
doxapram
doxycycline hyclate
Dramamine
Dristan
Drixoral
Dulcolax
Durmoplast
Dyazide

Eclipse
Efferdent
Elavil
elixir
Elixophyllin
Empirin
E-Mycin
endocrine

Enduron
Enfamil
Enovid
enzymes
ephedrine
epinephrine
Equagesic
Equanil
ergocalciferol
ergonovine
Ergostat
ergotamine
Erythrocin
erythromycin
Esidrix
esidrol
estradiol
estrogen
ether
ethinyl
ethyl alcohol
Etrafon
Evac-Q-Kit
Excedrin

Felsules
Femiron
Feosol
ferrous sulfate
fibrinolysin
Fiorinal
Flagyl
Fleet Bisacodyl
fluoride
fluorine
fluorouracil
formaldehyde
Formula 44
Fostex
Freezone
fructose
Furadantin
furosemide

gamma globulin
Gantanol

92

DRUGS AND REMEDIES

Gantrisin
Garamycin
Gaviscon
gelatin
Gelfoam
Gelusil
gentamicin
Geritol
globulin
glucagon
glucose
glutamic acid
glycerin
Glycoside
gonadotropins
griseofulvin

halothane
hashish
heparin
heroin
histamine
histoplasmin
hormone
Hycomine
Hydergine
hydralazine
hydrochlorothiazide
hydrocortisone
Hydrodiuril
Hydropres
Hygroton
Hyperstat

Ilosone
Imferon
Inderal
Indocin
Innovar
insulin
iodine
iodoform
Ionamin
iopanoic
ipecac

iron
isoniazid
isopropyl alcohol
Isopto Carpine
Isordil
Isuprel

kaolin
Kaon-Cl
Kaon Elixir
Kaopectate
Keflex
Kenalog
Kesso-Bamate
Kessodrate
Kesso-Pen
Kesso-Tetra
ketamine
K-Lyte
Komed
Komex
Kwell

lactic acid
Lactinex
lanolin
Lanoxin
Larotid
Lasix
lecithin
levodopa
Librax
Librium
Lidex
lidocaine
Lincomycin
Listerex
Listerine
lithium
Lomotil
Lo/Ovral
Lopurin
Lubriderm

Maalox
Macrodantin

magnesia
magnesium hydroxide
Mandelamine
Marax
marijuana
Massengill
Medrol
Mellaril
menthol
Mentholatum
meperidine
meprobamate
Meprospan
Meprotabs
mercurochrome
Merthiolate
mestranol
methadone
methamphetamine
methotrexate
methyldopa
methylene blue
methylprednisolone
methyltestosterone
Meticorten
Metrecal
metrizamide
Mexsana
Midol
Migral
Miltown
mineral oil
Minocin
Monistat
morphine
Motrin
Murine
Mycolog
Mycostatin
Mylanta
Mylicon
Mysteclin F

Naldecon
narcotic

DRUGS AND REMEDIES

Nembutal
Neodecadron
neomycin
Neosporin
neostigmine
Neo-Synephrine
niacin
Nico-400
Nicobid
nicotine
Nicotinex
nicotinic acid
Nitro-bid
Nitrobon
nitrofurantoin
nitroglycerin
Nitrol
Nitrospan
Nivea
Noctec
No Doz
Noludar
Norgesic
Norinyl
Norlestrin
Novahistine DH
Novocain
Noxzema
Nupercainal
Nyquil
nystatin
Nytol

Omnipen
opium
Orajel
Oretic
Orinase
Ornade
Ornex
Ortho-Novum
Ouabain
Ovral
Ovulen
oxytetracycline

Paba
Pamprin
Panmycin
Panwarfin
papaverine
parafon forte
parathyroid hormone
paregoric
Pavabid
pectin
Pediamycin
Pen-A
Penbriten
penicillamine
penicillin
Penobarbitul
Pentids
pentobarbital
Pen-Vee K
Pepto-Bismol
Percodan
Periactin
Peri-Colace
Peritrate
peroxide
Persantine
Pertussin
Pfizer-E
Pfizerpen G
phenacetin
Phenaphen
Phenergan
phenobarbital
phenolphthalein
phenothiazine
Phillips' Milk of
  Magnesia
pHisoDan
pHisoDerm
pHisoHex
pitressin
Placidyl
pneumococcal vaccine
poison ivy extract

Polaramine
Polident
poliomyelitis vaccine
Polycillin
polymyxin
Poly-Vi-Flor
potassium
prednisolone
prednisone
Preludin
Premarin
Preparation H
Primatene
Principen
Pro-Banthine
probenecid
procaine
progesterone
Proloid
Pronestyl
propoxyphene
propranolol
propylthiouracil
protamine sulfate
Provera
Psorex
Pyridium
pyridoxine

Qidpen G
Quāālude
Quibron
Quinacrine
Quinalor
Quinidex
quinidine
quinine
Quinora
Quinsana

Rau-Sed
Regitine
Regroton
reserpine

94

DRUGS AND REMEDIES

resorcinol
riboflavin
Riopan
Ritalin
Robaxin
Robaxisal
Robitet
Robitussin
Rolaids

salicylamide
salicylic acid
Salutensin
Sansert
scopolamine
Seconal
sedative
selenium
Selsun
Senokot
Sensodyne
Septra
Ser-ap-es
Serax
Serpasil
Serutan
silver nitrate
simethicone
Similac
Sinarest
Sinequan
Sinex
Singlet
Sinutab
SK-Bamate
SK-Chloral Hydrate
SK-Niacin
SK-Tetracycline
Slow-K
sodium chloride
Solarcaine
Solu-Medrol
Soma
somatropin

Sominex
Sorbitrate
Stelazine
Sucrets
Sudafed
sulfur
Sumycin
Synalar
Synalgos-DC
Synthroid

Talwin
tanac acid
Tandearil
tannic acid
Tedral
Teldrin
Telepaque
Tenuate Dospan
terpin hydrate
Terramycin
testosterone
tetracycline
Tetracyn
tetrahydrocannabinol (THC)
Tetrex
theophylline
thiamine
Thiosulfil
Thiuretic
Thorazine
Thylox
thyroglobulin
thyroid
thyroxine
Tigan
Tofranil
tolbutamide
Tolinase
Tranxene
Travasol
triamcinolone
Triavil

Tri-Vi-Flor
tuberculin
Tucks
Tuinal
Tums
Tuss-Ornade
Tylenol
typhoid vaccine

Unguentine
urokinase

Valisone
Valium
vancomycin
Vanquish
vaseline
Vasodilan
vasopressin
V-Cillin-K
Veetids
Vibramycin
Vicks Vaporub
vinblastine
Vioform-Hydrocortisone
Visine
Vistaril
vitamins

warfarin
wheat germ oil
Wigraine
witch hazel

Xylocaine

yeast
yellow fever vaccine

zinc gluconate
zinc oxide
zinc sulfate
Zinefrin
Zyloprim

95

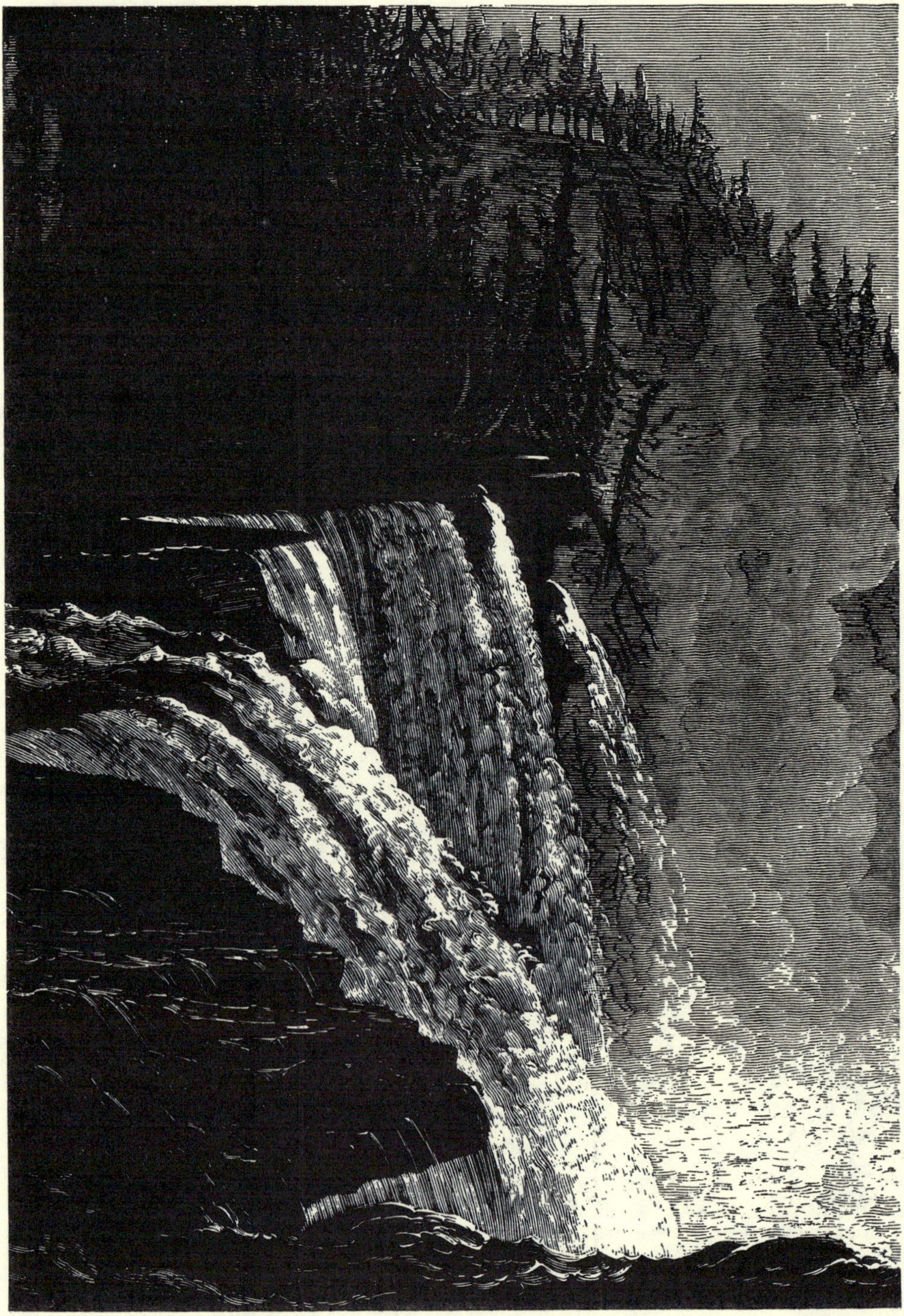

EARTH AND LANDFORMS

abrasion
abyssal
aggradation
alcove
alluvial
alp
andesite
anthracite
aquifer
archipelago
arête
arroyo
artesian
atmosphere
atoll
avalanche

bajada
basalt
basin
batholith
beach
biotite
bituminous
blowhole
bluff
braiding
breccia
butte

calcite
caldera
Cambrian
canal
canyon
capillarity
Carboniferous
cascade
cavity
Cenozoic
chalk
channel
chasm
chute

cirque
cleavage
cliff
col
conglomerate
continent
contour
coral
cordillera
core
crater
crescent
Cretaceous
crevasse
crust
crystal

degradation
delta
dendritic
desert
Devonian
dike
dolomite
drift
drumlin
dune

elevation
Eocene
erosion
eruption
escarpment
esker
estuary
evaporation
extrusive

fault
feldspar
felsite
fiord
fissure
flood plain
fossil

fracture
fumarole

gabbro
gap
geodesy
geological
geomorphology
geosyncline
geyser
glaciated
glacier
gneiss
gorge
graben
granite
gravitation
grotto
gulch
gully
gypsum

helictite
hematite
hemisphere
highland
hill
hogback
Holocene
homocline
horst
hydrosphere

intrusive
ionosphere
isostasy
isthmus

Jurassic

kame
karst
kettle
klippe

EARTH AND LANDFORMS

laccolith
lagoon
lava
levee
limestone
limonite
lithosphere
littoral
loess
lowland

magma
magnetism
magnetite
mantle
marble
meander
mesa
mesophere
Mesozoic
metamorphic
mica
Miocene
monocline
moor
moraine
moulin
mountain

nunatak

oasis
Oligocene
olivine
Ordovician
orogeny
orthoclase
oxbow lake

Paleocene
paleontology
Paleozoic

peak
pelagic
peneplain
peninsula
Permian
phyllite
pinnacle
plagioclase
plain
planet
plateau
playa
Pleistocene
Pliocene
pluton
prairie
Precambrian
precipice

Quartzite
Quaternary

ravine
ridge
rift

sandstone
schist
scoria
sculpturing
sedimentary
seismic
seismograph
sérac
serpentine
shale
shelf
shield
shoal
sial
sierra
silicate

sill
silt
Silurian
sima
slag
slate
slope
spit
spur
stalactite
stalagmite
steppe
strata
stratosphere
stria
swamp
syncline

taiga
talus
terminal moraine
terrace
terrestrial
tombolo
topography
travertine
Triassic
tributary
troposphere
trough
tsunami
tundra
turgite

uniformitarianism
uplift

valley
varve
vein
volcano

weathering

FLOWERS

abutilon
acacia
aconitum
adder's-tongue
African violet
ageratum
ajuga
alkanet
allheal
alyssum
amaryllis
anchusa
anemone
aquilegia
arabis
arbutus
armeria
arnica
aster
azalea

baby-blue-eyes
baby eyes
baby primrose
baby rambler
baby's-breath
baby tears
bachelor's-button
baneberry
banewort
baptisia
barren wort
basket flower
beardtongue
begonia
belladonna
bellflower
bird-of-paradise flower
bird's-foot trefoil
bird's-foot violet
bird's-tongue flower
bishop's cap
bitterroot
black-eyed Susan

bleeding heart
bluebell
bluebonnet
bluebottle
blue flag
blue flax
bluet
bloodroot
bouncing Bess
bunchberry
buttercup
butterfly lily
butterfly plant
butterfly weed

cactus
calceolaria
calendula
calla lily
camas
camellia
campanula
candytuft
canna
Canterbury bell
cardinal flower
carnation
catchfly
cattail
celandine poppy
celsia
centaurea
cereus
chaparral pea
checkerbloom
chicory
chrysanthemum
cineraria
clematis
clintonia
clover
cockscomb
coleus
columbine

coneflower
coreopsis
cornflower
corydalis
cosmos
cowherb
cowslip
creamcups
creeping Jennie
creeping strawberry
crocus
croton
cuckooflower
cup'-and-saucer
cyclamen

daffodil
dahlia
daisy
dandelion
day lily
delphinium
dewdrop
dianthus
dicentra
dodecatheon
dogtooth violet
Dutchman's-breeches

early saxifrage
edelweiss
eglantine
English daisy
eriogonum
eucharis
euphorbia

fleabane
foamflower
forget-me-not
four-o'clock
foxglove
fuchsia
fumewort

FLOWERS

gaillardia
gardenia
gaywings
gentian
geranium
gerbera
geum
gilia
gillyflower
ginger lily
gladiolus
globeflower
gloriosa
gloxinia
godetia
golden glow
goldenrod
gum plant
gypsophila

harebell
heather
helianthemum
helianthus
heliopsis
heliotrope
hellebore
hemerocallis
hepatica
hibiscus
hollyhock
horehound
horn poppy
horsemint
humble plant
huntsman's-cup
hyacinth

impatiens
Indian pipe
innocence
iris
ironweed
ixia

jacinth
jacket and breeches
jack-in-the-pulpit
jacobean lily
Japanese lantern
jasmine
Jerusalem artichoke
jessamine
jewelweed
joe-pye weed
jonquil

kalmia
knapweed
kochia

lady's slipper
lantana
larkspur
leopard plant
limonium
lobelia
loosestrife
lotus
lupine

mandrake
mare's tail
marguerite
marigold
mariposa lily
marshmallow
marsh marigold
marsh painted cup
marsh rosemary
maypop
meadow lily
mertensia
milkwort
mist flower
miterwort
moccasin flower
monkey flower
monkshood

montbretia
moonflower
morning-glory
morning star
mountain avens

narcissus
nasturtium
nemesia
nemophila

orchid
orchis
oriental poppy
Oswego tea
oxalis
oxeye daisy

paintbrush
painted cup
painted lady
pansy
partridgeberry
pasqueflower
pearly everlasting
peony
penstemon
periwinkle
petunia
phlox
pickerelweed
pipsissewa
pitcher plant
pitcher sage
plantain lily
poinsettia
poke
polemonium
poppy
portulaca
potentilla
prairie smoke
primrose

FLOWERS

primula
prince's-feather

quaker-ladies
Queen Anne's lace

ragwort
ranunculus
rattlesnake violet
red maids
rose campion
rose geranium
rose mallow
rudbeckia
rue anemone

safflower
salpiglossis
salvia
saxifrage
scabiosa
scarlet sage
schizanthus
scilla
sea lavender
sea pink

sedum
sego lily
Shasta daisy
shinleaf
shooting star
shortia
showy orchis
silverweed
snapdragon
snowdrop
snow lily
snow plant
soapwort
sparaxis
speedwell violet
spider orchid
spiderwort
spikenard
spring beauty
star-of-Bethlehem
statice
sticktight
stock
stokesia
stork's-bill
sunflower

sweet alyssum
sweet pea
sweet sultan
sweet william

tansy ragwort
thrift
tidytips
trillium
tuberose
tulip

valerian
vetch
violet

water lily
wild rose
wood sorrel

yarrow
yerba buena
yerba mansa
yerbarecuma
yucca

zinnia

FOOD

acorn squash
albacore
alfalfa
allspice
almond
amandine
anadama bread
anchovy
anise
antipasto
appetizer
applesauce
apricot
arrowroot
artichoke
asparagus
aspic
au gratin
avocado

baba
bacon
banana
barbecue sauce
barley
Bartlett pear
basil
bayberry
bay leaf
bean sprouts
béarnaise
béchamel
beet
benne
berries
Bibb lettuce
Bing cherry
biscuit
bisque
black-eyed peas
blade rib roast
blintz
Bok choy
bologna
bonbon

bonito
bordelaise
borscht
bouillon
boysenberry
bran
Brazil nuts
brewer's yeast
Brie cheese
brine
brioche
brisket
broccoli
brownies
Brussels sprouts
buckwheat
buffalofish
bulgur
buttermilk
butternut squash

cabbage
cacciatore
Caesar dressing
calf's liver
Camembert cheese
canapé
canneloni
cantaloupe
capers
capon
caramel
caraway
cardamom
carrot
casaba
cashew
casserole
catsup
cauliflower
caviar
cayenne
celeriac
celery

cereal
chard
Cheddar cheese
cheese
cherrystone
chervil
chestnut
chickpeas
chicory
chiffon pie
chili con carne
chitterling
chives
chocolate
chop suey
chowder
chow mein
chuck
chutney
cider
cinnamon
citron
citrus
cling peach
clove
club steak
cobbler
cocoa
coconut
codfish
coffee
coleslaw
collards
compote
condensed milk
condiment
cone
confectioner's
conserve
consommé
cookies
coriander
corned beef
Cornish hen
corn meal

103

FOOD

cornstarch
cortidos
cottage cheese
country ham
crabapple
crab meat
crackers
cracklins
cranberry
Cranshaw melon
cream
creole sauce
crescent
croissant
croquettes
crouton
cruller
crumbs
cucumber
cumin
curd
currant
curry
custard
cutlet

dandelion
Delmonico steak
dessert
deviled
dill
divinity
donut
doughnut
duck
dumpling
duxelles

éclair
Edam cheese
egg fu yung
eggnog
eggplant

Elberta peach
Emmenthaler cheese
enchilada
endive
escarole
espresso
evaporated milk
extract

farina
fatback
fava
fennel
feta cheese
fiddlehead
fig newton
figs
filbert
filet
finnan haddie
flank steak
flour
fondant
fondue
fontina cheese
frankfurter
freestone peach
fricassee
fritter
frosting
fryer
fudge

garbanzo
garlic
gazpacho
gelatin
gherkin
giblet
ginger
gingerbread
gingersnap
ginseng
glacé

glaze
gnocchi
goose
gooseberry
Gorgonzola cheese
Gouda cheese
goulash
granola
granulated
grapefruit
gratin
gravy
groats
Gruyère cheese
guava
gumbo

haddock
halibut
hamburger
hardtack
hazelnut
heel pot roast
herb
herring
hickory nut
hoagie
hollandaise
hominy
honeydew
hors d'oeuvres
horseradish
hubbard squash
hush puppies

iceberg
icicle
icing
iodized

jalapeño
jambalaya
johnnycake
jubilees
juice

FOOD

julienne
juniper

kale
kohlrabi
kumquat

lamb
lard
lasagna
leavening
lebkuchen
leek
legume
lemonade
lentil
lettuce
licorice
Liederkranz
limagrand
Limburger cheese
limeade
linguine
liptauer
liverwurst
lobster
loin

macadamia nuts
macaroni
macaroon
mace
mackerel
mandarin
mango
manicotti
maraschino cherry
marchand de vin
margarine
marinade
marjoram
marmalade
marron
marrow
marshmallow

marzipan
matzo
mayonnaise
Melba toast
melon
meringue
milk
mincemeat
minestrone
mint
mocha
molasses
monosodium glutamate
Monterey Jack cheese
Mornay sauce
moussaka
mousse
mousseline
mozzarella cheese
Muenster cheese
muffins
mulligatawny
muscat
mushroom
muskmelon
mussels
mustard greens

nachos
neapolitan
nectar
nectarine
Neufchâtel cheese
non-dairy
noodles
nougat
nutmeg

oatmeal
ocean perch
okra
oleomargarine
omelet
omelette

onion
orangeade
oregano
oxtail
oyster

paella
pancake
pandowdy
papaya
paprika
parfait
Parmesan cheese
parmigiana
parsley
parsnip
pasta
pastrami
pastry
pâté
pea
peanut butter
peanut brittle
pecan
penuche
pepper
peppercorns
peppermint
pepperoni
persimmon
petit four
pheasant
piccalilli
pickle
pickling spice
picnic ham
pilaf
pimiento
pinbone steak
pineapple
pinto
pistachio
pita bread
pizza
plantain

105

FOOD

polenta
pomegranate
pone
popcorn
poppy seed
porridge
porterhouse steak
potatoes
poultry seasoning
praline
preserves
pretzel
prosciutto
provolone cheese
prune
pudding
pumpernickel
pumpkin
punch
purée

quail
quiche
quince

rabbit
radish
ragout
raisin
rarebit
raspberry
ravioli
relish
rhubarb
rib roast
ricotta cheese
ripe olives
risotto
rock lobster
roe
romaine
Romano cheese
Roquefort cheese
rosemary

round steak
rump roast
rutabaga
rye

safflower
saffron
sage
salad
salami
salmon
salsify
saltine
salt pork
sandwich
sardine
sarsaparilla
sassafras
sauce
sauerbraten
sauerkraut
sausage
savarin
savory
scalloppini
scallops
scone
scrod
seafood
sea squab
serviche
sesame
shallots
shank
sherbet
shish kebab
shortening
short ribs
shoulder roast
sirloin steak
skimmed milk
sockeye
soft-shelled crab
sorghum

sorrel
soufflé
sour cream
sourdough
soy
soybean
spaghetti
spareribs
spinach
sprouts
spumoni
squab
squash
stew
strawberry
streusel
stroganoff
strudel
stuffed clams
stuffing
succotash
suet
sugar
sukiyaki
sultanas
sundae
sunflower
sweetbreads
syrup

Tabasco
tabbouleh
taco
taffy
tamale
tangerine
tapioca
tarragon
tartar sauce
T-bone steak
tenderloin
teriyaki
terrapin

106

FOOD

thyme	turnip	walnut
timbales	tutti-frutti	watercress
toffee		watermelon
Tokay grapes	vanilla	Welsh rarebit
tomatoes	veal	wheat germ
tongue	vegetable	wholewheat
torte	velouté sauce	Worcestershire
tortilla	venison	
tortoni	vermicelli	
tostadas	vichyssoise	yam
trifle	vinaigrette	yeast
tripe	vinegar	yogurt
tuna		Yorkshire pudding
turbot		
turkey	wafer	
turmeric	waffle	zucchini
	Waldorf salad	zwieback

FOREIGN WORDS AND PHRASES

à bientôt
ab initio
ab origine
adieu
ad infinitum
adios
ad nauseam
affaire d'honneur
Agnus Dei
áioli
à la carte
à la mode
alias
alibi
alma mater
aloha oe
alter ego
ambiance
amicus curiae
amigo
anno Domini
anno urbis conditae
  (a.u.c.)
annuit coeptis
anonymous
ante-bellum
antipasto
apartheid
apéritif
après moi le déluge
a priori
à propos
a rivederci
arpeggio
arrière-pensée
au courant
au fait
auf Wiedersehen
au gratin
au jus
au lait
au revoir
aurora borealis
avant-garde

à votre santé

bas-relief
basso profundo
beurre manié
bidet
bizarre
blasé
bon
bona fide
bon appétit
bonhomie
bonjour
bon mot
bonne amie
bonne nuit
bon soir
bon vivant
bon voyage
bouillabaisse
bouillon
bouquet
bourgeois
boutique
bueno
buenos dias
buffet
buon giorno

cabaña
café au lait
café noir
camaraderie
canapé
carafe
carte blanche
caveat emptor
c'est à dire
chacun à son goût
chaise longue
challah
chapeau
château
Châteaubriand

chauffeur
chauvinist
chef
chef d'oeuvre
chemin de fer
cherchez la femme
chutzpah
ciao
claque
cliché
cogito ergo sum
coiffure
concierge
consommé
contretemps
coq au vin
cornucopia
corpus delicti
coup de grâce
coup de main
coup d'état
crèche
crème de la crème
crêpe
crêpe de Chine
crêpe suzette
crochet
crouton
crudités
crux
cuisine
cum laude

dashiki
début
débutante
décolleté
de facto
dégagé
de gustibus non est
  disputandum
Dei gratia
déjà vu
delicatessen

FOREIGN WORDS AND PHRASES

demitasse
démodé
dénouement
Deo gratias
Deo volente
de profundis
déshabillé
dies irae
Dios Mio
discothèque
double entendre

eau de Cologne
eau de vie
ecce homo
éclair
éclat
élite
en avant
en famille
enfant terrible
enfin
en masse
ennui
en papillote
en passant
en rapport
en route
ensemble
ensuite
entente cordiale
entourage
entrée
entrepreneur
en vérité
e pluribus unum
errare humanum est
ersatz
español
espièglerie
esprit de corps
etcetera
ex cathedra
excelsior

exempli gratia (e.g.)
ex libris
ex officio
extempore

fait accompli
faux pas
fête
fiat lux
fiesta
filet mignon
fils
finis
fleur-de-lis
frappé
Frau
Fräulein

garçon
gauche
gaucho
geisha
gendarme
genius loci
gesundheit
gigolo
glacé
Gloria in Excelsis
gourmand
gourmet
gradus ad Parnassum
grand prix
guten Tag

habeas corpus
hacienda
hasta la vista
hasta mañana
Herr
hic jacet
hoi polloi
honi soit qui mal y pense
hors de combat
hors de saison

hors d'oeuvres
hôtel de ville
hôtel Dieu

ibidem (ibid.)
ici on parle français
idée fixe
id est (i.e.)
incommunicado
in perpetuum
in saecula saeculorum
in toto
ipso facto

jinrikisha
jujitsu

Kyrie eleison

labor omnia vincit
laissez faire
laissez passer
lapis lazuli
lapsus linguae
lederhosen
l'état c'est moi
lex talionis
lingerie

ma chère
macho
madame
mademoiselle
magna cum laude
maître d'
maître d' hôtel
mal de mer
mañana
mann spricht Deutsch
Mardi gras
marquis
mens sana in corpore
   sano
meringue

FOREIGN WORDS AND PHRASES

mesdames
messieurs
modus operandi
modus vivendi
mon cher
monsieur
mousse
mutatis mutandis

naïve
née
negligée
n'est-ce pas?
noblesse oblige
nolle prosequi
nolo contendere
nom de plume
non compos mentis
non sequitur
nouveau riche
nouvelle
nyet

où sont les neiges d'antan

panache
par excellence
parfait
passé
pâté de foie gras
paterfamilias
paternoster
Pater Patriae
pax vobiscum
per capita
per se
persona non grata
petite
petit four

pièce de résistance
pied à terre
pomme de terre
potage
potpourri
prima facie
primus inter pares
pro bono publico
prosit
protégé
pro tempore

queue
quien sabe?

ragoût
raison d'état
Rathaus
rathskeller
régime
rendezvous
répondez s'il vous plaît
requiescat in pace
résumé
robe-de-chambre
rôle
rôtisserie

salade niçoise
sanctum sanctorum
sans pareil
sans souci
sauté
savoir-faire
séance
semper fidelis
señorita
sic semper tyrannis
siesta

signor
s'il vous plaît
sine die
sine qua non
skaal
soirée
sotto voce
soufflé
status quo
subpoena
sub rosa
summa cum laude
sursum corda

table d'hôte
Te Deum
tempus fugit
terra firma
tête-à-tête
tout à fait
tout de suite
tout ensemble

veni, vidi, vici
via media
vice versa
vignette
vinaigrette
vis-à-vis
viva voce
vive le roi
voici
voilà
vox clamantis in deserto
vox populi

wie geht's?

yente

GAMES OF CHANCE AND SKILL

Abaca
acey-deucey
Acquire
acrostics
Ad-Dic'tion
Africa Korps
Aggravation
Al Pha Bet
Anaconda
anagrams
Anzio
Apollo Moon Flight
Astro Blitz
auction bridge
authors
Avalanche
Avante

baccarat
backgammon
bagatelle
Bali
Battle of the Bulge
Battleship
Battle Stations
Bazaar
Beeline
bergen
Bewilder
bézique
biliards
bingo
Bismarck
blackjack
blindman's buff
Blitzkrieg
Blockade
Blockhead
Booby Trap
boodle
Botticelli
Breakthrou
bridge

calabrasella
canasta
canfield
Careers
carom
casino
categories
caterpillar
charades
checkers
chemin de fer
chess
chessboard
chinese checkers
Chutzpah
cinch
clabber
Clue
comet
concentration
Conestoga
Confrontation
conquian
contract bridge
coon-can
coronet
corral
Count Down
Coup d'Etat
crapette
craps
Credibility Gap
cribbage
croquet
crossword

deuces wild
dice
dictionary
Diplomacy
dominoes
dom pedro
draughts
draw poker

duck-on-the-rock
duckpins
duplicate bridge

écarté
eights
euchre

fan-tan
faro
fish
five hundred
five-card stud
Focus
Foil
forfeit
frincy-francy

Gambit
german solo
Gettysburg
ghosts
gin
Go for Broke
Go Gin
Guadalcanal
guggenheim
Guru

Hannibal
hasenpfeffer
hazard
hearts
high-lo-jack
Hoodwink
hopscotch
horseshoes
hurricane

I doubt it
Infinity
Info-mania
Insight
I spy

GAMES OF CHANCE AND SKILL

jackstraws
Jai Alai
jamboree
Jotto

Kalah
keno
kickapoo
Kismet
klaberjass
klob
klondike
knucklebones
Krypto

Lingo
lotto
lowball

macao
mah-jongg
Management
marbles
Marco Polo
matadors
Maze
Mercer
Monard
Money Game
Monopoly
Movie Moguls
Mr. President
mumbletypeg
musical chairs

napoleon
newmarket
Numble

Oh-Wah-Ree
old maid
old sledge
omnibus

pachisi
panguingue
Parcheesi
Parlement
patience
Pegity
Pendulum
Penetration
Perquackey
Personality
piñata
pinochle
piquet
pitch
poker
Pollyanna
Probe
Psycho-Paths
Pyramid

quotations
quoits

rainbow
Randoo
Recall
Recognition
red dog
Regatta
ring toss
Risk
Roll-A-Par
rook
roulette
Royalty
rubicon bezique
rummy
Russian bank

sardines
scavenger hunt
Scotch whist
Scrabble
Scribbage

sebastopol
Secrecy
seven-card stud
seven up
Shakespeare
sheepshead
shuffleboard
Situation
sixty-six
skat
skittle
slapjack
Sleuth
smudge
snapdragon
solitaire
Speculation
Spill and Spell
Spinado
spin the bottle
Splurge
Squander
Stalingrad
statues
Stock Market
Stocks and Bonds
straight poker
Stratego
Student Survival
stud poker
Swahili

tableau
Tangle
tenpins
tick-tack-toe
Tic Tac Tower
tiddlywinks
towie
Traffic
Transaction
Trapola
trictrac
Tri-Nim

GAMES OF CHANCE AND SKILL

Tri-Ominos	twenty-one	Waterloo
Triple Junction	Twix	WFF'n Proof
triumph		whist
Troke	Venture	Whodunit
Tuf	vingt-et-un	
Tumble Numble	Vocabulary	yacht
Tumble Words		Yahtze
	war	

HUMAN BODY

abdomen
abducens nerve
accessory
Achilles tendon
Adam's apple
adenoids
adipose tissue
adrenal
alimentary canal
alveoli
amniotic fluid
ankle
anus
aorta
appendix
areola
artery
atrium
auditory
auricle
axillary

belly
biceps
bicuspid
biliary ducts
birthmark
bladder
blood
brachial
brain
breast
breastbone
bronchi
bursa
buttocks

cadaver
canines
capillary
carotid
carpal bone
cartilage
cecum

celiac
cerebellum
cerebrospinal
cerebrum
cervical
cervix
chest
clavicle
clitoris
cloaca
coccyx
cochlea
cochlear duct
collarbone
colon
cornea
coronary
cranial cavity
cranium
crural

deltoid
dermis
diaphragm
digestive tract
disc
dorsal
duodenum

ear
eardrum
earlobe
ejaculatory duct
elbow
endocardium
endocrine glands
enzymes
epicardium
epidermis
epididymis
epiglottis
epithelium
esophagus
eustachian tube

eyeball
eyelashes
eye teeth
excretory system

facial
Fallopian tube
femoral
femur
fetus
fibula
finger
fingernail
follicle
forehead
foreskin
frontal bone

gallbladder
gastric juice
gastroduodenal
genitalia
glandular
glans
globules
glossopharyngeal
glottis
gluteus
gums

hair
hand
head
heart
heel
hemoglobin
hepatic duct
hipbone
humerus
hymen
hypoglossal

ileum
iliac artery

117

HUMAN BODY

incisors
incus
innominate
insulin
intercostal
intestine
iris

jaw
jejunum
joint
jugular

kidney
knee
knuckle

labia majora
labia minora
lachrymal glands
lactiferous ducts
latissimus dorsi
lens
lids
ligament
lips
liver
lumbar
lung
lymphatic
lymph nodes

malleus
mammary
mandible
masseter
mastoid
maxilla
medulla oblongata
megaloblast
metacarpal bone
metatarsal
mitral
molars

mouth
mucous membrane
muscle
myocardium

nasal turbinate
navel
neck
nerve
nipple
nostril

occipital bone
oculomotor
olfactory
optic
orbicularis oris
orbit
ossicle
ovarian follicle
ovary
oviduct
ovum

palate
pancreas
papillary
parathyroid glands
parietal bone
parotid gland
patella
pectoralis
pelvis
penis
periodontal
peritoneum
peroneus longus
perspiration
pharynx
pineal body
pinna
pituitary gland
placenta
plasma

pleura
pons
pore
portal vein
prostate
pubic hair
pubis
pulmonary
pupil
pyloric canal
pylorus

radial
radius
rectum
renal
retina
rib cage

sacral plexus
sacroiliac
sacrum
salivary glands
saphenous
sartorius
scala cochlea
scalp
scapula
scrotum
sebaceous glands
seminal vesicle
septum
shinbone
shoulder
sigmoid
sinus
skin
skull
soleus
spermatic cord
spermatozoon
sphincter
spinal cord
spleen

HUMAN BODY

stapes
sternum
stomach
subclavian
sublingual
submaxillary
sweat
sympathetic nerve
symphysis pubis

tarsal bone
taste buds
teeth
temporal bone
tendon
testicle
testis
thighbone
thoracic
thorax
throat
thumb

thymus
thyroid
tibia
toe
toenail
tongue
tonsil
trachea
transverse colon
trapezius
triceps
tricuspid valve
trigeminal
trochlear
tympanic membrane

ulna
umbilical cord
umbilicus
ureter
urethra
urinary tract

uterine
uterus
uvula

vagina
vagus
vas deferens
veins
vena cava
ventricle
venule
vertebra
vestibule
viscera
vulva

waist
windpipe
wisdom teeth
wishbone
womb
wrist

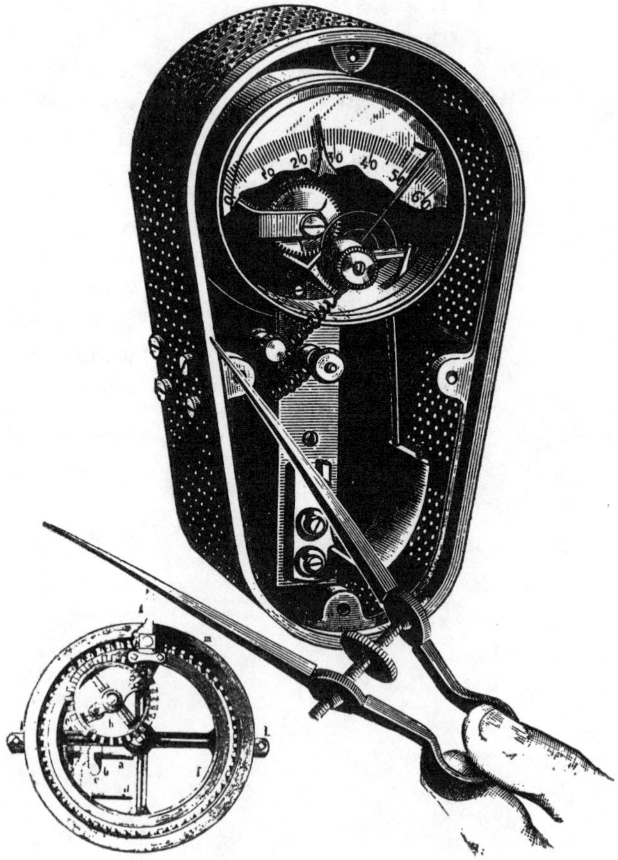
0 10 20 30 40 50 60

INSTRUMENTS FOR MEASURING, RECORDING, AND VIEWING

abacus
absorptiometer
accelerometer
acidimeter
acoumeter
actinograph
actinometer
adding machine
aerometer
aeroscope
aethrioscope
algometer
altimeter
altiscope
ammeter
amperemeter
anemograph
anemometer
anemoscope
aneroidograph
aneroid barometer
annunciator
arithmometer
astrolabe
astrometer
astroscope
atmidometer
atmometer
audiometer
auscultoscope
autoscope

balance
barograph
barometer
baroscope
bathometer
binocular
bioscope
bolometer
bronchoscope
brontograph
brontometer

calibrator
caliper
calorimeter
camera
cardiograph
cash register
chromatoscope
chromograph
chromometer
chromoscope
chronobarometer
chronograph
chronometer
chronoscope
clinometer
clock
coherer
colorimeter
colorimetric photometer
compass
computer
cyclometer
cyclonoscope
cymograph
cymoscope
cystoscope

declinograph
declinometer
dendrometer
densimeter
densitometer
dentiphone
detector
diagometer
diagrammeter
diagraph
dial
dichroscope
dipleidoscope
dipstick
divining rod
durometer

dynagraph
dynameter
dynamometer

electrocardiograph
electrodynamometer
electroencephalograph
electrograph
electrolytic hygrometer
electromagnet
electrometer
electron microscope
electron telescope
electroscope
embryoscope
endoscope
enteroscope
ergmeter
ergograph
ergometer
esophagoscope
extensometer

galvanometer
galvanoscope
gasometer
gauge
geodetist
geometer
glossograph
gnomon
goniometer
graphometer
gravimeter
gyrocompass
gyroscope
gyrostat

haploscope
heliometer
helioscope
hoppet
horoscope
hydrograph

INSTRUMENTS FOR MEASURING, RECORDING, AND VIEWING

hydrometer
hygrometer
hygroscope
hypsometer

indicator
inductometer
inductophone
inductoscope
interferometer
iris diaphragm
iriscope

kaleidoscope
kinetoscope
knockometer
koniscope
kymograph

lactometer
lactoscope
lead
level
log

macrometer
magnetograph
magnetometer
magnetophone
magnetoscope
manometer
measuring cup
meter
metrograph
metronome
microammeter
microbarograph
microdensitometer
micrograph
micrometer
micronometer
microphone
microphotometer
microscope

microtome
milliammeter
monochromator

nephelometer
nephelorometer
nepheloscope
nephoscope

odometer
odontoscope
ohmmeter
oleometer
ooscope
ophthalmoscope
optigraph
optometer
optophone
oscilloscope
otoscope

pantoscope
pantometer
pedometer
pendulum
perambulator
periscope
phacometer
phago-dynamometer
phantascope
pharyngoscope
phenakistoscope
philograph
phonautograph
phonendoscope
phonograph
phonoscope
phorometer
photometer
photoscope
planimeter
plastometer
plumb line
pluvioscope

polariscope
potentiometer
precipitation gauge
psychrometer
pulsimeter
pycnometer
pyrometer
pyrophotometer
pyroscope

quadrant
quantometer

radar
radarscope
radio beacon
radio compass
radiometer
radioscope
radiosonde
radio telescope
rain gauge
recorder
retinoscope
rheometer
rheoscope
rocketsonde
rod
roentgenoscope
ruler

saccharimeter
scale
seismograph
seismometer
seismoscope
selenoscope
semaphore
sensitometer
sextant
sideroscope
sniperscope
spectograph
spectrophone

INSTRUMENTS FOR MEASURING, RECORDING, AND VIEWING

spectroscope
speedometer
spherometer
spirograph
spirometer
stabilizer
stereoscope
stethoscope
stopwatch
stroboscope
surveyor
synchroscope

tachistoscope
tachometer
tape

taximeter
telemeter
telescope
thermobarometer
thermograph
thermometer
thermophone
thermophore
thermopile
thermoregulator
thermoscope
thermostat
ticket tape
T square

ureometer

vitascope
voltmeter

watch
water clock
wattmeter
weatherglass
wire recorder

X-ray spectrometer

yardstick

ymometer
ymoscope

ISLANDS

Adak
Admiralty Is.
Aland (Ahvenanmaa)
Alcatraz
Alderney
Aleutian Is.
Amchitka
Andaman Is.
Andros
Anglesey
Anguilla
Anticosti
Antigua
Antilles
Apostle Is.
Aquidneck (Rhode I.)
Aran Is.
Aruba
Ascension
Attu
Awaji
Axel Heiberg I.
Azores

Baffin I.
Bahamas
Bahrein
Bainbridge I.
Balearic Is.
Bali
Bangka
Barbados
Barbuda
Bathurst I.
Beaver I.
Belitung
Bermuda
Bikini
Bioko (Fernando Poo)
Block I.
Bonaire
Borneo (Kalimantan)
Bornholm
Bougainville

Campobello
Canary Is.
Canton I.
Cape Breton I.
Cape Verde Is.
Capri
Caroline Is.
Cayman Is.
Cebu
Celebes (Sulawesi)
Ceram
Ceylon (Sri Lanka)
Channel Is.
Chatham I.
Cheju
Chincoteague I.
Chios
Christmas I.
Comoro Is.
Cook Is.
Corfu (Kerkira)
Corsica (Corse)
Cos
Cozumel
Crete
Cuba
Curacao
Cyclades
Cyprus
Cythera

Dauphin I.
Devon I.
Djerba
Dodecanese
Dominica
Dry Tortugas

Easter I. (Isla de Pascua)
Elba
Eleuthera
Ellesmere I.
Enewetok
Euboea

Falkland Is.
Farne Is.
Faroe Is.
Fiji
Fire I.
Fishers I.
Flores
Florida Keys
Formosa (Taiwan)
Franz Josef Land
Frisian Islands
Fuerteventura
Fyn

Galápagos Is.
Gilbert Is.
Gotland
Gozo
Gran Canaria
Grand Bahama
Grand Manan
Great Britain
Greenland
Grenada
Grenadines, The
Guadalcanal
Guadeloupe
Guam
Guernsey

Hainan
Haiti
Halmahera
Hawaii
Hawaiian Is.
Hebrides (Inner and Outer)
Heimaey
Helgoland
Hilton Head I.
Hispaniola
Hokkaido
Hong Kong
Honshu

ISLANDS

Ibiza
Iceland
Iona
Ionian Is.
Ireland
Ischia
Isle of Pines (Isla de la Juventud)
Isle Royale
Iwo Jima

Jamaica
Japan
Java (Jawa)
Jersey
Juan Fernández

Kanaga
Kangaroo I.
Kauai
Key Largo
Kiska
Kodiak
Kuril Is.
Kwajalein
Kyushu

Labuan
Leeward Is.
Lesbos
Leyte
Lipari Is.
Lofoten Is.
Lombok
Long Island
Loyalty Is.
Lundy I.
Luzon

Mackinac I.
Madagascar
Madeira
Madura
Majorca (Mallorca)

Maldives
Malta
Manhattan
Man, Isle of
Manitoulin
Manus
Marajó
Mariana Is.
Marie-Galante
Marquesas
Marshall Is.
Martha's Vineyard
Martinique
Maui
Mauritius
Melville I.
Menorca
Midway Is.
Mindanao
Mindoro
Miquelon
Molokai
Moluccas (Maluku)
Montserrat
Mount Desert I.

Nantucket
Nauru
Naxos
Negros
Nevis
New Britain
New Caledonia
Newfoundland
New Guinea
New Hebrides
New Ireland
New Providence
New Zealand (North and South Islands)
Nicobar Is.
Niue
Norfolk I.
Novaya Zemlya

Oahu
Ocean I.
Okinawa
Orcas I.
Orkney Is.

Padre I.
Palau Is.
Palawan
Panay
Pantelleria
Pemba
Penang
Philippines
Pitcairn I.
Ponape
Pribilof Is.
Prince Edward I.
Prince of Wales I.
Puerto Rico

Queen Charlotte Is.
Quemoy (Chinmen)

Rarotonga
Réunion
Rhodes
Rügen
Ryukyu Is.

Saaremaa
Saba
Sable I.
Sado
Saint-Barthélemy
St. Croix
St. Eustatius
St. Helena
St. Kitts (St. Christopher)
St. Lawrence I.
St. Lucia
Saint-Pierre
St. Simons I.

ISLANDS

St. Thomas	South Orkney Is.	Tsushima
St. Vincent	South Shetland Is.	Tuamotu
Saipan	Spitsbergen (Svalbard)	Tutuila
Sakhalin	Sporades	
Salamis	Staten Island	Umnak
Samar	Stewart I.	Unalaska
Samoa	Stromboli	Unimak
Samos	Sulu Archipelago	Upolu
Samothrace	Sumatra (Sumatera)	
San Juan Is.	Sumbawa	Vancouver I.
Santa Catalina	Svalbard (Spitsbergen)	Vanua Levu
São Tomé	Sylt	Vashon I.
Sardinia (Sardegna)		Victoria I.
Sark	Tahiti	Virgin Is.
Savaii	Taiwan	Visayan Is.
Scilly Is.	Tanaga	Viti Levu
Sea Islands	Tarawa	
Seychelles	Tasmania	Wake I.
Shelter I.	Tenerife	Washington I.
Shetland Is.	Thera	West Indies
Shikoku	Thursday I.	Whidbey I.
Sicily (Sicilia)	Tierra del Fuego	Wight, Isle of
Singapore	Timor	Windward Is.
Skye	Tinian	Wrangel I.
Society Is.	Tobago	
Socotra	Tonga	Yap
Somerset I.	Trinidad	
Southampton I.	Tristan da Cunha	Zanzibar
South Georgia	Truk	Zeeland (Sjaelland)

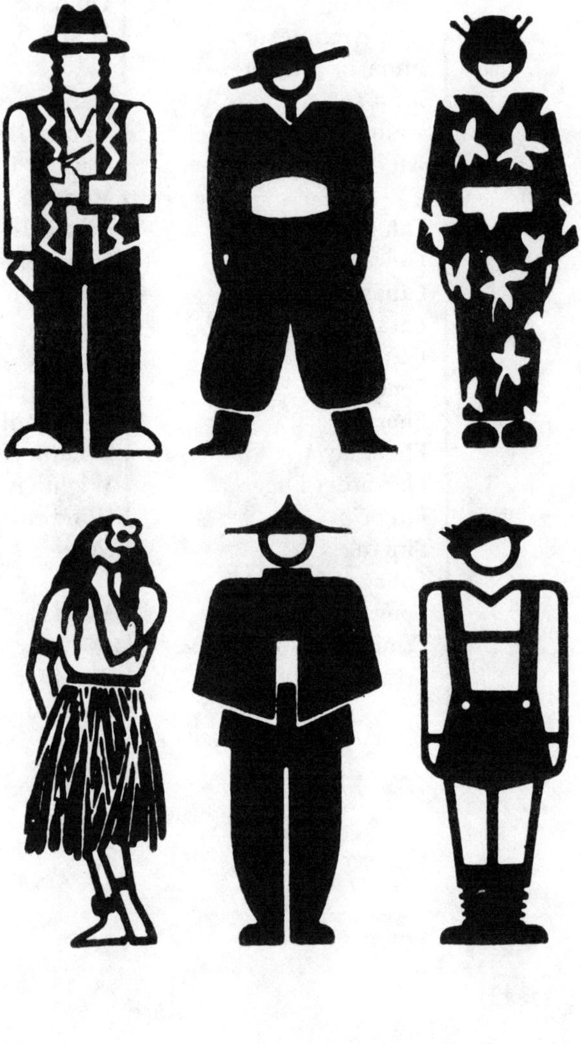

LANGUAGES

Abkhaz	Cambodian (Khmer)	Gaelic
Afrikaans	Cantonese	Galician
Ainu	Carib	Ganda (Luganda)
Akan (Twi)	Catalan	Gbaya
Akkadian	Cebuano	Georgian
Albanian	Chechen	German
Aleut	Cherokee	Gondi
Amharic	Chewa	Gothic
Anyi	Chibcha	Greek
Apache	Chin	Guaraní
Arabic	Chinese	Gujarati
Aramaic	Chokwe	Gullah
Armenian	Chuvash	
Assamese	Coptic	Hakka
Aymara	Cornish	Hausa
Azerbaijani	Czech	Hawaiian
		Hebrew
Bahasa Indonesia	Danish	Hindi
(Indonesian)	Dayak	Hindustani
Balinese	Dinka	Hittite
Baluchi	Dutch	Ho
Bamileke		Hopi
Bandi	Efik	Hottentot
Bantu	Egyptian	Hungarian
Bashkir	English	
Basque	Eskimo	Ibibio
Batak	Esperanto	Ibo (Igbo)
Baule	Estonian	Icelandic
Bemba	Etruscan	Ijo
Bengali	Ewe	Ilocano
Berber		Interlingua
Bhili	Fante	Irish (Irish Gaelic)
Bhotia	Faroese	Italian
Bihari	Fijian	
Bikol	Finnish	Japanese
Bodo	Flemish	Javanese
Brahui	Fon	
Breton	French	Kabardian (Circassian)
Bugi	Frisian	Kachin
Bulgarian	Friulian	Kafiri
Burmese	Fukienese	Kalenjin
Buryat	Fula (Peul)	Kalmyk
Bushman	Fulani	Kamba (Kikamba)
Byelorussian	Ful	Kanarese (Kannada)

LANGUAGES

Kanuri
Karelian
Kashmiri
Kazakh
Khalkha
Kherwari
Kikongo
Kikuyu
Kimbundu
Kirghiz
Komi (Zyryan)
Kongo
Konkani
Korean
Krio
Kuki
Kurdish
Kurukh (Oranon)

Lango
Lao
Lapp
Latin
Lettish (Latvian)
Lithuanian
Livonian
Loko
Luba (Chiluba)
Luhya
Lunda
Luo (Acholi)
Luri

Macedonian
Madurese
Makonde
Makua
Malagasy
Malay
Malayalam
Malinke
Maltese
Manchu
Mandarin

Mandingo (Bambara)
Manx
Maori
Marathi
Mari (Cheremis)
Masai
Maya
Mbundu (Kimbundu)
Mende
Miao
Micmac
Mina
Mishmi
Mixtec
Mohawk
Moldavian
Mon
Mongo
Mordvinian
More
Mossi
Mundari
Muong
Murmi

Naga
Nahuatl
Navaho
Ndebele
Nepalese (Nepali)
Newari
Ngala (Lingala)
Nkundo
Norwegian
Nubian
Nyamwezi
Nyanja

Ojibwa
Oriya
Oromo (Galla)
Ossetic
Otomi

Pahari
Papiamento
Persian (Farsi)
Pilipino (Tagalog)
Polish
Portuguese
Provençal
Punjabi
Pushtu (Afghan)

Quechua
Quiché

Rajasthani
Romansh
Romany (Gypsy)
Ruanda
Rumanian (Romanian)
Rundi
Russian
Rwanda

Samoan
Samoyed
Sango
Sanskrit
Santali
Sardinian
Scottish (Scottish Gaelic)
Senufo
Serbo-Croatian
Sesotho
Shan
Shona
Sindhi
Singhalese
Slovak
Slovenian (Slovene)
Somali
Songhai
Sorbian (Lusatian)
Sotho
Spanish
Sukuma

LANGUAGES

Sumerian	Tigre	Vai
Sundanese	Tigrinyna	Vietnamese
Swahili	Tiv	Visayan
Swazi	Tongan	Volapük
Swedish	Tsonga	
Syriac	Tswana	Welsh
	Tulu	Wolof
Tahitian	Tupí	Wu
Tajiki	Turkish	
Tamil	Turkoman	Xhosa
Tatar		
Telugu		Yao
Temne	Udmurt (Votyak)	Yiddish
Teso	Uighur	Yoruba
Thai (Siamese)	Ukrainian	
Thonga	Umbundu	Zande
Tibetan	Urdu	Zapotec
	Uzbek	Zulu

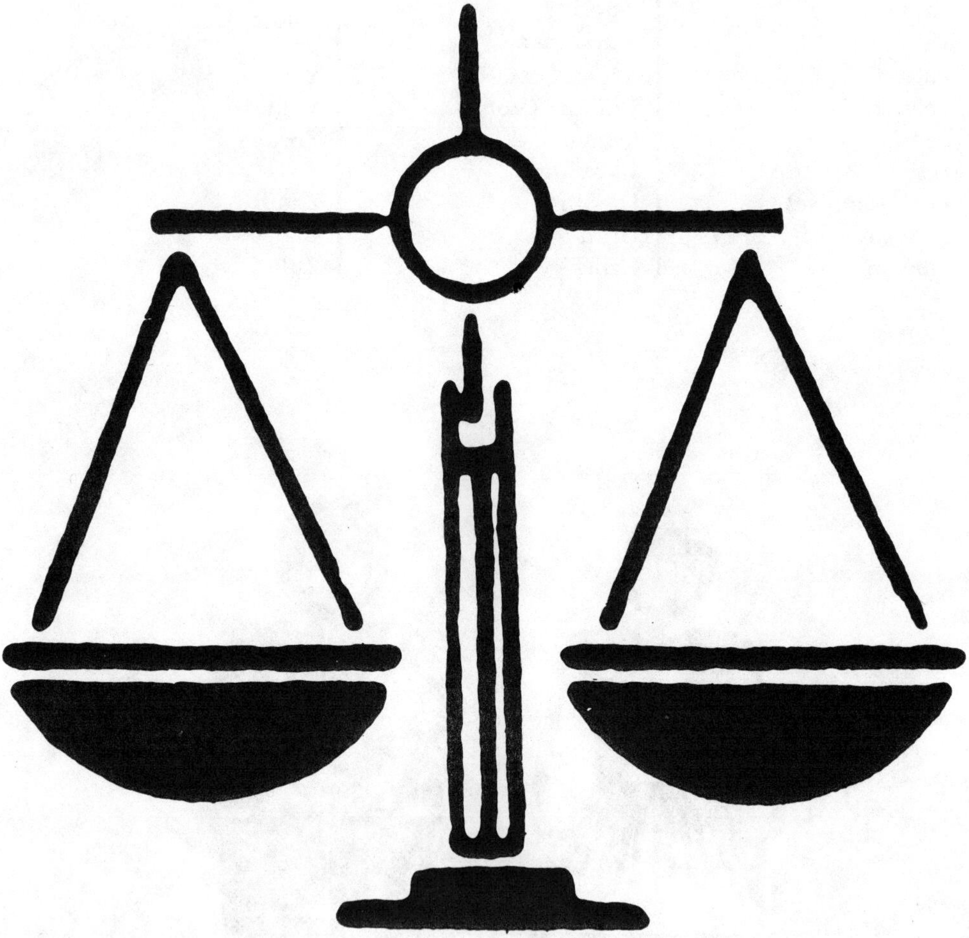

LAW

abandonment
abet
abeyance
abrogate
abscond
anbuttal
accessory
accomplice
accrue
acquittal
adjudicate
adultery
advocate
affidavit
alias
alibi
alimony
allegation
amalgamation
amicus curiae
annuitant
annuity
annulment
appeal
appellate
appellee
apprehend
appurtenance
a priori
arbitration
arraign
arrears
assault
assignor
attachment
attestation
attorney

bail
bailiff
bankruptcy
battery
bequeath

bigamy
bona fide
breach of contract
brief
burglary
bylaw

calendar
capitalization
cartel
caveat emptor
certified
chattel
circuit
clemency
codicil
cognizance
collusion
common law
complainant
condemnation
confession
confidential
conglomerate
consanguinity
consent
consignee
consolidation
conspiracy
contempt
copartnership
copyright
corespondent
coroner
corporation
corpus delicti
corpus juris
correspondent
counsel
counselor
covenant
creditor
cross-examination
custody

decedent
decree
deed
de facto
defamation
default
defendant
defraud
de jure
demise
demurrer
deponent
detainer
disclaimer
disclosure
disseise
dissipate
divestiture
divorce
docket
domicile
dower
duress

earnest
easement
elopement
embezzlement
eminent domain
endorse
endorsee
endorsement
endorser
equity
escrow
estoppel
executor
executrix
extempore
extortion
extradition

false pretense
felony

133

LAW

fiduciary
foreclosure
forgery
franchise
fraud
fraudulent

garnishment
grand larceny
grievance
guaranty
guardian

habeas corpus
heir
homicide

impanel
impeach
incorporeal
indemnity
indenture
indictment
infringement
inheritance
injunction
inquest
insolvent
interrogatory
intestate
ipso facto

jeopardy
joint tenants
judgment
judicial writ
jurisdiction
jurisprudence
jury

kidnaping

larceny
lease

legatee
legislation
lessee
lessor
liability
libel
license
lien
liquidation
litigation

malfeasance
malice
mandamus
mediation
merger
misdemeanor
modus operandi
monopoly
mortgage
mortgagee
mortgagor

negligence
negotiable
nolle prosequi
non sequitur
notary public
novation

obligee
obligor
option
outlawed

parole
partnership
patent
penal
perjury
persona grata
plagiarism
plaintiff
plea

power of attorney
precedents
prima facie
probate
promissory note
prosecute
pro tempore
protocol
proxy
punitive damages

quasi contract
quitclaim
quorum

ransom
ratification
real estate
receiver
recognizance
referee
regulation
rescission of contracts
residuary estate
respondent
restitution
retainer
royalty

search warrant
sheriff
sine die
sine qua non
slander
solvency
statute of limitations
subpoena
subrogation
subsidiary
summons
surrogate
syndicate
syndication

LAW

talesman	trademark	venue
tenant	trespass	verdict
tender	trustee	vest
tenement		voluntary conveyance
testament	underwriter	
testator	usury	waiver
testatrix		warrant
testimony	vagrancy	warranty
theft	vendee	without recourse
title	vendor	writ
tort	venire	writ of error

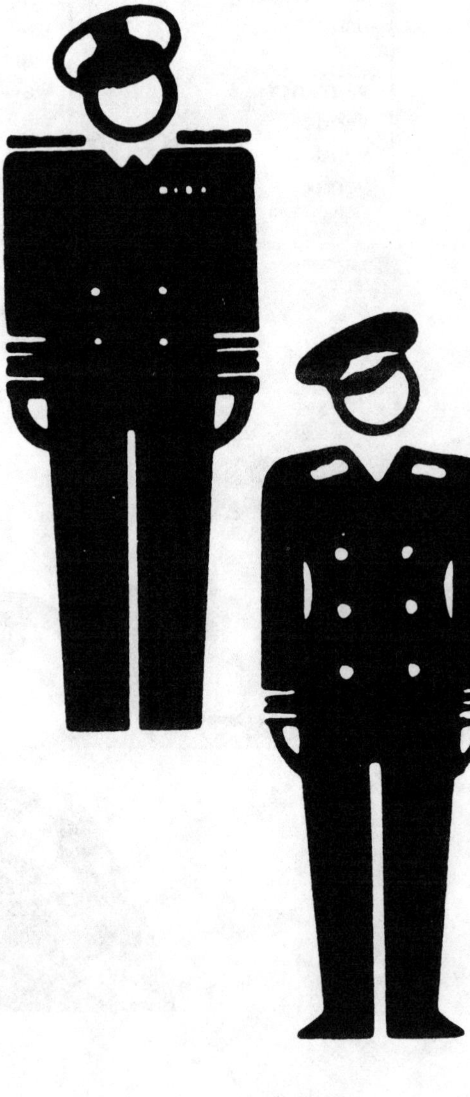

MILITARY AND NAVAL LEADERS

Abercrombie, James
Abrams, Creighton
Abruzzi, Duke of the
Adherbal
Aemilius
Aetius
Agricola
Agrippa, Marcus
Aguinaldo, Emilio
Akbar
Alcibiades
Alexander, Harold R.
Alexander Nevsky
Alexander the Great
Allen, Ethan
Allenby, Sir Edmund
Alva, Duke of
Alvarado, Pedro de
Amherst, Jeffrey
Anderson, Sir John
Anson, George
Antigonus
Antiochus
Antonius, Marcus
 (Mark Antony)
Arminius
Arnold, Benedict
Arnold, Henry H. (Hap)
Attila
Augustus

Baber
Barbarossa, Frederick
Barclay de Tolly,
 Mikhail
Barry, John
Batista y Zaldívar,
 Fulgencio
Beatty, David
Beauregard, Pierre
Belisarius
Blücher, Gebhard von
Bolívar, Simón
Bonaparte, Napoleon

Boulanger, Georges
Bourbon, Charles de
Boyle, William
Braddock, Edward
Bradley, Omar
Bragg, Braxton
Brauchitsch, Heinrich
 Alfred von
Brooke, Sir Alan
Broz, Josip (Tito)
Bruce, Robert
Brutus, Marcus Junius
Budënny, Semën
Buford, John
Bulganin, Nikolai
Bülow, Friedrich
 Wilhelm von
Burgoyne, John
Burnside, Ambrose
Byng, George

Caesar, Gaius Julius
Caligula
Camillus, Marcus
Cassius Longinus
Cavendish, William
Charlemagne (Charles I)
Chennault, Claire
Chiang Kai-shek
Christison, Sir Philip
Churchill, Winston
Cid, El
Cimon
Clausewitz, Karl von
Clay, Lucius
Clinton, Henry
Clive, Robert
Clovis
Constantine I
Cornwallis, Charles
Cortes, Hernando
Crazy Horse
Cromwell, Oliver

Custer, George A.
Cyrus

D'Annunzio, Gabriele
Darius
Darlan, Jean Louis
Dayan, Moshe
Decatur, Stephen
Decebalus
De Gaulle, Charles
De Grasse, Francois
Dempsey, Miles C.
Denikin, Anton
Dewey, George
Díaz, Armando
Doenitz, Karl
Donskoi, Dmitri
Doolittle, James
Dowding, Hugh C.
Drake, Francis

Early, Jubal A.
Easley, G.M.
Eichelberger, Robert
Eisenhower, Dwight D.
Ellington, Edward
Esarhaddon
Eugene of Savoy

Fabius Maximus
Farragut, David
Fisher, John Arbuthnot
Flaminius
Foch, Ferdinand
Forbes, John
Forrest, Nathan Bedford
Franco, Francisco
Frederick the Great

Gage, Thomas
Galba
Garibaldi, Giuseppe
Gasparri, Pietro
Gates, Horatio

MILITARY AND NAVAL LEADERS

Genghis Khan
Geronimo
Gneisenau, August von
Goering, Hermann
Gordon, Charles
Grant, Ulysses S.
Graziani, Rodolfo
Greene, Nathanael
Grenville, Richard
Gruenther, Alfred
Guderian, Heinz
Gustavus Adolphus
Gustavus Vasa

Haig, Douglas
Halleck, Henry
Halsey, William F.
Hamilcar Barca
Hamilton, Ian
Hammurabi
Hampton, Wade
Hannibal
Harold II of England
Harold Hardrada
Harris, Sir Arthur
Hastings, Francis
Hatshepsut
Hertzog, James Barry
Hindenburg, Paul von
Hipper, Franz
Hitler, Adolf
Hodges, C.H.
Hooker, Joseph
Horthy, Miklós
Howe, Richard
Howe, William
Hudson, Henry
Hulagu
Humphrey, Noel

Ironside, William Edmund

Jackson, Thomas (Stonewall)

Jehu
Jellicoe, John
Jeroboam
Joan of Arc
Jodl, Alfred
Johnston, Albert Sidney
Joffre, Joseph
Jones, John Paul
Judas Maccabaeus
Julian the Apostate

Kalb, Baron de
Kearny, Philip
Keitel, Wilhelm
Kesselring, Albert
King, Ernest Joseph
Kinkaid, Thomas
Kitchener, Horatio Herbert
Kluck, Alexander von
Kluge, Gunther von
Kolchak, Aleksandr
Konev, Ivan
Kornilov, Lavr
Kosciusko, Thaddeus
Kublai Khan
Kuribayashi, Tadamichi
Kutuzov, Mikhail
Kuznetsov, Nikolai

Lafayette, Marquis de
Lawrence, James
Lawrence, Thomas Edward (of Arabia)
Leahy, William D.
Leclerc, Jacques
Lee, Charles
Lee, Fitzhugh
Lee, Henry (Lighthorse Harry)
Lee, Robert E.
Leonidas
Longstreet, James
Lucius Tarquinius Priscus

Luckner, Felix von
Lucullus
Ludendorff, Erich
Luxembourg, François de
Lysander

MacArthur, Douglas
Macbeth
Mackensen, August von
Mangin, Charles Marie
Manstein, Erich von
Mao Tse-tung
Marlborough, John Churchill (Duke of)
Marshall, George C.
Martel, Charles
McAuliffe, Anthony
McClellan, George B.
Meade, George G.
Mikhailovich, Draja
Miltiades
Mitchell, William (Billy)
Mithridates
Mitscher, Mark
Model, Walter
Moltke, Helmuth von
Montcalm, Louis de
Montgomery, Bernard Law
Morgan, Daniel
Morgan, John Hunt
Moultrie, William
Mountbatten, Louis
Muhammad Ahmed
Murat, Joachim

Napier, Charles
Napier, Robert
Narses
Nebuchadnezzar
Nelson, Horatio
Nevsky, Alexander
Ney, Michel
Nimitz, Chester
Nivelle, Robert

MILITARY AND NAVAL LEADERS

Oglethorpe, James
Oyama, Iwao

Patton, George S.
Pericles
Perry, Matthew
Perry, Oliver H.
Pershing, John J.
Petain, Henri Philippe
Peter I, the Great
Philip Augustus
Philip II of Macedon
Pickett, George
Pisistratus
Pizarro, Francisco
Pompey
Pontiac
Potëmkin, Grigori
Powhatan
Ptolemy
Pulaski, Casimir
Pyrrhus

Radetzky, Joseph
Radford, Arthur
Raeder, Erich
Ramses
Rawlings, Sir Bernard
Razin, Stepan (Stenka)
Richard I, the Lion-Hearted
Rickenbacker, Edward Vernon
Rickover, Hyman
Ridgway, Matthew
Rodney, George
Rommel, Erwin

Rundstedt, Karl Rudolf Gerd von

Saladin
Sampson, William
Samsonov, Aleksandr
San Martin, José
Santa Anna, Antonio López de
Santander, Francisco
Sargon II
Saxe, Maurice de
Scipio, Publius
Scobie, Ronald
Scott, Winfield
Sennacherib
Shamshi-adad
Sheridan, Philip
Sherman, William T.
Sims, William
Simpson, William Hood
Slim, Sir William
Solomon
Solon
Spaatz, Carl
Spartacus
Spruance, Raymond
Steuben, Friedrich Wilhelm von
Stilwell, Joseph W.
Stuart, J.E.B. (Jeb)
Stülpnagel, Otto von
Sulla, Lucius
Sullivan, John
Supiluliu
Suvorov, Aleksandr

Tamerlane (Timur)
Taylor, Zachary
Tecumseh
Tedder, Sir Arthur
Themistocles
Theodosius
Thomas, George H.
Tiberius
Tiglath-pileser III
Tilly, Johann von
Timoshenko, Semën
Tirpitz, Alfred von
Tito (see Broz)
Togo, Heihachiro
Tojo, Hideki
Trajan

Vandenberg, Hoyt
Vercingetorix
Voroshilov, Kliment

Wainwright, Jonathan
Wallenstein, Albrecht von
Washington, George
Wavell, Archibald
Wayne, Anthony
Wellington, Arthur Wellesley (Duke of)
William I (the Conqueror)
Wolfe, James

Xerxes

Ypsilanti, Alexander

Zhukov, Georgi

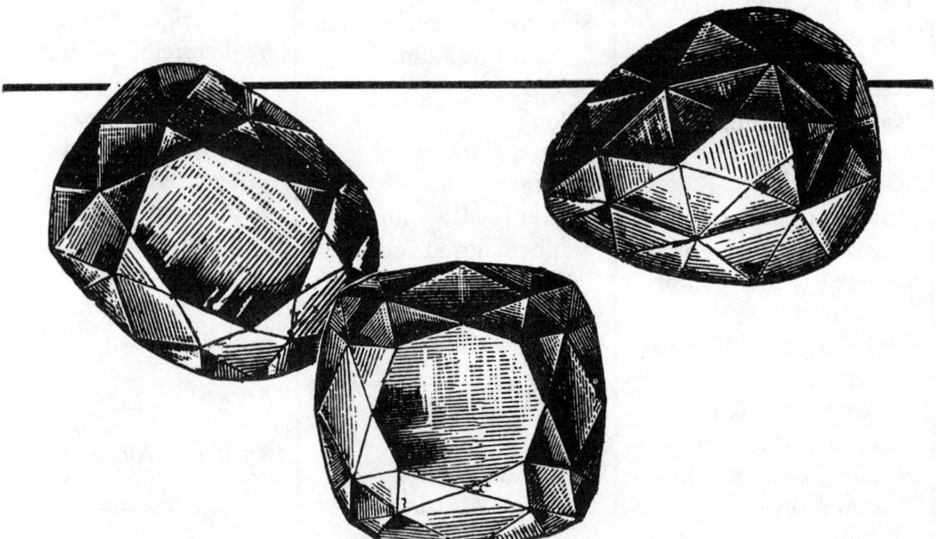

MINERALS, GEMS, AND ROCKS
(Chemical Elements are Listed Separately)

adamantine
adamite
agate
alabaster
albite
alexandrite
aluminum
amber
amethyst
amphibole
amphibolite
andalusite
andesite
andradite
anorthite
antimony
apatite
apophyllite
aquamarine
aragonite
argentite
arkose
arsenic
arsenopyrite
asbestos
ash
asphalt
augite
aurichalcite
axinite
azurite

barite
barium
basalt
bauxite
beryl
biotite
bismuth
bitumen
black opal
bloodstone
borax
breccia

calaverite
calcite
carnelian
carnotite
cassiterite
cat's-eye
celestite
cerargyrite
cerussite
chabazite
chalcanthite
chalcedony
chalcocite
chalcopyrite
chalk
chert
chondrite
chromite
chrysoberyl
chrysocolla
chrysolite
chrysoprase
cinnabar
citrine
clay
cobalt
cobaltite
colemanite
conglomerate
copper
cordierite
corundum
cristobalite
cryolite
cuprite
cyanite

demantoid
diamond
diaspore
diopside
diorite
dolerite
dolomite

emerald
enstatite
epidote
erythrite

feldspar
fire opal
fluorite

gabbro
galena
garnet
glacial ice
gneiss
gold
granite
granulite
graphite
gravel
graywacke
grossularite
gypsum

halite
harlequin opal
hematite
hornblende
hornfels

ilmenite
iron

jade
jasper
jet

kaolinite
kernite
kunzite
kyanite

lapis lazuli
lazulite
lazurite

141

MINERALS, GEMS, AND ROCKS

leucite
limestone
limonite
lodestone

magnetite
malachite
manganite
marble
marcasite
meerschaum
mica
microcline
millerite
millstone grit
mimetite
molybdenum
molybdenite
moonstone
morganite
muscovite

natrolite
nepheline
nickel

obsidian
onyx
opal
orthoclase

paraffin
pearl
pectolite
peridot
petroleum
phlogopite
phyllite
pitchblende

plagioclase
planoferrite
platinum
prehnite
proustite
psilomelane
pyrargyrite
pyrite
pyrope
pyroxene
pyrrhotite

quartz
quartzite

realgar
rhodonite
rhyolite
rose quartz
ruby
ruby spinel
rutile

salt
sandstone
sapphire
sard
sardonyx
scheelite
schist
serpentine
shale
siderite
silica
sillimanite
silver
slate
smithsonite
soapstone

sodalite
spessartite
sphaerite
sphalerite
spodumene
star sapphire
staurolite
stibnite
stilbite
sulfur
sylvanite
sylvite

tactite
talc
tetrahedrite
tiger's-eye
topaz
tourmaline
tremolite
tridymite
tuff
turquoise

ulexite
uraninite
uvarovite

vanadinite
variscite

water
wolframite
wollastonite
wulfenite

zaratite
zeolite
zircon

MOUNTAINS AND RANGES

Aconcagua
Adirondack Mountains
Ahaggar Mountains
Alphubel
Alps
Altai Mountains
Ancohuma
Andes Mountains
Aneto, Pico de
Annapurna
Apennines (Appennino)
Api
Apo
Appalachian Mountains
Ararat (Agri)
Ardennes
Athos
Atlas Mountains

Badrinath
Bandeira, Pico da
Batu
Bear
Ben Nevis
Bernina
Bierstadt
Big Horn Mountains
Black Forest
 (Schwarzwald)
Black Hills
Blanc, Mont
Blanca Peak
Bolívar
Breithorn
Brooks Range

Cameroun
Carmel (HarKarmel)
Carpathian Mountains
Cascade Range
Castor
Caucasus Mountains
 (Kavkaz)
Chimborazo

Cho Oyu
Clingman's Dome
Coast Mountains
Colima
Cook
Cotopaxi
Crestone Peak
Cristóbal Colón

Damavand
Dent Blanche
Dhaulagiri
Drakensberg

Egmont
Eiger
Elbert
Elbrus
Elburz Mountains
Elgon
Erebus
Etna (Mongibello)
Evans
Everest (Zhumulangma)

Finsteraarhorn
Foraker
Front Range
Fuji

Gannett Peak
Gardiner
Gasherbrum
Ghats
Godwin Austen (K2)
Grand Teton
Gran Paradiso
Great Dividing Range
Great Smoky Mountains
Green Mountains
Grizzly
Grossglockner
Grunhorn
Guna

Haleakala
Handies Peak
Harz
Hekla
Hermon
Himalaya Mountains
Hindu Kush
Hood
Huandoy
Huascarán
Huila
Humboldt

Illampu
Irazú
Ixtacihuatl

Jagerhorn
Jaya
Jongsang
Jungfrau

Kamet
Kanchenjunga
Karakoram Range
Karisimbi
Kashtan
Katahdin
Kazbek
Kenya (Kirinyaga)
Kerinci
Kilimanjaro
Kinabalu
Kommunizma, Pik
Kosciusko
Kunlun Mountains

La Plata
Lassen Peak
Lauteraarhorn
Llullaillaco
Logan
Longs Peak
Lucania

143

MOUNTAINS AND RANGES

Makalu
Marcy
Margherita Peak
Massive
Matterhorn
Mauna Kea
Mauna Loa
Mayon
McKinley (Denali)
Mercedario
Minya Konka
Mitchell
Mönch
Mont Blanc
Monte Rosa
Mulhacen

Nadelhorn
Nanda Devi
Nanga Parbat

Ojos del Salado
Olympic Mountains
Olympus (Olimbos)
Orizaba (Citlaltépetl)
Ouachita Mountains
Ouray
Owen Stanley Range
Ozark Plateau

Pamir
Parícutin
Parnassos (Parnassus)
Pelée
Perdido
Pidurutalagala
Pikes Peak
Pissis
Popocatépetl
Presidential Range
Pyramid Peak

Pyrenees

Quandary Peak

Rainier
Rakaposhi
Ras Dashen
Rhodope Mountains
Rimpfischhorn
Rocky Mountains

St. Elias
St. Helens
Sajama
San Gorgonio
Sangre de Cristo
  Mountains
San Juan Mountains
Sayan Mountains
Semeru
Serra da Estrela
Serra do Mar
Serra Pacaraima
Serra Parima
Shasta
Shavano
Shkhara
Sierra Blanca Peak
Sierra de Córdoba
Sierra de Gredos
Sierra de Guadarrama
Sierra Leone
Sierra Madre
Sierra Morena
Sierra Nevada
Sierra Nevada de Santa
  Marta
Sinai (Jabal Musa)
Snaefell
Snowdon
Snowmass

Soufrière
Steele
Sudeten Mountains

Tabeguache
Tajumulco
Taschhorn
Taurus Mountains
  (Toros)
Teide, Pico de
Tibesti Mountains
Tien Shan
Tirich Mir
Toubkal
Tres Cruces
Trikora
Tupungato
Tyndall

Uinta Mountains
Uncompahgre Peak

Vancouver
Vesuvius (Vesuvio)
Vignemale
Vindhya Range
Vinson Massif
Vosges

Wasatch Range
Washington
Weisshorn
Wetterhorn
White Mountains
Whitney
Wilhelm
Wrangell

Zagros
Zugspitze

MUSIC—Composers

Abel, Carl Friedrich
Adam, Adolphe
Ager, Milton
Agostini, Pietro
Albéniz, Isaac
Alfano, Franco
Allegri, Gregorio
Antheil, George
Arensky, Anton
Arlen, Harold
Arne, Thomas
Attwood, Thomas
Auber, Daniel
Austin, Frederick
Ayer, Jakob

Bach, Johann Christian
Bach, Johann Sebastian
Bach, Karl Philipp
  Emanuel
Bach, Wilhelm
  Friedemann
Balakirev, Mili
Balfe, Michael
Ball, Ernest
Barber, Samuel
Bartók, Béla
Bax, Arnold
Beach, Amy
Beethoven, Ludwig van
Bellini, Vincenzo
Bennett, Robert Russell
Berg, Alban
Berio, Luciano
Berlin, Irving
Berlioz, Hector
Bernstein, Leonard
Biber, Heinrich von
Billings, William
Bizet, Georges
Bland, James A.
Bliss, Sir Arthur
Bloch, Ernest
Blow, John

Boccherini, Luigi
Bock, Jerry
Boieldieu, François
Boito, Arrigo
Bond, Carrie Jacobs
Borodin, Alexander
Bossi, Marco Enrico
Boyce, William
Brahms, Johannes
Bretón, Tomás
Bridge, Frank
Britten, Benjamin
Brown, Herb
Bruch, Max
Bruckner, Anton
Bruneau, Alfred
Bull, John
Burke, Joe
Burleigh, Henry T.
Busoni, Ferruccio
Bussotti, Sylvano
Buxtehude, Dietrich
Byrd, William

Cage, John
Cahn, Sammy
Caldara, Antonio
Campra, André
Caplet, André
Carissimi, Giacomo
Carmichael, Hoagy
Casella, Alfredo
Castelnuovo-Tedesco,
  Mario
Catalani, Alfredo
Cavalli, Pietro Francesco
Cesti, Marc Antonio
Chabrier, Alexis
  Emmanuel
Chadwick, George
Charpentier, Gustave
Charpentier, Marc-
  Antoine
Chausson, Ernest

Chavez, Carlos
Cherubini, Luigi
Chopin, Frédéric
Cilea, Francesco
Cimarosa, Domenico
Clementi, Muzio
Coccia, Carlo
Cohan, George M.
Coleridge-Taylor,
  Samuel
Copland, Aaron
Corelli, Arcangelo
Cornelius, Peter
Couperin, François
Coward, Noel
Creston, Paul
Cui, César
Czerny, Carl

Dallapiccola, Luigi
Damase, Jean Michel
Damrosch, Walter
David, Félicien
Dawson, William
Debussy, Claude
De Koven, Reginald
Delibes, Léo
Delius, Frederick
Dello Joio, Norman
Dessau, Paul
de Sylva, George G.
  (Buddy)
Diamond, David
D'Indy, Vincent
Ditters von Dittersdorf,
  Karl
Dohnányi, Ernst von
Donaldson, Walter
Donizetti, Gaetano
Dopper, Cornelius
Dowland, John
Draghi, Antonio
Dresser, Paul
Dubin, Al

MUSIC—Composers

Dubois, Pierre Max
Dukas, Paul
Duparc, Henri
Dussek, Jan Ladislav
Dvořák, Antonin
Dylan, Bob

Edwards, Gus
Einem, Gottfried von
Elgar, Edward
Emmett, Dan
Enesco, Georges
Ernst, Heinrich
Etler, Alvin

Falla, Manuel de
Fauré, Gabriel
Feo, Francesco
Fibich, Zdeněk
Field, John
Finck, Heinrich
Fisher, Fred
Flotow, Friedrich von
Foss, Lukas
Foster, Stephen C.
Franchetti, Alberto
Franck, Cesár
Franz, Robert
Frescobaldi, Girolamo
Friedman, Leo
Friml, Rudolf

Gabrieli, Giovanni
Gade, Niels
Gallet, Louis
Galuppi, Baldassare
Gaubert, Philippe
Gay, John
German, Edward
Gersł.win, George
Gesualdo, Carlo
Gibbons, Orlando
Gilbert, Henry F.
Giordani, Tommaso

Giordano, Umberto
Glazunov, Alexander
Glière, Reinhold
Glinka, Mikhail
Gluck, Christoph Willibald
Goddard, Benjamin
Goldmark, Karl
Gossec, François
Gould, Morton
Gounod, Charles
Grainger, Percy
Granados, Enrique
Graun, Karl
Graupner, Christopher
Grétry, André
Grieg, Edvard
Griffes, Charles T.
Grofé, Ferde

Hahn, Reynaldo
Halévy, Jacques
Handel, George Frederick
Handy, W.C.
Hanson, Howard
Harris, Roy
Harburg, E.Y.
Hart, Lorenz
Hasse, Johann Adolph
Hassler, Hans Leo
Haydn, Franz Joseph
Haydn, Michael
Heiden, Bernhard
Heller, Stephen
Henderson, Ray
Henschel, George
Henze, Hans Werner
Herbert, Victor
Hérold, Ferdinand
Hewitt, John Hill
Hill, Edward Burlingame
Hiller, Johann

Hindemith, Paul
Hoffmann, Ernst
Holst, Gustav
Honegger, Arthur
Hopkinson, Francis
Hummel, Johann
Humperdinck, Engelbert

Ibert, Jacques
Ives, Charles

Janáček, Leoš
Jensen, Adolph
Joachim, Joseph
Jones, Isham
Joplin, Scott
Juon, Paul

Kalinnikov, Vasili
Karg-Elert, Sigfrid
Keiser, Reinhard
Kern, Jerome
Kodály, Zoltán
Korngold, Erich Wolfgang
Křenek, Ernst
Kuhlau, Friedrich
Kuhlau, Johann

Laderman, Ezra
Lalo, Edouard
Lassus, Orlandus
Leclair, Jean Marie
Lecocq, Charles
Lehar, Franz
Lekeu, Guillaume
Lennon, John
Leoncavallo, Ruggiero
Lerner, Alan Jay
Lesueur, Jean François
Liadov, Anatol
Liszt, Franz
Locke, Matthew
Loeffler, Charles Martin
Loewe, Frederick

MUSIC—Composers

Loewe, Johann Karl
Loesser, Frank
Lully, Jean Baptiste
Lutoslawski, Witold

MacDowell, Edward
Mackenzie, Alexander
Maderna, Bruno
Mahler, Gustav
Malipiero, Francesco
Mancini, Henry
Marcello, Benedetto
Martin, Frank
Martinu, Bohuslav
Mascagni, Pietro
Massenet, Jules
McHugh, James
Méhul, Etienne Henri
Mendelssohn, Felix
Menotti, Gian-Carlo
Mercer, John
Meyer, G.W.
Messager, André
Meyerbeer, Giacomo
Miaskovsky, Nikolai
Milhaud, Darius
Moniuszko, Stanislaus
Monte, Philippe de
Monteverdi, Claudio
Morley, Thomas
Mozart, Wolfgang
  Amadeus
Musgrave, Thea
Mussorgsky, Modest

Nápravnik, Eduard
Neilsen, Carl
Nevin, Ethelbert
Nicolai, Otto

Obrecht, Jakob
Offenbach, Jacques
Olcott, Chauncey
Orff, Carl

Paganini, Niccolò
Paine, John Knowles
Palestrina, Giovanni
Parker, Horatio W.
Parry, C. Hubert
Pergolesi, Giovanni
Persichetti, Vincent
Piccinni, Niccolò
Pijper, Willem
Piston, Walter
Ponchielli, Amilcare
Porter, Cole
Poston, Elizabeth
Poulenc, Francis
Previn, Andre
Prokofiev, Sergei
Puccini, Giacomo
Purcell, Henry

Rachmaninoff, Sergei
Raff, Joachim
Rameau, Jean Philippe
Ravel, Maurice
Reger, Max
Reinecke, Karl
Reznicek, Emil von
Riegger, Wallingford
Rieti, Vittorio
Resphighi, Ottorino
Rigel, Henry
Rimsky-Korsakov,
  Nikolai
Rodgers, Richard
Romberg, Sigmund
Rome, Harold
Root, George Frederick
Rorem, Ned
Rossini, Gioacchino
Roussel, Albert
Rubinstein, Anton
Ruby, Harry
Russell, Henry

Sachs, Hans

Saint-Saëns, Camille
Salieri, Antonio
Sarasate, Pablo de
Satie, Erik
Scarlatti, Alessandro
Scarlatti, Domenico
Schickele, Peter
Schönberg, Arnold
Schreker, Franz
Schubert, Franz
Schuller, Gunther
Schuman, William
Schumann, Robert
Schütz, Heinrich
Schwartz, Arthur
Scriabin, Alexander
Seeger, Ruth Crawford
Sekles, Bernhard
Shostakovich, Dmitri
Sibelius, Jean
Silvers, Louis
Smetana, Bedrich
Sousa, John Philip
Sowerby, Leo
Spohr, Louis
Spontini, Gasparo
Stainer, John
Stamitz, Karl
Stanford, Charles
Stanley, John
Still, William Grant
Straus, Oskar
Strauss, Johann
Strauss, Richard
Stravinsky, Igor
Sullivan, Arthur
Suppé, Franz von
Svendsen, Johan
Sweelinck, Jan
Szymanowski, Karol

Tansman, Alexander
Tartini, Giuseppe
Taylor, Deems

MUSIC—Composers

Tchaikovsky, Peter Ilyich
Tcherepnin, Alexander
Telemann, Georg
Thomas, Ambroise
Thomson, Virgil
Tilzer, Albert von
Tilzer, Harry von
Toch, Ernest
Tosti, Francesco
Turina, Joaquin

Van Alstyne, Egbert
Van De Vate, Nancy
Van Heusen, James

Varèse, Edgard
Verdi, Giuseppe
Vierne, Louis
Villa-Lobos, Heitor
Vivaldi, Antonio
Volkmann, Robert

Wagner, Richard
Walton, William
Ward, Robert
Warren, Harry
Wayne, Mabel
Weber, Karl Maria von
Webern, Anton von
Weelkes, Thomas

Weill, Kurt
Weinberger, Jaromir
Wenrich, Percy
Whiting, Richard
Widor, Charles Marie
Wieniawski, Henri
Williams, John
Williams, Ralph Vaughan
Wolf, Hugo
Wolf-Ferrari, Ermanno
Work, Henry Clay

Youmans, Vincent

MUSIC—Operas

Aegyptische Helena (The Egyptian Helen)
Africaine, l' (The African Girl)
Aida
Albert Herring
Alceste
Amahl and the Night Visitors
Amelia al Ballo (Amelia Goes to the Ball)
Amore dei Tre Re, l' (The Love of Three Kings)
Andrea Chénier
Anna Bolena (Anne Boleyn)
Apotheker, Der (The Apothecary)
Arabella
Ariadne auf Naxos (Ariadne on Naxos)
Armide

Ballad of Baby Doe, The
Ballo in Maschera, Un (A Masked Ball)
Barbiere di Siviglia, Il (The Barber of Seville)
Barbier von Bagdad, Der (The Barber of Bagdad)
Bartered Bride, The
Bastien und Bastienne
Béatrice et Bénédict
Beggar's Opera, The
Belle Hélène, La (The Beautiful Helen)
Benvenuto Cellini
Billy Budd
Bluebeard's Castle
Bohème, La (The Bohemians)
Bohemian Girl, The
Boris Godunov

Capriccio
Carmen
Carmina Burana
Cavalleria Rusticana (Rustic Chivalry)
Cenerentola, La (Cinderella)
Christophe Colomb
Cid, Le
Clemenza di Tito, La (The Mercy of Titus)
Comte Ory, Le (Count Ory)

Consul, The
Contes d'Hoffmann, Les (The Tales of Hoffmann)
Coq d'Or, Le (The Golden Cockerel)
Cosi fan Tutte (Women Are Like That)
Cunning Little Vixen, The

Devil and Daniel Webster, The
Dialogues des Carmélites, Les (The Dialogues of the Carmelites)
Dido and Aeneas
Don Carlos
Don Giovanni (Don Juan)
Don Pasquale
Don Rodrigo
Dreigroschenoper, Die (The Threepenny Opera)

Elektra
Elisir d'Amore, l' (The Elixir of Love)
Enchantress, The
Enfant et les sortilèges, l' (The Bewitched Child)
Enfant prodigue, l' (The Prodigal Son)
Entführung aus dem Serail, Die (The Abduction from the Seraglio)
Ernani
Eugene Onegin

Fair at Sorochinsk, The
Falstaff
Fanciulla del West, La (The Girl of the Golden West)
Faust
Favorita, La (The Favored One)
Fidelio
Fille du Regiment, La (The Daughter of the Regiment)
Fledermaus, Die (The Bat)
Fliegende Holländer, Der (The Flying Dutchman)
Forza del Destino, La (The Force of Destiny)
Four Saints in Three Acts

MUSIC—Operas

Frau ohne Schatten, Die (The Woman without a Shadow)
Freischütz, Der (The Free-Shooter)

Gianni Schicchi
Gioconda, La
Giojelli Della Madonna (The Jewels of the Madonna)
Giulio Cesare in Egitto (Julius Caesar in Egypt)
Good Soldier Schweik, The
Götterdämmerung (The Twilight of the Gods)

Hänsel und Gretel
Heure Espanole, l' (The Spanish Hour)
Histoire du Soldat, l' (The Soldier's Tale)
Huguenots, Les

Idomeneo
Incoronazione di Poppea, l' (The Coronation of Poppaea)
Intermezzo
Iphigénie en Aulide
Iris
Italiana in Algeri, l' (The Italian Woman in Algiers)

Jonny Spielt Auf
Juive, La (The Jewess)

Khovantchina

Lakmé
Le Prophetè (The Prophet)
Lohengrin
Louise
Love for Three Oranges, The
Lucia di Lammermoor
Lucrezia Borgia
Luisa Miller
Lulu
Lustigen Weiber von Windsor, Die (The Merry Wives of Windsor)
Macbeth

Madama Butterfly (Madame Butterfly)
Makropoulos Affair, The
Manon
Manon Lescaut
Maria Golovin
Maria Stuarda (Mary Stuart)
Martha
Mathis der Maler (Mathias the Painter)
Médée (Medea)
Medium, The
Mefistofele
Meistersinger von Nurnberg, Die (The Mastersingers of Nuremberg)
Mignon
Mikado, The
Mother of Us All, The
Mourning Becomes Electra

Nabucco
Nebuchadnezzar
Norma
Nose, The
Noye's Fludde (Noah's Flood)
Nozze di Figaro, Le (The Marriage of Figaro)

Oberon
Oedipus Rex
Old Maid and the Thief, The
Orfeo ed Euridice (Orpheus and Eurydice)
Orphée aux Enfers (Orpheus in the Underworld)
Otello

Pagliacci, I
Parsifal
Pêcheurs de Perles, Les (The Pearlfishe
Pelléas et Mélisande (Pelleas and Melisande)
Périchole, La
Peter Grimes
Pinafore, H.M.S.
Pique Dame, La (The Queen of Spade

MUSIC—Operas

Porgy and Bess
Prince Igor
Princess Jaune, La
Princess on the Pea, The
Puritani, I (The Puritans)

Queen of Spades

Rake's Progress, The
Rape of Lucretia, The
Rheingold, Das (The Rhinegold)
Rienzi
Rigoletto
Ring des Nibelungen, Der
  (The Ring of the Nibelungs):
  Götterdämmerung (The Twilight of the Gods)
  Rheingold, Das (The Rhinegold)
  Siegfried
  Walküre, Die (The Valkyrie)
Robert le Diable (Robert the Devil)
Roberto Devereux
Romeo et Juliette (Romeo and Juliet)
Rosenkavalier, Der (The Knight of the Rose)
Rusalka
Russlan and Lyudmilla
Sadko
Saint of Bleecker Street, The
Salome
Samson et Dalila (Samson and Delilah)
Schauspieldirektor, Der (The Impresario)
Schweigsame Frau, Die (The Silent Woman)
Semele

Serva Padrona, La (The Maid Mistress)
Siegfried
Simon Boccanegra
Sonnambula, La (The Sleepwalker)
Suor Angelica (Sister Angelica)
Susannah
Sweet Bye-and-Bye, The

Tabarro, Il (The Cloak)
Tannhäuser
Telephone, The
Tender Land, The
Thaïs
Tiefland
Tosca
Tote Stade, Die (The Dead City)
Traviata, La
Tristan und Isolde
Trouble in Tahiti
Trovatore, Il (The Troubadour)
Turandot
Turco in Italia, Il (The Turk in Italy)
Turn of the Screw, The

Vanessa
Vida Breve, La (The Brief Life)

Walküre, Die (The Valkyrie)
Wally, La
Werther
Wozzeck

Zampa
Zauberflöte, Die (The Magic Flute)
Zaza
Zigeunerbaron, Der (The Gypsy Baron)

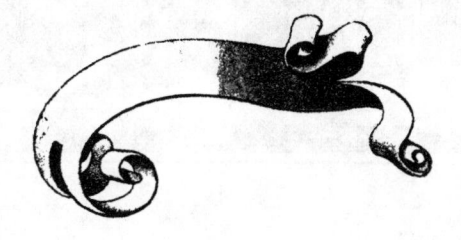

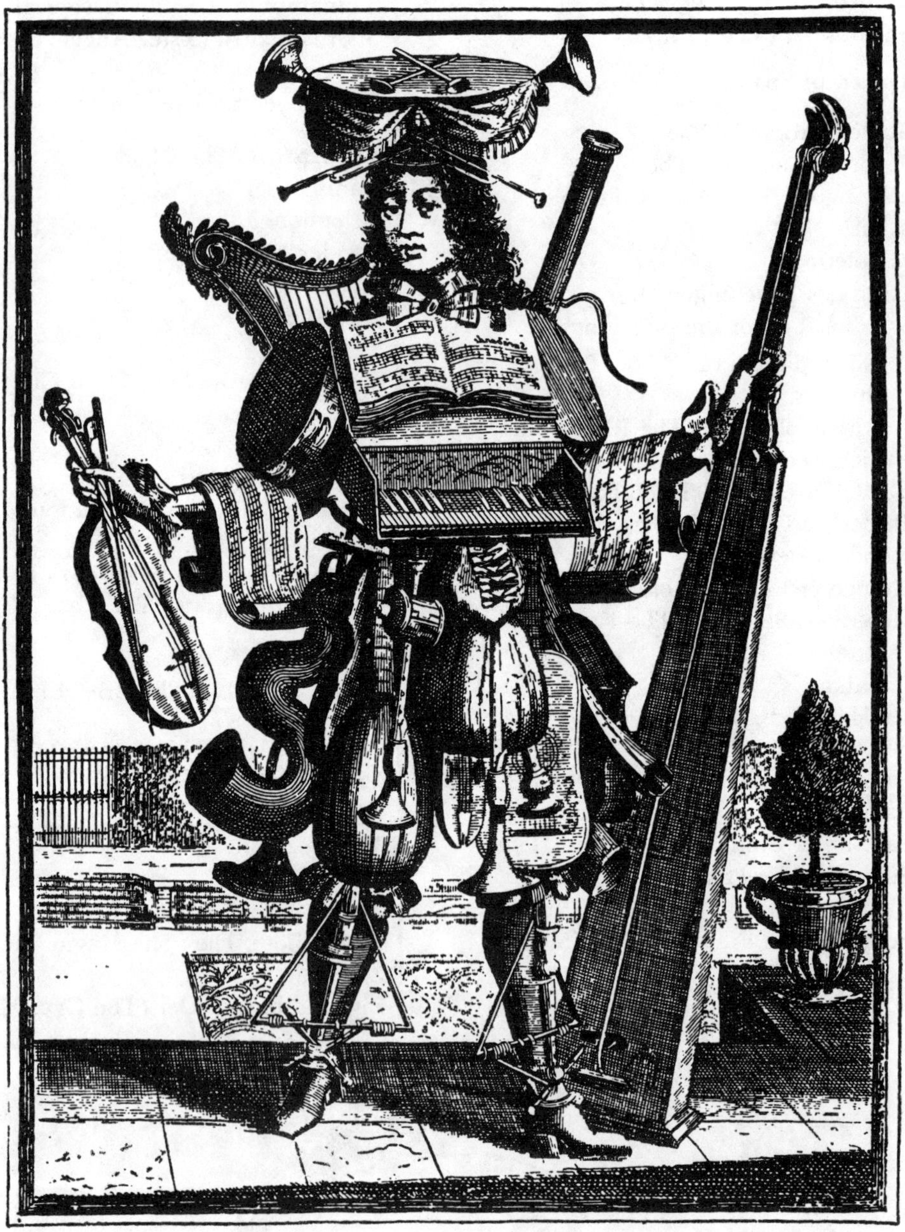

MUSICAL TERMS

a cappella
accelerando
accompaniment
accordion
acoustics
adagio
air
allargando
allegretto
allegro
allemande
alto
andante
andantino
anthem
antiphonal
aperture
appoggiatura
arco
aria
arpeggio
articulation
a tempo
atonality
aubade
avant-garde

bagatelle
bagpipe
balafon
balah
balalaika
ballad
ballet
bamboli
bamboula
banjo
baritone
baroque
bass clef
bass drum
basset horn
bassoon
bass viol

baton
beat
bel canto
bitonality
bluegrass
bolero
boogie-woogie
bop
bourrée
bouzouki
brass
bratsche
bravura

cabaletta
cadence
cadenza
calliope
calypso
canon
cantabile
cantata
cantor
cantus firmus
canzone
capriccio
carillon
carillonneur
carol
cassette
castanet
castrato
celesta
cello
chaconne
chamber music
chanson
chant
chantey
chiaroscuro
chimes
choir
chorale
chord

chorus
chromatic
clarinet
classicism
claves
clavichord
clavier
clef
coda
col legno
coloratura
concertina
concertino
concerto grosso
conductor
con moto
consonance
continuo
contrabass
contralto
cornet
counterpoint
crescendo
cue
cymbal

da capo
dal segno
descant
diapason
diatonic
diminuendo
dirge
dissonance
divertimento
dolce
double bar
double stop
duet
dulcimer
duple
duplet

elegy
embellishment

MUSICAL TERMS

embouchure
encore
English horn
enharmonic
ensemble
espressivo
étude
euphonium

falsetto
fantasia
fermata
fiddle
fife
finale
fioritura
flageolet
flamenco
flat
flautando
flute
folk song
form
forte
fortissimo
fugue
funk
furioso

gamelan
gavotte
gigue
glissando
glockenspiel
gong
gloria
guitar

harmonica
harmonics
harmony
harp
harpsichord
hautboy

hemiolia
homophony
hornpipe
hurdy-gurdy
hymn

impressionism
impromptu
instrumentation
interlude
intermezzo
interval
intonation
ipopa

jazz

kalimba
kettledrum
keyboard
keynote
key signature
kora

larghetto
largo
legato
leitmotif
lento
lieder
liturgical
lullaby
lute
lyre
lyric

madrigal
maestoso
maestro
Magnificat
major
mandolin
marcato
marimba

mazurka
melisma
melodic
melodion
melody
meter
metronome
mezza voce
mezzo-soprano
minor
minstrel
minuet
modal
mode
moderato
modulation
mordent
motet
motif
moto perpetuo
movement

neoclassical
nocturne
nonet

obbligato
oboe
octave
octet
opera
opéra bouffe
opera buffa
opéra comique
operetta
ophicleide
opus
oratorio
orchestra
orchestration
organ
overtone
overture

MUSICAL TERMS

partita
passacaglia
percussion
phonograph
phrase
pianissimo
pianist
piano
pianoforte
piatti
piccolo
pitch pipe
pizzicato
plain song
poco
polonaise
polyphony
ponticello
portamento
prelude
presto
prima donna
psaltery

quartet
quintet

recapitulation
recitative
recorder
requiem
resonance
rhapsody
rhumba
rhythm
ripieno
ritardando
rock
rococo
romanticism
romanza
rondo
rubato

sansa
saraband
saxophone
scale
scherzo
score
segue
semitone
septet
sequence
serenade
serialism
sextet
sforzando
sharp
siciliana
sinfonia
snare drum
solfeggio
soloist
sonata
sopranino
soprano
sostenuto
sotto voce
spiccato
spinet
spiritual
Stabat Mater
staccato
staff
subito
suite
symphony
syncopation

tambourine
tarantella
Te Deum
tempo
tenor
terzetto
tessitura

theme
timbre
timpani
toccata
tonality
tone poem
tonic
transcription
treble clef
tremolo
triad
triangle
trill
trio
triplet
tritone
trombe
trombone
troubadour
trumpet
tuba
tubular bells
tuning fork
tutti
twelve-tone

ukulele
unison

variation
vibrato
viola
viola da gamba
violin
violoncello
virtuoso
vivace
vocalize

waltz
whistle

xylophone

zither

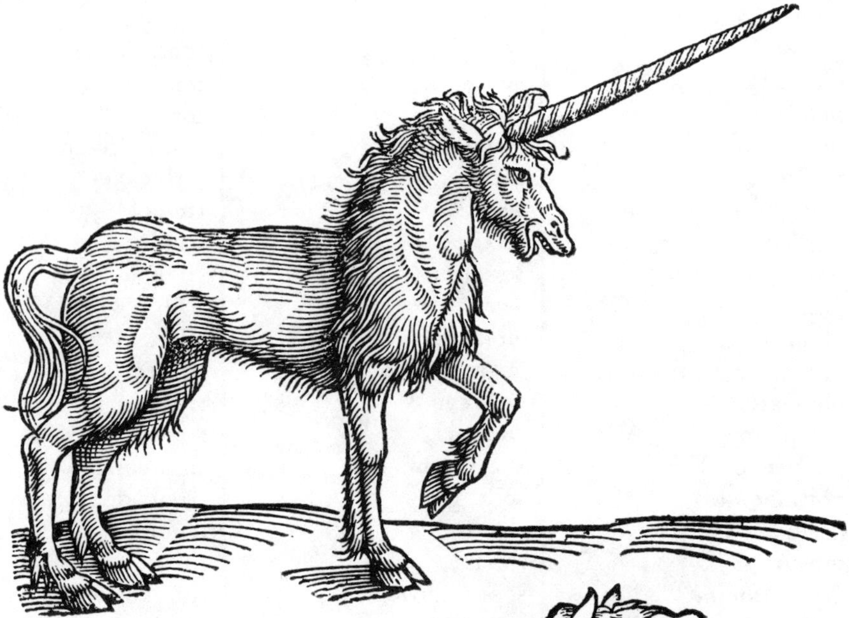

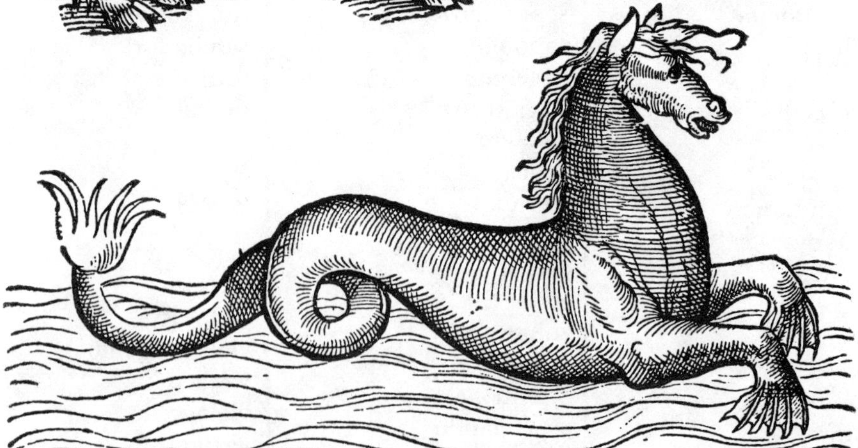

MYTHOLOGY

Abydos
Achelous
Acheron
Achilles
Acis
Acrisius
Actaeon
Adad
Adissechen
Admetus
Adonis
Adrammelech
Aeacus
Aegeus
Aegir
aegis
Aegisthus
Aegle
Aegyptus
Aeneas
Aeolus
Aesacus
Aesculapius
Aesir
Aeson
Aethra
Agamemnon
Aganippe
Agni
Ahriman
Ajax
Akuman
Alcestis
Alcinous
Alecto
Alectryon
Alfadur
Allatu
Alpheus
Althaea
Amaterasu
Amalthea
Amazon
ambrosia

Amen
Amen-Ra
Amida
Ammon
Amphion
Amphitrite
Anat
Ancaeus
Anchises
Andromache
Andromeda
anemone
Angana
Anshar
Antaeus
Antigone
Anu
Anubis
Aphrodite
Apis
Apollo
Arachne
Aralu
Ares
Arethusa
Argo
Argonauts
Argus
Ariadne
Arion
Artemis
Aruru
Asgard
asphodel
Astarte
Atalanta
Ate
Aten
Athamas
Athena
Atlantis
Atlas
Aton
Atreus

Atropos
Attis
Atum
Aurae
Aurora
Avatar
Avernus
Azrael

Baal
Baba Yaga
Bacchus
Balder
Balmung
Barguest
Beelzebub
Befana
Bellerophon
Bellona
Belus
Beowulf
Berenice
Bhima
Bia
Bladud
Boreas
Bragi
Brahma
Bran
Briareus
Brigit
Brunhild
Bukadawin

Cacus
Cadmus
caduceus
Calliope
Callisto
Calpe
Calydon
Calypso
Camelot
Camenae

157

MYTHOLOGY

Camilla
Cassandra
Cassiopeia
Castalia
Castor
Cauther
Cecrops
centaur
Cephalus
Cepheus
Cerberus
Ceres
Chaos
Charon
Charybdis
Chimera
Chloe
Chou
Chryseis
Circe
Clio
Clotho
Clytemnestra
Clytie
Cocytus
Comus
Coronis
Corybantes
Cottus
Coxcox
Creon
Cressida
Creusa
Cronus
Cupid
Cybele
Cyclops
Cygnus

Daedalus
Dag
Dagan
Dagda
Daikuku

Damayanti
Danae
Danaides
Daphne
Daphnis
Deianira
Deiphobus
Deirdre
Delos
Delphi
Demeter
Demogorgon
Dercoto
Deucalion
Diana
Dido
Dike
Diomedes
Dione
Dionysus
Dodona
Donar
Dragon
Droma
druid
dryad
Durga

Echo
Edda
Egia
Eira
Elbegast
Electra
elf
Elinas
Elivagar
Elysian Fields
Enceladus
Endymion
Enipeus
Enki
Eos
Epaphus

Epimetheus
Erato
Erebus
Eridanus
Eris
Eros
Erytheia
Eumaeus
Euphorbus
Euphrosyne
Europa
Euryale
Eurydice
Eurylochus
Eurynome
Eurystheus
Euterpe
Evander

Fafnir
Fata Morgana
Fates
faun
Felicitas
Feng
Fenris
Feronia
Flora
Fortuna
Freki
Frey
Freya
Frigga
Frodi
Furies

Gaea
Galatea
Gangler
Ganymede
Gautama
Geb
Gemini
genie

158

MYTHOLOGY

Gerda
giant
Gitch'i Manito
Gladsheim
Glooskap
gnome
goblin
Golden Fleece
Gorgon
Graces
Graeae
Grendel
Grid
griffin
Guinevere
Gunther

Hades
Hagen
Harmachis
Harmonia
Harpy
Haskah
Hathor
Hebe
Hecate
Hecatoncheires
Hector
Hecuba
Hel
Helen
Helenus
Helice
Helicon
Helios
Hellas
Helle
Hemerax
Hephaestus
Hera
Heracles
Heraclidae
Hercules
Hermes

Hermione
Hesperides
Hesperus
Hestia
Hippolyta
Hippomenes
Hobomoko
Hoder
Homer
Honos
Horus
Hou Chi
Hours
Hyacinthus
Hyades
Hydra
Hygeia
Hylas
Hymen
Hymir
Hyperion
Hypnos

Iapetus
Icarius
Icarus
Ida
Idomeneus
Iduna
Indra
Io
Iolaus
Iole
Ion
Iona
Iphigenia
Irene
Ishtar
Isis
Ismene
Israfel
Italapas
Ithaca
Ixion

Jamshid
Janus
Jason
Jizo
Jocasta
Jord
Jove
Juggernaut
Juno
Jupiter

Kali
Kama
Kami
Kaswa
kelpie
Khepera
kobold
Koppenberg
Kriemhild
Krishna
Krita Yuga
Kubera

Lachesis
Laertes
Laestrygonians
Laius
Lamia
Laocoön
Laodamia
Laomedon
Lapithae
Latinus
Latona
Lavinia
Leander
Leda
leprechaun
Lethe
Leto
Loki
Lorelei
Lotis

159

MYTHOLOGY

lotus-eaters
Lucifer
Luna
Lycomedes
Lynceus
Lyonesse

Maia
Mammon
manitou
Marduk
Mars
Marsyas
Medea
Medusa
Megaera
Melanthus
Meleager
Melia
Melicertes
Melissa
Melpomene
Melusina
Memnon
Mendes
Menelaus
Menoeceus
Mentor
Mephistopheles
Mercury
mermaid
Metis
Midas
Milo
Mimir
Min
Minerva
Minos
Minotaur
Mithras
Mnemosyne
Moakkibat
Momus
Morpheus

muses
Myrmidon

naiad
Nala
Namtaru
Nanna
Naraka
Narcissus
Nausicaa
Naxos
Nebo
nectar
Negus
Neleus
Nemesis
Neoptolemus
Nephthys
Neptune
Nereid
Nereus
Nestor
Nibelungs
Nickar
Niflheim
Nike
Nina
Ningal
Niobe
Nithogg
Nokomis
Norn
Nox
Nut
nymph
Nyx

oceanids
Oceanus
Odin
Odysseus
Oedipus
ogre
Olympia

Olympus
Omphale
Ops
Orestes
Orion
Orlog
Orpheus
Osiris
Ostara
Otus

Pachacamac
Palaemon
Palamedes
Pales
Palladium
Pallas Athena
Pan
Panacea
Pandora
Panx
Paris
Parnassus
Pasiphaë
Pasht
Patroclus
Pauguk
Paupukkeewis
Pax
Pegasus
Peleus
Pelias
Pelops
Penelope
Penthesilea
peri
Perse
Persephone
Perseus
Phaeacia
Phaedra
Phaëton
Phaon
Philemon

MYTHOLOGY

Philoctetes
Philomela
Phoebe
Phoebus
Phoenix
Phosphor
Phyllis
Pirene
Pleiad
Pluto
plutus
Pollux
Polydorus
Polyhymnia
Polyphemus
Polyxena
Poseidon
Pressima
Priam
Priapus
Procris
Procrustes
Prometheus
Proserpine
Proteus
Psyche
Ptah
Pukwana
Pygmalion
Pylades
Pyramus
Pyrrhus
Pythia
Python

Ra
Ragnarok
Rahu
Rakshasas
Rama Chandra
Re
Remus
Rhadamanthus

Rhea
Romulus
Rumpelstiltskin

Salmoneus
Saturn
satyr
Scylla
Sekhet
Selene
Semele
Semiramis
Serapis
Set
Shamash
sibyl
Siegfried
Sieglinde
Sigmund
Sigurd
Sinon
siren
Sirius
Sisyphus
Siva
Skirnir
Sol
Somnus
Sphinx
Styx
Surya

Tantalus
Tartarus
Telamon
Telemachus
Tellus
Terpsichore
Thalia
Thanatos
Thea
Themis
Thersites

Theseus
Thetis
Thisbe
Thor
Tiresias
Tisiphone
Titan
Tithonus
Triton
troll
Troy
Tyche
Typhon
Tyr

Ulysses
unicorn
Urania
Uranus
Urdur
Utnapishtim

Valhalla
valkyrie
Vayu
Venus
Vesta
Vishnu
Vulcan

Woden

Xipe

yacatecutli
Yama
Yima
Ymir

Zenobia
Zephyrus
Zethus
Zeus

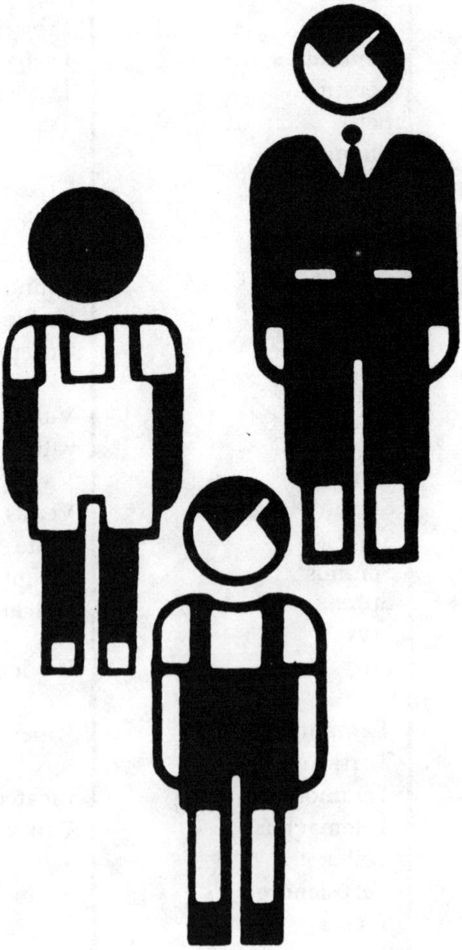

NAMES—Boys

Aaron
Abraham
Adam
Adolf
Adolph
Adrian
Alan
Alban
Alben
Albert
Albin
Alden
Alec
Aleck
Alexander
Alfonse
Alfred
Allan
Allen
Aloysius
Alvan
Alvin
Amos
André
Andrew
Andy
Anthony
Antoine
Archie
Archibald
Arnold
Arthur
Artie
Augustus
Austin
Avery

Barney
Barry
Bartholomew
Basil
Bayard
Benjamin
Bennett

Benny
Bernard
Bert
Bertram
Billie
Billy
Blair
Bobbie
Bobby
Boyd
Brett
Brian
Brice
Bruce
Bruno
Bryan
Bryce
Burt
Butch
Byron

Calvin
Carey
Carl
Carol
Carroll
Cary
Casey
Caspar
Cecil
Charles
Charlie
Chauncey
Chester
Christopher
Chuck
Clarence
Claude
Clayton
Clement
Cliff
Clifford
Clifton
Clint

Clinton
Clive
Clyde
Colin
Conrad
Conroy
Constantine
Cornelius
Curt
Curtis
Cy
Cyril
Cyrus

Daniel
Danny
Darrell
Davey
Davy
Dean
Denis
Dennis
Denny
Derek
Dexter
Dick
Dominick
Donald
Donnie
Douglas
Drew
Dudley
Duke
Duncan
Dwight

Earl
Eddie
Eddy
Edmond
Edmund
Edward
Edwin
Egbert

163

NAMES—Boys

Elbert
Eli
Eliot
Elliot
Elliott
Elmer
Emanuel
Emil
Emile
Erastus
Eric
Ernest
Ernie
Erwin
Ethan
Eugene
Evan
Everett

Felix
Ferdinand
Floyd
Francis
Frank
Franklin
Freddie
Freddy
Frederic
Frederick
Fritz

Garrett
Garry
Garth
Gary
Gene
Geoffrey
George
Gerald
Gerard
Gerry
Gilbert
Glen
Godfrey

Gordon
Graham
Grant
Gregory
Gus
Guy

Hal
Hale
Harold
Harry
Harvey
Henry
Herbert
Herman
Hiram
Homer
Horace
Howard
Hoyt
Hubert
Hugh
Humphrey

Ian
Immanuel
Ira
Irvin
Irving
Irwin
Isidore
Ivan

Jackson
Jacob
Jacques
James
Jason
Jasper
Jay
Jed
Jeff
Jeffrey
Jerome

Jerry
Jess
Jesse
Jimmie
Jimmy
Joe
Joel
Joey
Johnnie
Johnny
Jon
Jonathan
Joseph
Joshua
Jules
Julian
Julius

Karl
Keith
Kenneth
Kent
Kevin
Konrad
Kirk
Kit
Kris

Lance
Larry
Laurence
Lawrence
Lee
Lemuel
Leo
Leon
Leonard
Leroy
LeRoy
Lesley
Leslie
Lester
Lew
Lewis

NAMES—Boys

Llewellyn	Nathan	Reuben
Lloyd	Nathanael	Rhett
Lou	Nathaniel	Rob
Louis	Neal	Robbie
Lowell	Neil	Robert
Luke	Neville	Roderick
Luther	Newton	Rodney
Lyle	Nicholas	Roland
Lynn	Nick	Rolf
	Nicky	Rollo
Mac	Norman	Rolph
Mack	Norton	Ronald
Malcolm		Ronnie
Manny	Olaf	Roscoe
Marc	Oliver	Ross
Marcus	Omar	Roy
Mario	Oscar	Rudolf
Marion	Oswald	Rudolph
Mark	Otto	Russell
Marshal	Owen	Rusty
Marshall		
Martin	Patrick	Samuel
Marty	Paul	Sandy
Marvin	Pearce	Saul
Matt	Percival	Scott
Matthew	Percy	Sean
Matty	Perry	Seymour
Maurice	Pete	Shawn
Max	Phil	Sheldon
Maynard	Philip	Sid
Meredith	Phillip	Sidney
Michael	Pierce	Simon
Mick		Solomon
Mickey	Quentin	Stanley
Micky		Stephen
Miles	Ralph	Steve
Milton	Randal	Steven
Mitchell	Randall	Stewart
Monty	Randolph	Stuart
Morris	Randy	
Mortimer	Raoul	Tad
Morton	Raymond	Ted
Murray	Reginald	Terrence
Myron	Reid	Terry

NAMES—Boys

Theodore	Valentine	Warren
Thomas	Vaughn	Wayne
Timothy	Vergil	Wesley
Tobias	Vernon	Wilbur
Toby	Victor	Willard
Tod	Vincent	William
Tommie	Vinny	Willie
Tommy	Virgil	Willis
Tony		Winnie
Tyrone	Waldo	Winston
	Wallace	Winthrop
Ulysses	Walter	Wyatt

NAMES—Girls

Abby
Abigail
Ada
Adah
Addie
Adela
Adelaide
Adele
Adeline
Agatha
Aggie
Agnes
Aileen
Aimee
Alberta
Alexandra
Alfreda
Alice
Alison
Allison
Allyson
Alma
Althea
Alvera
Alvina
Alvira
Amanda
Amelia
Amy
Andrea
Angela
Angelina
Angeline
Anita
Ann
Anna
Annabel
Annabella
Annabelle
Anne
Anne Marie
Annette
Annie
Antoinette

Arabel
Arabella
Arlene
Audrey
Augusta
Avis

Babs
Barbara
Beatrice
Becky
Belle
Bernice
Bertha
Bess
Bessie
Beth
Betsey
Betsy
Betty
Beulah
Beverly
Birgit
Blanche
Bobbie
Bobby
Bobette
Bonnie
Brenda
Bridget
Bunnie
Bunny

Candace
Candie
Candy
Carla
Carlotta
Carmelita
Carmen
Carol
Carola
Carole
Carolyn

Carrie
Cassandra
Catherine
Cathleen
Cathy
Cecile
Cecilia
Cecily
Charlene
Charlotte
Cherry
Cheryl
Chloe
Chris
Christina
Christine
Cindy
Claire
Clara
Clare
Clarice
Clarissa
Clarisse
Claudette
Claudia
Cleo
Colette
Colleen
Conchita
Connie
Constance
Cora
Cordelia
Corinna
Corinne
Cornelia
Cynthia

Daisy
Daphne
Darlene
Dawn
Debbie
Debby

NAMES—Girls

Debora
Deborah
Deirdre
Della
Denise
Diana
Dinah
Dolly
Dolores
Donna
Dora
Doris
Dorothea
Dorothy
Dotty

Eadie
Edith
Edna
Edwina
Effie
Eileen
Elaine
Elberta
Eleanor
Eleanora
Elinore
Elizabeth
Ella
Ellen
Ellie
Eloise
Elsa
Elsie
Elspeth
Elva
Elvira
Emily
Emma
Enid
Erica
Erma
Ernestine
Essie

Estella
Estelle
Esther
Ethel
Eugenia
Eunice
Eva
Evangeline
Eve
Evelyn
Evelyne

Faith
Fannie
Fanny
Fay
Felicia
Fifi
Flo
Flora
Florence
Flossie
Frances
Freda
Frederica

Gabrielle
Gail
Gay
Genevieve
Georgia
Georgiana
Geraldine
Gertrude
Gerty
Gilda
Gisele
Gladys
Gloria
Grace
Greta
Gretchen
Gussie
Gwendolyn

Hannah
Harriet
Hattie
Hatty
Hazel
Heather
Helen
Helena
Helga
Heloise
Henrietta
Hermione
Hetty
Hilda
Hildegarde
Hope
Hortense
Hulda

Ianthe
Ida
Imogene
Inez
Irene
Iris
Irma
Isabel
Isabelle
Isadora
Isobel
Ivy

Jacqueline
Jane
Janet
Janice
Jean
Jeanne
Jeannette
Jemima
Jennifer
Jenny
Jessica
Jessie

NAMES—Girls

Jewel
Jill
Jo
Joan
Joanie
Joanna
Johanna
Josephine
Joy
Joyce
Juanita
Judith
Judy
Julia
Julie
June
Justine

Karen
Karol
Kate
Katherine
Kathleen
Kathrine
Kathy
Katrina
Kay
Kirsten
Kit
Kitty

Laura
Lauretta
Laverne
Lavinia
Leah
Leila
Lena
Leonora
Lesley
Letitia
Letty
Libby
Lillian

Lily
Linda
Lisa
Lise
Liz
Lizbeth
Lizzy
Lois
Lola
Lolita
Lolly
Loretta
Lorna
Lottie
Lotty
Lou
Louise
Lucille
Lucinda
Lucy
Lulu
Lydia

Mabel
Madeleine
Madge
Mae
Mag
Magdalen
Maggie
Maggy
Maisie
Malvina
Mamie
Marcella
Marcia
Margaret
Marge
Margie
Margo
Margot
Marguerite
Maria
Marian

Marianne
Marie
Marietta
Marilyn
Marina
Margery
Marj
Marjorie
Martha
Mary
Matilda
Matty
Maud
Maude
Maura
Maureen
Mavis
Maxine
May
Meg
Mehetabel
Melanie
Melissa
Mercedes
Mignon
Mildred
Millicent
Mina
Minna
Minnie
Miranda
Miriam
Moira
Molly
Mona
Mora
Muriel
Myra
Myrtle

Nadine
Nan
Nancy
Nanette

NAMES—Girls

Natalie
Nell
Nelly
Nettie
Nina
Nita
Nona
Nora
Noreen
Norena
Norma

Olga
Olive
Olivia
Opal

Pamela
Pansy
Pat
Patience
Patricia
Patty
Paula
Pauline
Pearl
Peg
Peggy
Penelope
Penny
Phoebe
Phyllis
Polly
Priscilla
Prudence
Prue

Rachel
Ramona
Rebecca
Regina

Rhoda
Rita
Roberta
Rosa
Rosabel
Rosalie
Rosamund
Rose
Roseanna
Roselind
Rosemary
Rosetta
Rosina
Rowena
Roxana
Ruby
Ruth

Sabena
Sadie
Sally
Samara
Sandra
Sara
Sarah
Selma
Shirley
Sibyl
Sidney
Sigrid
Silvia
Sonia
Sophia
Stella
Stephanie
Stephie
Sue
Susan
Susannah
Susie
Suzanne

Suzy
Sylvia

Teresa
Tess
Tessie
Thelma
Theodora
Theresa
Tilda
Tillie
Tilly
Trudy

Una
Ursula

Valerie
Vera
Verna
Veronica
Vicky
Victoria
Viola
Violet
Virginia
Vivian

Wanda
Wendy
Wilma
Winifred
Winnie

Yolanda
Yolande
Yvette
Yvonne

Zenia
Zoe

OCCUPATIONS

- abstractor
- accountant
- account executive
- acrobat
- actor/actress
- actuary
- addresser
- adjuster
- administrative assistant
- administrator
- ad-taker
- advertising account executive
- advertising salesman
- aerialist
- aerial photographer
- aeronautical engineer
- aerospace engineer
- agricultural engineer
- agronomist
- airbrush artist
- air-conditioning mechanic
- aircraft mechanic
- air director
- airline hostess
- airplane pilot
- air-traffic controller
- allergist
- ambulance driver
- analytical statistician
- anesthesiologist
- anesthetist
- animal boarder
- answering-service operator
- anthropologist
- antique dealer
- apothecary
- appraiser
- apprentice
- archeologist
- architect
- artisan

- artist
- assayer
- assembler
- astrologer
- astronomer
- athlete
- athletic trainer
- attorney
- auctioneer
- audiologist
- audiovisual specialist
- auditor
- author
- automobile dealer
- automobile engineer
- automobile mechanic
- automobile wrecker

- baby-sitter
- back-order clerk
- baggageman
- bagger
- bailiff
- baker
- ballet dancer
- ballistic expert
- band-saw operator
- banker
- bank examiner
- bank teller
- barber
- barmaid
- bartender
- beautician
- bellhop
- biochemist
- biologist
- biophysicist
- boat builder
- bodyguard
- bookbinder
- booking clerk
- bookkeeper
- bookmaker

- book salesman
- botanist
- brazier
- brewer
- bricklayer
- broker
- builder
- bureaucrat
- busboy
- bus driver
- butcher
- butler
- buyer

- cabinetmaker
- caddie
- calibrator
- campaign manager
- cantilever-crane operator
- cardiologist
- carhop
- caricaturist
- carpenter
- carpet installer
- cartographer
- cartoonist
- cashier
- caterer
- certified public accountant
- chain-saw operator
- chambermaid
- chauffeur
- checker
- cheesemaker
- chef
- chemical engineer
- chemist
- child psychologist
- chiropodist
- chiropractor
- choir director
- choreographer
- civil engineer

OCCUPATIONS

claim adjuster
clergyman
clerical worker
coach
cobbler
coin dealer
collector
columnist
composer
compositor
comptroller
computer programmer
computing-systems
   analyst
concierge
conductor
congressman
congresswoman
construction consultant
construction inspector
construction worker
consultant
contractor
cook
copilot
copyist
copywriter
coroner
correspondent
cosmetic consultant
cosmetologist
cost analyst
costumer
counselor
counter clerk
courier
crabber
crane operator
credit analyst
credit clerk
cremator
criminalist
criminal lawyer
criminologist

critic
curator
custodian
customs inspector

dairy helper
dance instructor
deckhand
decorator
delegate
deliveryman
demographer
demonstrator
dental hygienist
dentist
deputy sheriff
dermatologist
derrick operator
designer
desk clerk
detective
dietitian
direct-mail clerk
director
dishwasher
dispatcher
distiller
district attorney
diver
dock hand
doctor
dogcatcher
domestic helper
door-to-door salesman
draftsman
dramatic coach
draper
drapery estimator
dressmaker
driver
driving instructor
druggist
dry cleaner
drywall installer

ecologist
economist
editor
editorial assistant
editorial writer
educational consultant
electrical engineer
electrician
elevator operator
embalmer
embosser
embroiderer
encyclopedia salesman
endocrinologist
engineer
engraver
entertainer
entomologist
estate planner
ethnologist
examiner
excavator
exchange clerk
expediter
exporter
exterminator

farmer
fence erector
ferryboat operator
field representative
file clerk
film cutter
film developer
financial analyst
fire fighter
fireman
fire ranger
first-aid attendant
fisherman
floral designer
florist
food technologist
foreign-student adviser

OCCUPATIONS

foreman
forester
forest-fire fighter
foster parent
foundry worker
Four-H club agent
free-lance artist
fumigator
fund raiser
funeral director
furrier

gambler
game warden
garage worker
garbage collector
gardener
gas-station attendant
gastroenterologist
gem cutter
genealogist
general manager
geneticist
geodesist
geographer
geologist
geometrician
geophysicist
gigolo
girl Friday
glazier
golf-course ranger
governess
government employee
governor
grader
graphic artist
graphologist
greenskeeper
grill cook
grocer
grouter
guard
guidance counselor

guide
gunsmith
gymnast
gynecologist

haberdasher
hairdresser
hair stylist
handyman
harbor master
harvest worker
health officer
heating contractor
heavy-equipment
 operator
hematologist
historian
hoist operator
home economist
horse trader
horticulturist
hosteler
hostess
hotel clerk
housecleaner
housekeeper
humorist
hustler
hydrologist
hygienist
hypnotist

illustrator
impersonator
importer
impresario
industrial engineer
inspector
insurance adjuster
interior decorator
intern
internist
interpreter
investigator

investment advisor

janitor
jeweler
jobber
jockey
joiner
journeyman
judge

keypunch operator
kitchen helper

laboratory technician
landscape architect
landscape gardener
laryngologist
lather
lawyer
leasing agent
librarian
librettist
lifeguard
linguist
literary agent
lithographer
loan counselor
lobbyist
locksmith
locomotive engineer
logger
longshoreman
lyricist

machinist
magazine dealer
magician
magistrate
maid
mailman
maintenance mechanic
makeup artist
management analyst
managing editor

OCCUPATIONS

manicurist
mannequin
manufacturers' representative
marine engineer
marriage counselor
mason
masseur/masseuse
material inspector
mechanical engineer
medical assistant
medical-laboratory technician
merchandise manager
merchant
messenger
metallurgical engineer
meteorologist
meter reader
microbiologist
midwife
migrant worker
miller
miner
mineralogist
mining engineer
model
mortgage arranger
mortician
motion-picture projectionist
mover
music conductor
musician
music supervisor
mycologist

naprapath
narrator
navigator
nephrologist
neurologist
newsboy
newscaster

nuclear engineer
nurse
nurseryman
nutritionist

obstetrician
occupational therapist
oceanographer
office manager
oil driller
oncologist
opera singer
operating-room assistant
ophthalmologist
optician
optometrist
oral hygienist
oral surgeon
orderly
orthodontist
orthopedic specialist
osteopath
otologist
otorhinolaryngologist

packer
page
painter
paleontologist
paperhanger
parasitologist
parking-lot attendant
park ranger
pathologist
pawnbroker
pediatrician
pedicurist
pedodontist
perfumer
periodontist
personal shopper
personnel manager
petrologist
pharmacist

pharmacologist
philologist
photoengraver
photographer
physical therapist
physician
physicist
piano tuner
pilot
pipefitter
plastic surgeon
playwright
plumber
podiatrist
poet
policeman
police officer
political scientist
political worker
porter
postal employee
practical nurse
precision machine operator
press operator
priest
principal
printer
private eye
private secretary
proctologist
production manager
programmer
prompter
proofreader
property assessor
prospector
psychiatrist
psychologist
public relations advisor
publisher
punch-press operator
puppeteer

OCCUPATIONS

purchasing agent
purser

quality control engineer
quilt maker

racehorse trainer
radiographer
radiologist
radio repairer
radio-television
  announcer
railroad engineer
reader
real estate agent
realtor
receptionist
record clerk
recreational therapist
recruiter
registered nurse
registrar
religious worker
repairman
reporter
representative
research analyst
restaurant employee
restaurateur
revenue agent
reviewer
rheumatologist
rhinologist
roofer
room clerk
room maid

saddler
safety inspector
sailmaker
sailor
sales clerk
salesman
school administrator

scientist
screen printer
screen writer
script reader
scuba diver
sculptor
seamstress
secretary
securities trader
security officer
seismologist
senator
sergeant-at-arms
service manager
sexton
sheetmetal worker
sheriff
ship chandler
shop supervisor
short-order cook
show girl
silversmith
singer
social worker
sociologist
soil conservationist
solicitor
spectroscopist
state trooper
statistician
stenographer
stenotypist
stevedore
steward
stewardess
stitcher
stonecutter
stonemason
storekeeper
supervisor
supply clerk
surgeon
surveyor
switchboard operator

tailor
taxidermist
taxi driver
teacher
teamster
technician
telephone operator
telephone installer
  and repairer
teller
theater manager
therapist
ticket agent
timekeeper
time-study engineer
tire mounter
title attorney
title searcher
toll collector
tool-and-die maker
tour counselor
town clerk
township supervisor
tractor operator
traffic clerk
trainman
translator
travel agent
treasurer
truck driver
trust officer
tutor
typesetter
typist
typographer

umpire
underwriter
upholsterer
urologist
usher

vendor
ventriloquist

OCCUPATIONS

veterinarian
vocational counselor

waiter/waitress
warden
weatherman

welder
well-drill operator
wholesaler
window dresser
wrapper
writer

X-ray technician

yard worker

zoologist

OCEANS, SEAS, GULFS, AND LAKES

Adriatic Sea
Aegean Sea
Andaman Sea
Aqaba, Gulf of
Arabian Sea
Arafura Sea
Aral Sea
Arctic Ocean
Atlantic Ocean, North and South
Azov, Sea of

Baffin Bay
Baltic Sea
Barents Sea
Beaufort Sea
Bengal, Bay of
Benin, Bight of
Bering Sea
Biscay, Bay of
Black Sea
Bothnia, Gulf of

California, Gulf of
Caribbean Sea
Carpentaria, Gulf of
Caspian Sea
Chesapeake Bay
Coral Sea

Dead Sea

East China Sea
East Siberian Sea

Fundy, Bay of

Great Australian Bight
Guinea, Gulf of

Hudson Bay

Indian Ocean
Inland Sea (Seto-naikai)
Ionian Sea
Irish Sea

Japan, Sea of

Kara Sea

Labrador Sea
Laptev Sea

Marmara, Sea of
Mediterranean Sea
Mexico, Gulf of
Molucca Sea

North Sea

Okhotsk, Sea of
Oman, Gulf of

Pacific Ocean, North and South
Persian Gulf

Red Sea
Ross Sea

St. Lawrence, Gulf of
South China Sea
Suez, Gulf of
Sulu Sea

Tasman Sea
Tatary, Gulf of
Thailand, Gulf of
Timor Sea
Tonkin, Gulf of
Tyrrhenian Sea

White Sea

Yellow Sea

Zuyder Zee (IJsselmeer)

LAKES

Albano
Albert (Mobutu Sese Seko)
Athabasca

Baikal
Balaton
Balkhash
Bangweulu
Biwa

Canandaigua

Cayuga
Chad
Champlain
Chapala
Chautauqua
Como
Constance (Bodensee)

Edward
Erie
Eyre

Finger Lakes

Garda
George
Geneva
Great Bear L.
Great Lakes
Great Salt L.
Great Slave L.
Green Lake

Hemlock
Huron

Ilmen

LAKES

Issyk-Kul
Itasca

Kariba
Keuka
Koko Nor

Ladoga
Lake of the Woods
Lomond, Loch
Lucerne (Vierwaldstät-
 tersee)
Lugano

Maggiore
Manitoba
Maracaibo
Michigan
Minnetonka
Moosehead L.
Muskoka

Neagh, Lough
Ness, Loch

Neuchâtel
Nicaragua
Nipigon
Nyasa (Malawi)

Okeechobee
Onega
Oneida
Onondaga
Ontario
Owasco

Peipus
Pend Oreille
Pontchartrain

Rangeley Lakes
Rudolf (Turkana)

Sabine
St. Clair
Seneca
Simcoe
Skaneateles

Superior

Tahoe
Tanganyika
Tiberias (Galilee, Sea of)
Titicaca
Tonle Sap
Torrens

Urmia

Van
Vänern
Victoria
Volta

Winnebago
Winnipeg
Winnipegosis
Winnipesaukee

Yellowstone

Zürich

PAINTERS, SCULPTORS, AND ARCHITECTS

Adam, Robert
Agasias
Aitken, Robert I.
Albers, Joseph
Albright, Malvin M.
Alkamenes
Altdorfer, Albrecht
Angelico, Fra
Apelles
Archipenko, Alexander
Arp, Jean (Hans)
Audubon, John James

Baldovinetti, Alesso
Baldung, Hans
Bannister, Edward M.
Barbari, Jacopo de
Barlach, Ernst
Barthé, Richmond
Bartholdi, Frédéric
Bartolommeo, Fra
Bayer, Herbert
Bearden, Romare
Beardsley, Aubrey
Beckman, Max
Bellini, Giovanni
Bellows, George Wesley
Benton, Thomas Hart
Bernini, Giovanni
Berruguete, Alonso Pedro
Biddle, George
Bingham, George
Blake, William
Boilly, Louis
Bonheur, Rosa
Bonington, Richard Parkes
Bonnard, Pierre
Bordone, Paris
Borglum, Gutzon
Bosch, Hieronymus
Botticelli, Sandro
Boucher, François

Bramante (Donato d'Agnolo)
Braque, Georges
Breton, André
Breuer, Marcel
Brouwer, Adriaen
Brueghel, Pieter
Brunelleschi, Filippo
Bulfinch, Charles
Burchfield, Charles
Burnham, Daniel Hudson

Cadmus, Paul
Cadorin, Ettore
Calder, Alexander
Callot, Jacques
Cambiaso, Luca
Canale, Antonio
Caravaggio, Michelangelo
Carlin, John
Carpaccio, Vittore
Carpeaux, Jean-Baptiste
Cassatt, Mary
Castagno, Andrea del
Catlin, George
Caton, Richard
Cecere, Gaetano
Cellini, Benvenuto
Cézanne, Paul
Chagall, Marc
Chardin, Jean-Baptiste
Chirico, Giorgio di
Church, Frederick
Churriguera, José
Chu Ta
Cimabue, Giovanni
Cima da Conegliano, Giovanni Batista
Clark, Claude
Clodion, Claude
Cole, Thomas
Constable, John

Copley, John Singleton
Corbino, Jon
Corot, Jean-Baptiste
Correggio, Antonio Allegri da
Courbet, Gustave
Cranach, Lucas
Crivelli, Carlo
Crome, John
Currier, Nathaniel
Curry, John Steuart

Dali, Salvador
Dalou, Jules
Daubigny, Charles François
Daumier, Honoré
David, Jacques Louis
Davidson, Jo
Davies, Arthur
Degas, Edgar
Dehn, Adolf
Delacroix, Eugène
Delaroche, Paul
Donatello
Douglas, Aaron
Dubuffet, Jean
Dufy, Raoul
Duncanson, Robert
Dupré, Jules
Dürer, Albrecht

Eakins, Thomas
Edmonds, Francis W.
Ehninger, John
El Greco
Elsheimer, Adam
Ensor, James
Epstein, Jacob
Ernst, Max
Eyck, Jan van

Fantin-Latour, Ignace
Foppa, Vincenzo

PAINTERS, SCULPTORS, AND ARCHITECTS

Fouquet, Jean
Fragonard, Jean
Franceschi, Pietro
Frémiet, Emmanuel
French, Daniel Chester
Frishmuth, Harriet W.
Fuseli, Henry

Gainsborough, Thomas
Gaudi, Antonio
Gauguin, Paul
Géricault, Jean-Louis
Ghiberti, Lorenzo
Giacometti, Alberto
Giorgione (Giorgio
   Barbarelli)
Giotto di Bondone
Girtin, Thomas
Goes, Hugo van der
Gogh, Vincent van
Goujon, Jean
Goya, Francisco
Grafly, Charles
Greenough, Horatio
Greuze, Jean-Baptiste
Gropius, Walter
Grosz, George
Grünewald, Matthias
Guardi, Francesco

Hals, Frans
Harnett, William
Hassam, Childe
Hayden, Palmer
Hébert, Louis
Hiler, Hilaire
Hobbema, Meindert
Hoffman, Malvina
Hofman, Hans
Hogarth, William
Holbein, Hans
Homer, Winslow
Hooch, Pieter de
Hopper, Edward

Hosmer, Harriet G.
Houdon, Jean-Antoine
Hunt, William Holman

Ingres, Jean-Auguste
Inman, Henry
Inness, George

Johnson, Eastman
Johnson, William H.
Jones, Lois M.

Kallimachos
Kandinsky, Wassily
Kent, Rockwell
Kirchner, Ernst Ludwig
Kiprensky, Orest
Klee, Paul
Kokoschka, Oskar
Kollwitz, Käthe
Kooning, Willem de
Korin, Ogata
Krimmel, John L.
Kritios
Kroll, Leon
Kupka, Frank

La Farge, John
La Tour, Georges de
Latrobe, Benjamin
Lawrence, Thomas
Le Corbusier (Charles
   Edouard Jeanneret)
Léger, Fernand
Leonardo da Vinci
Lescaze, William
Leutze, Emanuel
Liebermann, Max
Lion, Jules
Lippi, Fra Filippo
Longman, Evelyn B.
Lorrain, Claude
Lotto, Lorenzo
Lucas van Leyden

Lysippos

Macintire, Samuel
MacNeil, Herman A.
Maderno, Carlo
Magnasco, Allessandro
Maillol, Aristide
Manet, Edouard
Mansart, François
Manship, Paul
Marc, Franz
Marin, John
Marsh, Reginald
Martini, Simone
Masaccio (Tommaso
   Guidi)
Massys, Quentin
Matisse, Henri
McKenzie, Robert T.
Memling, Hans
Mena, Pedro de
Mendelsohn, Erich
Mestrovic, Ivan
Michelangelo Buonarroti
Mies van der Rohe,
   Ludwig
Milles, Carl
Millet, Jean-François
Miró, Joan
Modigliani, Amedeo
Mondriaan, Pieter
Monet, Claude
Moore, Henry
Moreau, Gustave
Morelli, Domenico
Morse, Samuel F.B.
Moses, Anna Mary
   (Grandma)
Motherwell, Robert
Motley, Archibald
Mount, William S.
Munch, Edvard
Murillo, Bartolomé
Myron

PAINTERS, SCULPTORS, AND ARCHITECTS

Nash, John
Nervi, Pier Luigi
Neutra, Richard
Niehaus, Charles H.
Niemeyer, Oscar

O'Keeffe, Georgia
Orozco, José
Ostade, Adriaen van
Ostade, Isaac van

Palladio, Andrea
Parmigianino, Il
Paxton, W.M.
Peale, Charles Wilson
Peirce, Waldo
Perugino (Pietro Vannucci)
Phidias
Picasso, Pablo
Piccirilli, Attilio
Piero di Cosimo
Pippin, Horace
Piranesi, Giovanni Battista
Pisanello, Antonio
Pissarro, Camille
Pollaiuolo, Antonio
Pollock, Jackson
Polykleitos
Pontormo, Jacopo da
Porter, James
Poussin, Nicolas
Praxiteles
Prud'hon, Pierre-Paul

Quercia, Jacopo della
Quidor, John
Quin, Edmond T.

Raeburn, Henry
Raphael (Raffaello Sanzio)
Redon, Odilon

Rembrandt van Rijn
Remington, Frederic
Renoir, Pierre Auguste
Reynolds, Joshua
Ribera, Jusepe
Richardson, Henry Hobson
Riemenschneider, Tilman
Rivera, Diego
Robbia, Andrea della
Robbia, Luca della
Rodgers, John
Rodin, Auguste
Romney, George
Rosa, Salvator
Rossetti, Dante Gabriel
Rossi, Giovanni
Rouault, Georges
Rousseau, Henri
Rubens, Peter Paul
Rush, William
Russell, Charles
Ruysdael, Jacob van

Saarinen, Eliel
Saint-Gaudens, Augustus
Sample, Paul
Sangallo, Antonio
Sargent, John Singer
Sarto, Andrea del
Savage, Edward
Schongauer, Martin
Sert, José Luis
Sesshu
Seurat, Georges
Shahn, Ben
Sheeler, Charles
Signorelli, Luca
Siqueiros, David
Skopas
Sloan, John
Sluter, Claus

Sodoma, Il (Giovanni Bazzi)
Speicher, Eugene
Steen, Jan
Stevens, Alfred
Strickland, William
Stuart, Gilbert
Sullivan, Louis Henry
Sully, Thomas

Taft, Lorado
Tait, Arthur F.
Tanguy, Yves
Tanner, Henry O.
Tarbell, Edmund C.
Terborch, Gerard
Thomas, Alma
Tibaldi, Pellegrino
Tiepolo, Giovanni
Tintoretto (Jacopo Robusti)
Titian (Tiziano Vecellio)
Toulouse-Lautrec, Henri de
Trumbull, John
Tung Yuan
Tura, Cosimo
Turner, J.M.W.

Uccello, Paolo
Upjohn, Richard
Utrillo, Maurice

Vanbrugh, John
Van Dyck, Anthony
Vasari, Giorgio
Velazquez, Diego
Vermeer, Jan
Veronese, Paolo
Verrocchio, Andrea del
Vignola, Jacopo Barozzi da
Vlaminck, Maurice de
Vuillard, Edouard

PAINTERS, SCULPTORS, AND ARCHITECTS

Wang Hui	Weyden, Rogier van der	Wu Tao-Tzu
Watteau, Antoine	Whistler, James McNeill	Wyeth, Andrew
Watts, George	White, Charles	
Waugh, Frederick	Wilson, Richard	Yumedono
Weber, Max	Wood, Grant	
Weinman, A.A	Woodruff, Hale	Zadkine, Ossip
Weir, J.A.	Wren, Christopher	Zorach, William
West, Benjamin	Wright, Frank Lloyd	Zurbarán, Francisco de

PHILOSOPHERS, THEOLOGIANS, AND OTHER FAMOUS THINKERS

Abélard, Pierre
Adler, Felix
Ailly, Pierre d'
Albertus Magnus
Alcott, Bronson
Alexander, Samuel
Algarotti, Francesco
Anaxagoras of Clazomenae
Anaximander of Miletus
Anaximenes
Anselm, Saint
Antisthenes
Aquinas, Thomas, Saint
Aristippus
Aristotle
Arius
Arnauld, Antoine
Athanasius, Saint
Augustine, Saint
Averroës
Avicenna
Ayer, Alfred Jules

Baader, Franz X.
Bacon, Francis
Barth, Karl
Baur, Ferdinand C.
Bayle, Pierre
Bede, The Venerable
Bennett, John Coleman
Bentham, Jeremy
Bentley, Arthur
Berdyaev, Nikolai
Bergson, Henri
Berkeley, George
Besant, Annie
Blanshard, Brand
Boëthius
Bonaventure, Saint
Bonhoeffer, Dietrich
Bosanquet, Bernard
Boutroux, Etienne
Bradley, Francis Herbert

Bridgman, Percy W.
Broad, Charlie D.
Brunner, Heinrich E.
Bruno, Giordano
Buber, Martin
Büchner, Ludwig
Buddha, Gautama
Bukhari, Muhammad ibn
Bultmann, Rudolf
Burke, Edmund
Butler, Joseph

Calvin, John
Campanella, Tommaso
Camus, Albert
Carnap, Rudolf
Carneades
Cassirer, Ernst
Chrysippus
Chrysostom
Chuang Chou
Chu-hsi
Cicero, Marcus Tullius
Clarke, Samuel
Cleanthes
Cohen, Hermann
Colet, John
Collier, Jeremy
Comte, Isidore Auguste
Condorcet, Marquis de
Confucius
Cournot, Antoine A.
Cranmer, Thomas
Croce, Benedetto

Darwin, Charles R.
Democritus of Abdera
Demosthenes
Descartes, René
Dewey, John
Diderot, Denis
Diogenes
Ducasse, Curt John
Duns Scotus, John

Durant, Will
Durkheim, Emile

Eckhart, Johannes
Eddy, Mary Baker
Edwards, Jonathan
Einstein, Albert
Emerson, Ralph Waldo
Empedocles of Acragas
Engels, Friedrich
Epictetus
Epicurus
Erasmus, Desiderius
Erigena, Johannes Scotus
Eucken, Rudolf
Eusebius of Caesarea

Fechner, Gustav T.
Feuerbach, Ludwig
Fichte, Johann Gottlieb
Fischer, Kuno
Fisher, George Park
Fleury, Claude
Fouillée, Alfred Jules
Fourier, François
Franklin, Benjamin
Fraser, Alexander Campbell
Frauenstädt, Christian
Freud, Sigmund
Fries, Jacob

Galen
Galluppi, Pasquale
Gandhi, Mohandas
Gassendi, Pierre
Gerson, Jean de
Gilbert, William
Gilson, Etienne Henry
Gioberti, Vincenzo
Gorgias
Green, Thomas Hill

Haeckel, Ernst H.
Hamann, Johann G.

PHILOSOPHERS, THEOLOGIANS, AND OTHER FAMOUS THINKERS

Han Fei Tzu
Harnack, Adolf von
Harris, William T.
Hartmann, Eduard von
Hartmann, Nicolai
Hegel, Georg Wilhelm Friedrich
Heidegger, Martin
Helvétius, Claude
Heraclitus of Ephesus
Herbart, Johann F.
Herder, Johann G. von
Hillel
Hobbes, Thomas
Höffding, Harald
Holbach, Paul Henri Dietrich, Baron d'
Humboldt, Karl Wilhelm
Hume, David
Husserl, Edmund
Huxley, Thomas Henry

Ibn Hazm, Abu Muhammad
Ibn Muhammad
Ibn Tufayl, Abu Bakr Muhammad
Ibn Tumart, Muhammad

James, William
Jaspers, Karl
Jesus
Joachim, Harold
Jouffroy, Theodore S.
Jung, Carl G.
Justin

Kant, Immanuel
Kempis, Thomas à
Kierkegaard, Sören
Knox, John
Krishnamurti, Jiddu
Kropotkin, Petr A.
Kung-Sun Lung

La Mettrie, Julien Offray de
Lanfranc
Lao-Tsu or Lao-tzu
Leibniz, Gottfried von
Lenin, Nikolai
Leucippus
Lévy-Bruhl, Lucien
Lewis, Clarence L.
Locke, John
Lombard, Peter
Lotze, Rudolf
Lucretius
Lull, Ramon
Luther, Martin

Mach, Ernst
Machiavelli, Niccolò
Mahavira, Vardhamana
Maimonides, Moses
Malebranche, Nicholas de
Marcel, Gabriel
Marcus Aurelius
Marcuse, Herbert
Maritain, Jacques
Marx, Karl
McCosh, James
Mead, George Herbert
Melanchthon, Philipp
Mencius
Mendelssohn, Moses
Mill, John Stuart
Mohammed
Montague, William
Montaigne, Michel F. de
Montesquieu, Charles
Moore, George Edward
More, Thomas
Morris, Charles W.
Moses

Nanak
Nazzam, al-
Nestorius

Newman, John H.
Newton, Isaac
Nicholas of Cusa
Niebuhr, Reinhold
Nietzsche, Friedrich

Occam, William of
Origen
Ortega y Gasset, José
Otto, Rudolf

Paley, William
Parker, De Witt Henry
Parmenides of Elea
Pascal, Blaise
Peirce, Charles Sanders
Perry, Ralph Barton
Plato
Plotinus
Poincaré, Jules Henri
Pratt, James B.
Price, Henry H.
Protagoras
Proudhon, Pierre
Pythagoras

Radhakrishnan, Sarvepalli
Ramanuja
Reid, Thomas
Renouvier, Charles B.
Rosenzweig, Franz
Ross, W. David
Rousseau, Jean-Jacques
Royce, Josiah
Russell, Bertrand A.
Ryle, Gilbert

Santayana, George
Sartre, Jean-Paul
Schelling, Friedrich
Schleiermacher, Friedrich
Schlick, Moritz
Schopenhauer, Arthur

PHILOSOPHERS, THEOLOGIANS, AND OTHER FAMOUS THINKERS

Schweitzer, Albert
Sellers, Roy Wood
Seneca, Lucius Annaeus
Sextus Empiricus
Shankaracharya
Sharp, Frank Chapman
Sidgwick, Henry
Smith, Adam
Smith, Joseph
Socrates
Spencer, Herbert
Spengler, Oswald
Spinoza, Baruch
Stevenson, Charles Leslie
Strauss, David
Suárez, Francisco
Suzuki, Daisetz
Swedenborg, Emanuel
Syed Ahmed Khan

Tabari, al-
Tagore, Rabindranath
Tarski, Alfred
Tawney, Richard Henry
Teilhard de Chardin, Pierre
Thales of Miletus
Theophrastus
Theresa of Avila, Saint
Thoreau, Henry David
Tillich, Paul
Tischendorf, Lobegott von
Tocqueville, Alexis de
Tolstoy, Leo
Toynbee, Arnold J.

Veblen, Thorstein
Vico, Giovanni Battista
Voltaire (Francois Marie Arouet)

Weber, Max
Wesley, John
Whitehead, Alfred North
William of Ockham
Windelband, Wilhelm
Wisdom, John
Wittgenstein, Ludwig
Woodbridge, Frederick James

Xenocrates
Xenophanes

Yasin, Abdullah ibn
Young, Brigham

Zeno
Zoroaster (Zarathustra)
Zwingli, Ulrich

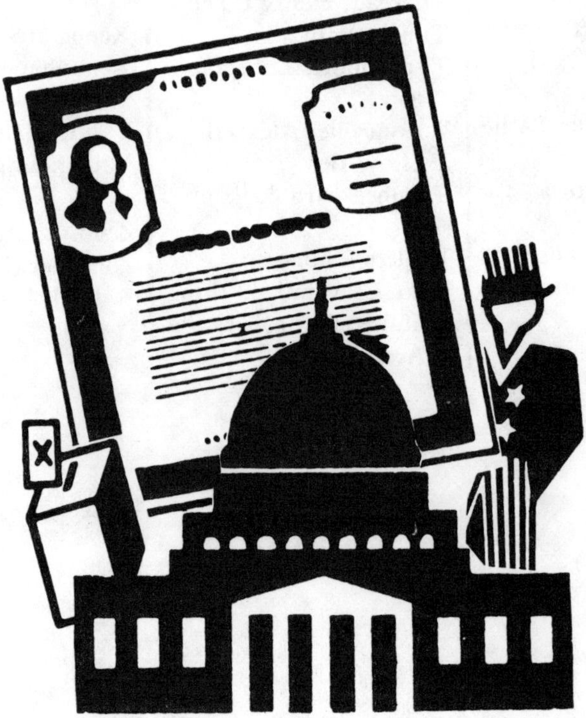

POLITICS AND GOVERNMENT

abdicate
abolish
abrogation
absolutism
ad hoc
administration
admiralty
adjourn
adopt
adversary
advisory
agenda
aggression
alien
allegiance
alliance
allied
ambassador
amendment
amnesty
anarchy
annexation
annul
appeal
appoint
appropriation
arbitration
aristocracy
armistice
arsenal
assembly
assent
attainder
attorney general
authoritarian
authority
autocracy
autonomy

bail
ballot
battle line
belligerency
bicameral

bloc
blockade
bolshevism
boodle
boondock
boondoggle
bossism
boundary
bounty
budget
buncombe
bureaucracy

cabal
cabinet
campaign
candidate
capture
caucus
cede
census
chancellery
chancellor
charter
citizenship
civil disobedience
civil service
cloture
coalition
collectivism
collegial
colonial
commission
commitment
committee
commonweal
commonwealth
communal
communism
compulsory voting
concurring opinion
confederation
confrontation
congress

congressional
congressman
congresswoman
conscientious objector
conscription
consensus
consent
conservative
constituency
constituent
constitution
constitutional monarchy
consul
consulate
contraband
convene
convention
corruption
council
counter
counterfeit
coup
coup d'etat
credential
czar

debate
decree
de facto government
defensive
delegation
democracy
democratic socialism
deputy
despotism
dictatorship
dictum
diet
dilatory motion
diplomacy
diplomat
discrimination
disenfranchisement
disfranchisement

POLITICS AND GOVERNMENT

dispute	gerrymandering	legislation
dissent	government	legislator
dissolve	governor	legislature
district	ground rules	liberal
doctrine	guerrilla warfare	lieutenant governor
dominion	gynarchy	lobby
dynasty		logrolling
	habeas corpus	
election	hegemony	majority
elector	hostage	mandate
electoral college	hostility	maneuver
embargo		manor
embassy	immigration	Marxism
eminent domain	immunity	mayor
emirate	impeachment	militia
emperor	imperialism	minister
empire	implied powers	ministry
enumerated powers	import	minority
envoy	inauguration	mint
exacerbate	in camera	missile
execute	incumbent	mobocracy
executive	indemnity	mock trial
exile	infiltrate	moderator
expatriate	influence	modus vivendi
export	independence	monarchy
expunge	initiative	monopoly
extradition	insurrection	muckrake
extraterritoriality	international	mugwump
	interposition	municipal
fascism	interstate commerce	
federal	intervention	nationality
federalism	intrastate	naturalization
feudal system	invasion	negotiate
fiat	isolate	neutrality
fiefdom	issue	nihilism
filibuster		nonbelligerent
fiscal year	judge	noninterference
foreign minister	judicial	nullification
forum	judiciary	
franchise	junta	obstructing
freedom	jurisdiction	official
	jurisprudence	oligarchy
geopolitical	jury	ombudsman
general welfare	justice	opinion

188

POLITICS AND GOVERNMENT

opposition
ordinance
overrule

pacifism
pact
parliamentary
participant
particularism
partisan
partition
passport
paternalism
patronage
peer
peonage
perfidy
persona non grata
Pharaoh
pigeonholing
plebiscite
plenary
plurality
plutocracy
pocket veto
police state
policy maker
political
politics
poll
populism
pork barrel
pourparler
precedence
prefect
prefecture
preferential voting
premier
preside
president
presidential
presidium
primary
prime minister

principality
privy council
promulgate
propaganda
proportional
  representation
proposition
prorogue
protectorate
pro tempore
protocol
provincial
provisional
proxy
public record

quadripartite
quasilegislative
quorum

radical
rajah
rally
ratify
reactionary
reapportionment
rebellion
recall
reciprocity
referendum
regency
regime
reign
repeal
representative
republic
republican
rescind
resolution
retroactive
revolution
revolutionary council
rider
rightist

roll call
roorback
royalty

secession
secretary
secret ballot
security
self-determination
senate
senatorial
separation
serfdom
session
sheikdom
siege
slavery
slush fund
socialism
sovereign
soviet
speaker
splinter
stalemate
state
statutes
statutory
steering
subversive
suffrage
sultan
summary jurisdiction
summit
superior court
superpower
supreme
surrogate
suzerainty
syndicalism

tactical
taxation
tenure
theocracy

POLITICS AND GOVERNMENT

totalitarian	unanimous decision	vizier
town meeting	underground	vote
treason	unicameral	voter
treaty	universal suffrage	
trial by jury		warrant
tribunal	vacancy	welfare
tripartite	vest	whip
troika	veto	whitewash
tyranny	vice president	wirepulling
	viceroy	
ultraconservative	victory	yeas and nays
ultraliberal	visa	yield

PRESIDENTS, THEIR WIVES, AND VICE-PRESIDENTS

Adams, John (Abigail Smith)
Adams, John Quincy (Louisa Catherine Johnson)
Arthur, Chester A. (Ellen L. Herndon)

Buchanan, James (none)

Carter, James Earl "Jimmy" (Rosalynn Smith)
Cleveland, Grover (Frances Folsom)
Coolidge, Calvin (Grace Anna Goodhue)

Eisenhower, Dwight David (Mamie G. Doud)

Fillmore, Millard (Abigail Powers, Caroline McIntosh)
Ford, Gerald Rudolph (Elizabeth B. Warren)

Garfield, James Abram (Lucretia Rudolph)
Grant, Ulysses Simpson (Julia Dent)

Harding, Warren Gamaliel (Florence DeWolfe)
Harrison, Benjamin (Caroline L. Scott, Mary Scott Dimmick)
Harrison, William Henry (Anna Symmes)
Hayes, Rutherford Birchard (Lucy Webb)
Hoover, Herbert Clark (Lou Henry)

Jackson, Andrew (Rachel Donelson Robards)
Jefferson, Thomas (Martha Wayles Skelton)
Johnson, Andrew (Eliza McCardle)

Johnson, Lyndon Baines (Claudia A. "Lady Bird" Taylor)

Kennedy, John Fitzgerald (Jacqueline L. Bouvier)

Lincoln, Abraham (Mary Todd)

Madison, James (Dorothea "Dolley" Payne Todd)
McKinley, William (Ida Saxton)
Monroe, James (Elizabeth Kortright)

Nixon, Richard Milhous (Thelma "Pat" Ryan)

Pierce, Franklin (Jane Means Appleton)
Polk, James Knox (Sarah Childress)

Reagan, Ronald Wilson (Nancy Davis)
Roosevelt, Franklin Delano (Anna Eleanor Roosevelt)
Roosevelt, Theodore (Alice H. Lee, Edith K. Carow)

Taft, William Howard (Helen Herron)
Taylor, Zachary (Margaret Smith)
Truman, Harry S. (Elizabeth V. Wallace)
Tyler, John (Letitia Christian, Julia Gardiner)

Van Buren, Martin (Hannah Hoes)

Washington, George (Martha Dandridge Custis)
Wilson, Woodrow (Ellen L. Axson, Edith B. Galt)

VICE-PRESIDENTS

Adams, John
Agnew, Spiro T.
Arthur, Chester A.

Barkley, Alben W.
Breckinridge, John C.
Burr, Aaron
Bush, George Herbert

Calhoun, John C.
Clinton, George
Colfax, Schuyler
Coolidge, Calvin
Curtis, Charles

Dallas, George M.
Dawes, Charles G.

Fairbanks, Charles W.
Fillmore, Millard

Ford, Gerald R.

Garner, John Nance
Gerry, Elbridge

Hamlin, Hannibal
Hendricks, Thomas A.
Hobart, Garret A.
Humphrey, Hubert H.

Jefferson, Thomas
Johnson, Andrew
Johnson, Lyndon Baines
Johnson, Richard M.

King, William R.

Marshall, Thomas R.
Mondale, Walter F.

Morton, Levi P.

Nixon, Richard

Rockefeller, Nelson A.
Roosevelt, Theodore

Sherman, James S.
Stevenson, Adlai E.

Tompkins, Daniel D.
Truman, Harry S.
Tyler, John

Van Buren, Martin

Wallace, Henry Agard
Wheeler, William A.
Wilson, Henry

PSYCHOLOGY AND PSYCHIATRY

acrophobia
adaption
adolescence
affect
aggression
agoraphobia
alter ego
ambivalence
amnesia
anaclisis
anaesthesia
anal
analysis
analytical
analyze
anima
animus
annihilation
anorexia
anticathesis
antidepressant
anxiety
aphasia
apraxia
archetype
ataxia
attitude
autism
autoeroticism
autonomy

behaviorism
bisexuality

castration complex
catalepsy
catatonia
catharsis
cathexis
causation
chemotherapy
climacteric
cognition
complex

compulsion
conditioned reflex
congruence
conscious
constriction
contiguity
coprophilia
cretin
crisis

déjà vu
delirium tremens
delusion
depersonalization
depression
dissociation
dyslexia
dysphasia
dysphoria

echolalia
echopraxia
ecstasy
ectomorphy
ego
egocentrism
ego ideal
egoist
egomania
electroencephalography
electroshock
empathy
empiricism
enuresis
equivalence
erogenous
eroticism
etiology
euphoria
exhibitionism
existentialism
experiential
extinguishing
extraversion

fetishism
fixation
folie à deux
fragmentation
Freudian slip
frigidity
frustration

generativity
Gestalt therapy
glossolalia
grandiose
guilt

hallucination
hallucinogen
hedonism
hermaphrodite
heterosexuality
holistic
homosexuality
hyperkinesis
hypertension
hypnosis
hypnotize
hypochondria
hysteria

id
idealization
identification
imago
individuation
inferiority complex
inhibition
instinct
intellectualization
intelligence quotient (IQ)
introvert
intuition
isomorphism

kinesthesia
kleptomania

PSYCHOLOGY AND PSYCHIATRY

latency	phenylketonuria (PKU)	sadism
libidinal	phobia	sadomasochism
libido	pica	schizoid
logorrhea	placebo	schizophrenia
	polarity	sedative
manic-depressive	posthypnotic suggestion	sensation
masochism	preconscious	somnambulism
memory	projection	Stanford-Binet test
migraine	psyche	stimulus
motivation	psychiatric	subconscious
	psychic	sublimation
narcissism	psychoanalysis	subrogate
narcotic	psychogenic	superego
necrophilia	psychological	symbiotic
negativism	psychometry	symbolization
neurosis	psychoneurosis	synchronism
neurotic	psychopath	
nymphomania	psychopathology	taboo
	psychopharmacology	therapeutic
obsession	psychophysiological	tic
Oedipus complex	psychosis	tranquilizer
omnipotent	psychosomatic	transactional
oral	psychotherapy	transcendent
organismic	pyromania	transfer
		traumatic
paranoia	rapport	
paranoid	rapprochement	unconscious
parapraxis	rationalization	
pathological	recall	vertigo
pederasty	recognition	vicarious
perception	regression	voyeurism
personification	reinforcement	
perversion	repression	withdrawal
phallic	response	
	Rorschach test	xenophobia

RACES, TRIBES, AND PEOPLES

Abnaki	Breton	Dorian
Achaean	Briton	Dravidian
Aeolian	Bulgar	Druse
Afghan	Burgundian	
Afrikaner	Burmese	Egyptian
Ainu	Buryat	Eskimo
Albanian	Bushman	Ethiopian
Aleut		Etruscan
Algonkin	Caddo	
Alpine	Cajun	Filipino
Andaman	Cantonese	Finn
Angle	Cape African	Flathead
Annamese	Cape Verdean	Fon
Apache	Carib	Formosan
Apalachee	Catawba	Fox
Arab	Caucasian	Frank
Arakanese	Cayuga	Frisian
Arapaho	Cayuse	Fuegian
Araucanian	Celt	Fulani
Arawak	Chemehuevi	
Arikara	Cherokee	Gosiute
Armenian	Chibcha	Goth
Aryan	Chickasaw	Gros Ventre
Ashanti	Chimu	Guaraní
Assamese	Chin	Gurkha
Assiniboin	Chinese	Gypsy
Assyrian	Chinook	
Aymara	Chippewa	Haida
Azorean	Choctaw	Hakka
Aztec	Chukchi	Hamite
	Circassian	Han
Bakhtiari	Coeur d'Alene	Hausa
Baluchi	Comanche	Havasupai
Bambara	Copt	Hawaiian
Bannock	Cossack	Helvetian
Bantu	Coushatta	Hindu
Basque	Cree	Hoh
Bedouin	Creek	Hoopa
Bellacoola	Croatian	Hopi
Bengali	Crow	Hottentot
Berber	Cypriot	Hualapai
Bhil		Hun
Bhotiya	Dakota	Huron
Blackfeet	Digger	Hutu

RACES, TRIBES, AND PEOPLES

Ibo
Inca
Indian
Ionian
Iranian
Irish
Iroquois

Japanese
Jívaro
Jute

Kabyle
Kachin
Kalmyk
Kanikkaran
Kara-Kalpak
Karamajong
Karen
Kashmirian
Kaskaskia
Kaw
Kazakh
Khalkha
Khasi
Khmer
Kickapoo
Kikuyu
Kiowa
Kirghiz
Klamath
Kootenai
Korean
Koryak
Kurd
Kwakiutl

Ladakh
Lao
Lapp
Lebanese
Lepcha
Lombard
Lumbee

Lummi
Luri
Lushai

Magyar
Maidu
Malay
Manchu
Mandan
Maori
Maricopa
Masai
Mashona
Matabele (Ndebele)
Mattapony
Maya
Mede
Mediterranean
Melanesian
Menominee
Miao
Micmac
Micronesian
Mishmi
Miwok
Mixtec
Modoc
Mohave
Mohawk
Mohegan
Moi
Mongol
Montagnais
Montagnard
Moor
Mossi
Mulatto
Munsee
Muria

Naga
Nahuatl
Nanticoke
Narraganset

Natchez
Navaho (Navajo)
Nazca
Negrito
Nez Percé
Nilote
Nisqually
Nootka
Nordic
Norman

Ojibwa
Olmec
Omaha
Oneida
Onondaga
Osage
Ostrogoth
Ostyak
Otoe

Paiute
Pamunkey
Papago
Parsee
Passamaquoddy
Pathan
Pawnee
Pequot
Persian
Philistine
Phoenician
Pict
Pima
Polynesian
Pomo
Ponca
Potawatomi
Powhatan
Pueblo
Pygmy

Quapaw
Quinault

RACES, TRIBES, AND PEOPLES

Rajput
Romanian
Ruthenian
Ryukyuan

Salish
Samoan
Samoyed
Santal
Sardinian
Sauk
Saxon
Scot
Scythian
Seminole
Semite
Seneca
Senoi
Serb
Shan
Shawnee
Sherdukpen
Sherpa
Shinnecock
Shoshone
Sicilian
Sikh
Siletz
Singhalese
Sioux

Slav
Slovene
Snake
Snohomish
Sotho
Sudanese
Swazi
Swinomish
Syrian

Tartar (Tatar)
Tibetan
Tiv
Tlingit
Toda
Toltec
Tonkawa
Tonkinese
Totonac
Tsimshian
Tswana
Tuareg
Tungus
Tunica
Tupí
Turk
Tuscarora
Tutsi
Tuvinian
Twa

Uighur
Ute
Uzbek

Vandal
Vedda
Visigoth

Wa
Walloon
Wampanoag
Washo
Welsh
Wichita
Winnebago
Wolof
Wyandotte

Yao
Yakima
Yakut
Yavapai
Yeshkun
Yoruba
Yuma
Yurok

Zapotec
Zulu
Zuni (Zuñi)

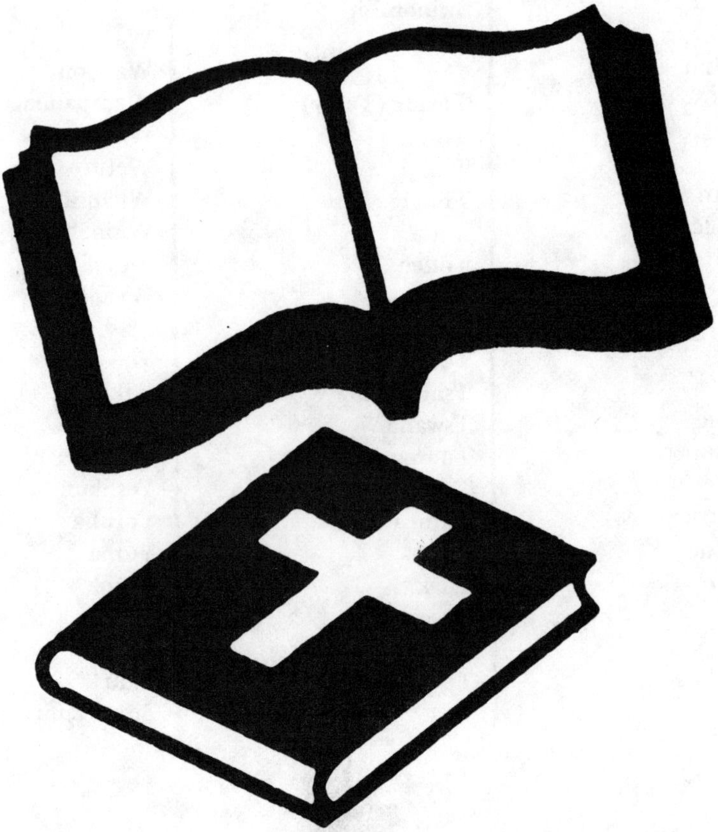

RELIGION—Biblical Names and Places
(of the many only a few have been chosen)

Aaron	Berea	Ecclesiastes
Abednego	Besara	Eden
Abel	Bethany	Edom
Abilene	Bethel	Egypt
Abraham	Bethesda	Elam
Absalom	Bethlehem	Elijah
Achor	Bezetha	Elisha
Actium	Bosphorus	Enoch
Adam	Byzantium	Enos
Adonai		Ephesians
Adria	Caesar	Ephesus
Alexandria	Caiaphas	Ephraim
Amalek	Cain	Ephron
Ammon	Caleb	Esau
Amos	Calvary	Esdras
Andrew	Cana	Esther
Antichrist	Canaanites	Eucharist
Antioch	Capernaum	Euphrates
apocalypse	Cappadocia	Eve
Arabah	Carmel	Exodus
Arabia	Caspian	Ezekiel
Ararat	Chaldea	Ezra
Ark	Chanukah	
Armageddon	Cherubim	Gabriel
Armenia	Chronicles	Galatia
Asshur	Claudius	Galatians
Assyria	Colossians	Galilee
Azariah	Corinth	Gaza
	Corinthians	Genesis
Baal	Cos	Gethsemane
Babel	Cyprus	Gideon
Babylon	Cyrenaica	Gilead
Balaam		Gilgal
Barabbas	Dalmatia	Golan
Barnabas	Damascus	Golgotha
Bartholomew	Daniel	Gomorrah
Baruch	David	Gordian
Bashan	Delilah	
Bathsheba	Deuteronomy	Habakkuk
Beelzebub	Doriscus	Hagar
Beersheba		Haggai
Behemoth	Easter	Hannah
Bel	Ebal	Hannathon
Belshazzar	Ebenezer	Hanukkah
Benjamin		

RELIGION—Biblical Names and Places

Haran	Judea	Mesopotamia
Hebrews	Judges	Messiah
Hebron	Judith	Methuselah
Hellespont	Julian	Micah
Heptateuch		Mizpah
Hermon	Kabul	Moab
Herod	Kabzeel	Moriah
Herodias	Kedah	Moses
Herodium	Kedron	Myra
Hezekiah	Kings	
Hittites		Nahum
Horeb	Lamentations	Nathanael
Hosea	Last Supper	Nazareth
	Lazarus	Nebo
Immanuel	Leah	Nebuchadnezzar
Ionia	Lebanon	Negeb
Isaac	Lesbos	Nehemiah
Isaiah	Levi	Nicaea
Ishmael	Leviticus	Nicene
Israel	Libya	Nicodemus
Issus	Lucifer	Nicopolis
Ituraea	Luke	Nineveh
	Lycia	Nippur
Jacob	Lydia	Noah
James		Numbers
Jehovah	Maacah	
Jeremiah	Maccabees	Obadiah
Jericho	Macedonia	Orontes
Jerusalem	Magdalene	
Jesse	Magnificat	Palestine
Jesus Christ	Malachi	Palmyra
Jezebel	Malta	Parthia
Jezreel	Manasseh	Passover
Job	Mare Nostrum	Patriarch
Joel	Mark	Paul
John	Martha	Peloponnesus
Jonah	Mary	Pentateuch
Jonas	Mary Magdalene	Pentecost
Jordan	Matthew	Persepolis
Joseph	Matthias	Peter
Joshua	Mecca	Pharaoh
Judah	Mediterranean	Pharisee
Judas Iscariot	Megiddo	Philemon
Jude	Memphis	Philip

200

RELIGION—Biblical Names and Places

Philippians
Philistine
Phoenicia
Phoenix
Phrygia
Pisgah
Pontius Pilate
Proverbs
Psalms
Purim
Pyramids

Raamses
Rabbah
Rachel
Ravenna
Rebekah
Redeemer
Revelation
Romans
Rosh Hashanah
Ruth

Saab
Sabbath
Sadducee
Salamis
Salem
Salome

Samaria
Samaritan
Samos
Samothrace
Samuel
Sanhedrin
Sarah
Sardis
Satan
Saul
Scopus
Scriptures
Seleucia
Semite
Sennacherib
Sharon
Sheba
Shechem
Shiloh
Sidon
Simeon
Simon Peter
Sinai
Sirach
Smyrna
Sodom
Solomon
Suez
Susanna

Tabor
Tarshish
Tarsus
Thaddaeus
The Acts
Thebes
Thermopylae
Thessalonians
Thessalonica
Thessaly
Thomas
Tiberius
Tigris
Timothy
Titus
Tobit
Tyre
Tyrrhenian

Vashti

Yehem
Yishub

Zacchaeus
Zanoah
Zechariah
Zephaniah
Zerubbabel
Zion

RELIGIONS, FAITHS, GROUPS, AND ISMS

Adventism
ageism
agnosticism
Anglicism
animism
anthropomorphism
antidisestablishmentarianism
Arminianism
Aryanism
asceticism
atheism

Baalism
Bahá'í
Baptist
Birchism
Brahmanism
Buddhism

Calvinism
Catholicism
chauvinism
chiliasm
Christianity
Christian Science
Confucianism
congregationalism
Coptic

deism
demonism
dharma
Donatism
dualism
Dunker

ecclesiasticism
episcopalism
Episcopalianism
equalitarianism
evangelicalism

fatalism
fetishism
Friends
fundamentalism

Gnosticism

hagiocracy
heathenism
hedonism
Hinayana
Hinduism
Huguenot
humanism

Islam

Jainism
Jehovah's Witnesses
Jesuitism
Judaism

Lutheranism

Mahayana
Maoism
maraboutism
materialism
Mennonitism
Methodism
Mohammedanism
monasticism
monism
Monophysitism
monotheism
Mormonism
Moslemism

neologism
Neoplatonism
nihilism

pacifism

paganism
pantheism
parochialism
Pelagianism
Pentecostalism
Platonism
pluralism
polytheism
predestinarianism
Protestantism
Pythagoreanism

Quakerism

rationalism
reformation
ritualism
Roman Catholicism

Salvation Army
Shintoism
Sikhism
spiritualism
Stoicism
supernaturalism
Swedenborgianism

Taoism
theocracy
theosophism
totemism
Tractarianism
transcendentalism

Unitarianism
Universalism

Waldensian

Yogism

Zen
Zoroastrianism

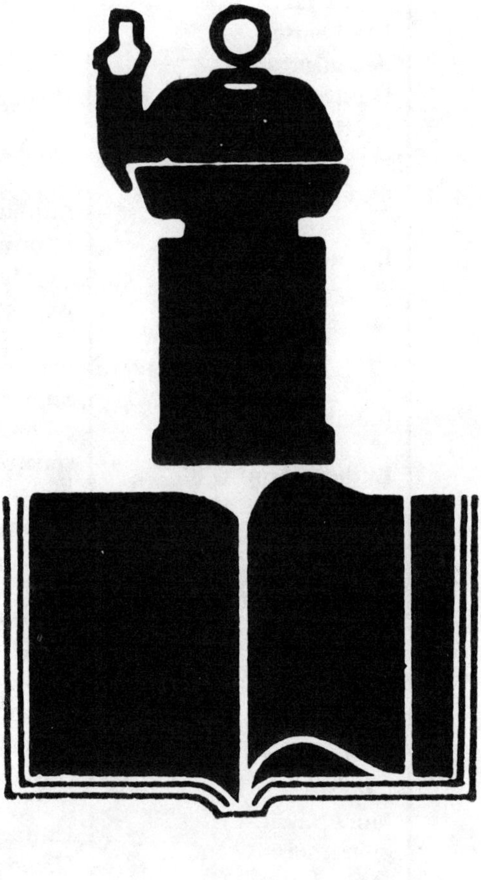

RELIGIOUS TERMS

abbess
abbot
ablution
absolution
abstinence
acolyte
A.D. (anno Domini)
affusion
alleluia
alpha and omega
altar
amen
anchorite
angel
anoint
Antichrist
antinomian
apocalypse
apocrypha
apostasy
apostle
Apostles' Creed
apostolic succession
archangel
archbishop
archdeacon
atonement
Avesta

baptism
bar mitzvah
beatitudes
belief
benediction
beneficent
blasphemy
bodhi
bodhisattva

cabala
caliph
canon
Capuchin
cardinal
carillon

cassock
catechism
cathedral
catholic
celibate
cenacle
cenobite
censer
chalice
chancel
Chanukah
chaplain
chastity
chrism
circumcision
clergyman
collect
commandment
communion
conciliar
concordat
concubine
confession
confirmation
congregation
consecration
contrition
coronation
covenant
creation
crèche
credence
creed
cross
crucifixion
crusader
curate

deacon
Decalogue
demon
dervish
devil
disciples
divine

divorce
doctrine
dogma
donation

Easter
ecumenical
elder
elevation
epiphany
episcopal
episcopate
epistle
Eucharist
eunuch
evangelist
everlasting
excommunication
exorcist
expiation

faithfulness
fakir
fast
forgiveness
frankincense

Gemara
gentile
genuflect
golden rule
gospel
grace
Gregorian

Hades
hallelujah
Hanukkah
hassock
heaven
hierarch
hosanna
hymnal
hyssop

RELIGIOUS TERMS

icon
iconoclast
idolatry
image
imam
immortality
impanation
incarnation
indulgence
Inquisition
inspiration
intinction
investiture

judgment
justification

Kaaba
Kaddish
kalpa
Karma
khalif
Koran
kosher

laity
Lateran
lavabo
lector
leper
litany
liturgical
liturgy

mammon
manna
marabout
marriage
martyr
meditation
mendicant
millennium
minister
miracle

Mishnah
Monophysite
mosque
mullah
myrrh
mysticism

Nicene Creed
nimbus

obedience
oblation
ordination

papacy
parable
paradise
Passover
pastor
patriarch
penance
penitent
pilgrimage
polity
prayer
preacher
predestination
presbyter
priest
priesthood
primate
prophecy
prophet
Protestant
providence
psalm
psalter
purgatory
Purim

rabbi
Ramadan
redemption
Reformation

repentance
resurrection
revelation
rite
ritual
rosary
Rosh Hashanah

Sabbath
sacrament
sacrifice
saint
salvation
samadhi
samsara
sanctify
sanctuary
Sanhedrin
Satan
savior
Scriptures
sepulcher
seraphim
sermon
Shakta
shepherd
shittah
shofar
simony
skeptic
skullcap
solitary
spiritual
stewardship
supplication
sura
sutra
synagogue

tabernacle
Talmud
temple
theological
Torah

206

RELIGIOUS TERMS

Transfiguration	unleavened	Yahrzeit
transmigration	usher	Yahweh
transubstantiation		Yin and Yang
Trinity	versicle	Yom Kippur
triptych	vestment	
triquetrous	vicar	Zealot
		Zen
unction	Whitsunday	Zend
unicorn	worldliness	Zend-Avesta

RIVERS

Adige
Aisne
Aldan
Allegheny
Amazon
Amu Darya
Amur (Heilong)
Angara
Apalachicola
Araguaia
Aras (Araks)
Arkansas
Assiniboine
Atchafalaya
Athabasca
Attawapiskat
Avon

Balsas
Beaver
Benue
Boyne
Brahmaputra (Jamuna)
Brazos
Bug

Canadian
Cape Fear
Casiquiare
Cauca
Cauvery
Chao Phraya
Chari
Chattahoochee
Chaudière
Cheyenne
Chubut
Churchill
Cimarron
Clyde
Colorado
Columbia
Conemaugh
Congo (Zaire)

Connecticut
Coosa
Cowlitz
Cumberland
Cuyahoga

Danube
Darling
Dee
Delaware
Des Moines
Dnieper (Dnepr)
Dniester (Dnestr)
Don
Donets
Dordogne
Douro (Duero)
Drava
Dvina

Ebro
Elbe
Escambia
Euphrates (Al-Furat)

Fox
Fraser
French Broad

Gambia
Ganges (Ganga)
Garonne
Gila
Godavari
Guadalquivir
Guadiana

Holston
Hong-ha (Red)
Hooghly
Housatonic
Huang (Hwang Ho)
Hudson
Humboldt

Iguaçu
Illinois
Indus
Inn
Irrawaddy
Irtysh

James
Japura
John Day
Jordan
Juniata

Kama
Kanawha
Kankakee
Kansas
Kaskaskia
Kennebec
Kiskiminetas
Kolyma
Kootenai
Krishna (Kistna)
Kuskokwim
Kura

Lackawanna
Lehigh
Lena
Liard
Licking
Liffey
Limpopo
Loire
Lualaba

Mackenzie
Madeira
Magdalena
Mahanadi
Mahoning
Main
Marañón
Maritsa

RIVERS

Marne
Maumee
Meander (Menderes)
Mekong
Meramec
Merrimack
Mersey
Meuse
Miami
Minnesota
Mississippi
Missouri
Mohawk
Monongahela
Moselle (Mosel)
Moskva
Murray
Muskingum
Musselshell

Narmada (Narbada)
Neches
Neckar
Negro
Nelson
Nemunas (Niemen)
Neosho
Neuse
Neva
Niger
Nile (An-Nil)
Niobrara
Nueces

Ob
Oconee
Oder
Ohio
Oise
Oka
Okanogan
Orange
Orinoco
Orontes (Al-Ahsi)

Osage
Ottawa
Ouachita

Paraguay
Paraíba
Paraná
Parnaíba
Patuxent
Peace
Pearl
Pechora
Pecos
Pee Dee
Pend Oreille
Penobscot
Pilcomayo
Platte
Po
Potomac
Prut
Purus
Putumayo

Rappahannock
Red
Republican
Rhine
Rhône
Richelieu
Río de la Plata
Rio Grande
Roanoke
Rock
Roosevelt
Ruhr

Saale
Saar
Sabine
Sacramento
Saguenay
St. Croix
St. Francis

St. John
St. Lawrence
Saint-Maurice
Salmon
Salween
San Joaquin
Santee
São Francisco
Saône
Saskatchewan
Sava
Savannah
Schelde (Escaut)
Scioto
Seine
Senegal
Severn
Shannon
Shatt al-Arab
Shenandoah
Smoky Hill
Snake
Somme
Sungari (Songhua)
Susquehanna
Sutlej
Suwannee
Syr-Darya

Tagus (Tajo)
Tallahatchie
Tallapoosa
Tanana
Tapajós
Tarim
Tennessee
Thames
Tiber (Tevere)
Ticino
Tigris (Dijlah)
Tisza
Tocantins
Tombigbee
Trent

210

RIVERS

Trinity
Tuscarawas
Tyne

Ubangi
Ucayali
Ural
Uruguay
Ussuri (Wusuli)

Vaal
Vistula (Wisla)

Vltava (Moldau)
Volga
Volta

Wabash
Weser
Willamette
Wisconsin

Xi (Si)
Xingu

Yadkin

Yakima
Yalu (Amnok)
Yamuna (Jumna)
Yangtze (Chang)
Yazoo
Yellowstone
Yenisei
York
Youghiogheny
Yukon

Zambezi

SCALE OF MILES.

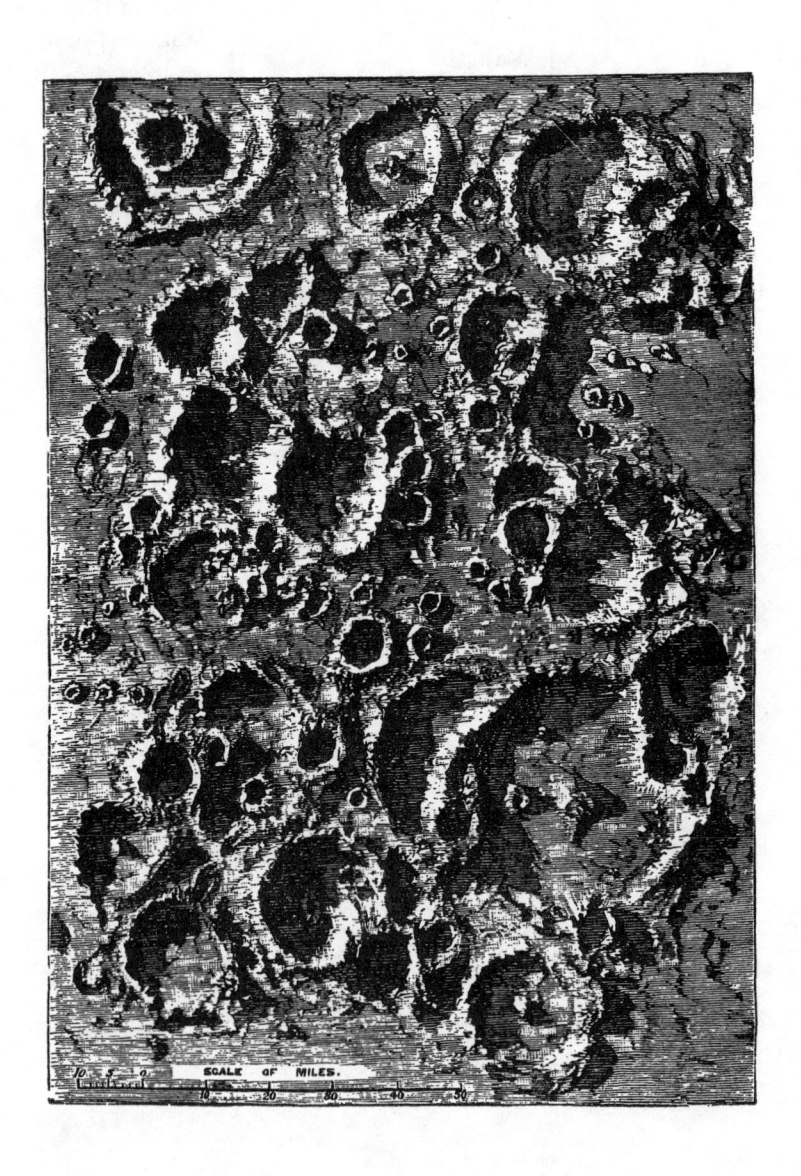

SCIENCES

acoustics
aerobatics
aerodynamics
aeronautics
agriculture
agrobiology
agronomy
algology
analytical chemistry
anatomy
anthropology
archaeology
astrodynamics
astrogeology
astronautics
astronomy
astrophotography
astrophysics
atomic physics
atomics

bacteriology
ballistics
bibliography
biochemistry
biodynamics
bioecology
biogeography
biology
biomathematics
biometrics
bionics
biophysics
biosciences
biotechnology
botany

carcinology
chemistry
chemurgy
climatology
computer technology
cosmography

cosmology
cryogenics
crystallography
cytology

dermatology
domestic science
dynamics

earth science
ecology
economics
electrochemistry
electronics
embryology
energy technology
engineering
entomology
epistemology
ethnology
ethnomusicology
etymology
eugenics

forestry

genealogy
genetics
geochemistry
geodesy
geography
geology
geophysics
geriatrics
glossology

helminthology
herpetology
histology
husbandry
hydrology

ichnology
ichthyology

ideology
immunohematology
immunology
inorganic chemistry
invertebrate zoology

lexicology
library science
life science
linguistics
logic

magnetics
magnetism
mammalogy
mathematics
mechanics
medicine
metallurgy
metaphysics
meteorology
metrology
microbiology
microchemistry
mineralogy
molecular biology
morphology
musicology
mycology
mythology

neurobiology
neurology
neuroscience
nuclear physics
nutrition

oceanography
ontology
optics
orchidology
organic chemistry
organology
ornithology

213

SCIENCES

paleobiology
paleobotany
paleogeography
paleogeology
paleontology
pantology
parapsychology
particle physics
pathology
pharmacodynamics
pharmacology
pharyngology
phenology
phenomenology
philosophy
phonemics
phonetics
phonology
phorometry
photobiology
photogeology
photogrammetry
photography
photometry

phylogeny
physical chemistry
physics
physiography
physiology
phytogeography
phytosociology
plant pathology
political economy
political science
psychiatry
psychoacoustics
psychobiology
psycholinguistics
psychology
psychopathology
psychophysiology

quantum mechanics

radiation
radiogoniometry
radiology
rhetoric

seismology
social science
sociology
solid state physics
spectroscopy
statistics
symbology
symptomatology
synecology
systematics

taxonomy
teleology
theology
thermodynamics
toxicology
typology

vertebrate zoology
veterinary medicine
virology

zoology

SCIENTISTS AND EXPLORERS

Achillini, Alessandro
Adler, Alfred
Agassiz, (Jean) Louis
Agricola, Georg (Bauer)
Aiken, Howard
Aldrin, Edwin Eugene
Aldrovandi, Ulisse
Alembert, Jean Le Rond d'
Alfven, Hannes Olof
Alvarez, Louis Walter
Ampère, André Marie
Anaximander
Anderson, Carl David
Anderson, Philip Warren
Andrews, Roy Chapman
Apollonius Pergaeus
Appleton, Edward
Archimedes
Aristarchus of Samos
Aristotle
Armstrong, Neil Alden
Ashley, William Henry
Aston, Francis W.
Audubon, John James
Avogadro, Amedeo

Bacon, Francis T.
Bahaim, Martin
Balboa, Vasco de
Bardeen, John
Barth, Heinrich
Bartram, John
Bartram, William
Basov, Nikolai
Bates, Henry Walter
Battani, al-
Baumé, Antoine
Beckford, William
Becquerel, Antoine Henri
Becquerel, Antoine César
Beebe, (Charles) William
Beekman, Isaac
Behring, Emil von
Bekesy, Georg von

Belon, Pierre
Bell, Alexander Graham
Benalcázar, Sebastian de
Bergius, Friedrich
Bering, Vitus
Bernard, Claude
Bernoulli, Daniel, Jacques, and Jean
Bertillon, Alphonse
Berzelius, Jöns Jakob
Bessemer, Sir Henry
Biringuccio, Vanoccio
Blériot, Louis
Bloch, Felix
Bloch, Konrad
Boas, Franz
Bodoni, Giambattista
Boone, Daniel
Bordet, Jules
Borlaug, Norman Ernest
Born, Max
Borodin, Aleksandr
Bosch, Karl
Bose, Jagadis
Bothe, Walter
Bowditch, Nathaniel
Boyle, Robert
Bradley, Henry
Bradley, James
Bragg, Sir William
Brahe, Tycho
Brattain, Walter Houser
Braun, Karl
Braun, Wernher von
Bridger, James
Briggs, Lyman James
Brown, Herbert
Bruce, Sir David
Bruno, Giordano
Buchner, Eduard
Bunsen, Robert Wilhelm
Burbank, Luther
Burroughs, John

Burton, Richard Francis
Byrd, Richard Evelyn

Cabeza de Vaca, Alvar
Cabot, John
Cabral, Pedro Alvares
Caillié, Auguste René
Caius, John
Calvin, Melvin
Camerarius, Rudolf Jakob
Carrel, Alexis
Carson, Christopher
Carson, Rachel Louise
Carter, Howard
Cartier, Jacques
Carver, George Washington
Cassini, Jean Dominique
Catesby, Mark
Cavendish, Henry
Caxton, William
Celsius, Anders
Celsius, Olaf
Chadwick, Sir James
Chamberlain, Thomas Crowder
Champlain, Samuel de
Chancellor, Richard
Cherenkov, Pavel
Childe, Vere Gordon
Clark, Kenneth Bancroft
Clark, William
Claude, Albert
Coale, Ansley
Cockcroft, Sir John Douglas
Cohn, Ferdinand
Collins, Michael
Columbus, Christopher
Colt, Samuel
Commoner, Barry

215

SCIENTISTS AND EXPLORERS

Compton, Arthur Holly
Comte, Auguste
Cook, James
Conant, James Bryant
Cooper, Leon
Copernicus, Nicolaus
Córdoba, Francisco
　Fernández de
Cordus, Valerius
Cornforth, John
Coronado, Francisco
　Vásquez de
Corte Real, Gaspar and
　Miguel
Coryat, Thomas
Cournand, André
Cousteau, Jacques
Croll, James
Crookes, William
Cunha, Tristão da
Curie, Marie
Curie, Pierre
Curtiss, Glen
Curtius, Ernst
Cuvier, Georges
　Léopold (Baron)

Daguerre, Louis
Daimler, Gottlieb
Dakin, Henry
Dale, Sir Henry
Dalton, John
Dampier, William
Dana, Edward
Dana, James Dwight
Darwin, Charles Robert
Davis, John
Davy, Sir Humphrey
Debierne, André
Deere, John
De Forest, Lee
de Kruif, Paul
Delbrück, Max
De Long, George

Deniker, Joseph
Descartes, René
De Soto, Hernando
Dias, Bartholomeu
Díaz del Castillo, Bernal
Diesel, Rudolf
Digges, Leonard
Digges, Thomas
Dioscorides, Pedanius
Dirac, Paul
Doisy, Edward
Dooley, Thomas
Doppler, Christian
Drake, Sir Francis
Draper, Henry
Draper, John William
Du Bois-Reymond, Emil
Duve, Christian

Eastman, George
Eddington, Sir Arthur
Edelman, Gerald
Edison, Thomas Alva
Ehrlich, Paul Ralph
Einstein, Albert
Ellis, Alexander
Ellsworth, Lincoln
Enders, John
Eratosthenes
Ericson, Leif
Ericsson, John
Erlanger, Joseph
Esaki, Leo
Euclid
Euler, Leonhard
Eustachio, Bartolomeo
Evans, Sir Arthur
Evans, Herbert McLean

Faber, Jean Henri
Fahrenheit, Gabriel
　Daniel
Fairchild, David
Faraday, Michael

Fermat, Pierre de
Fernel, Jean
Fernandez, Juan
Fetchnev, Gustav
Feynman, Richard
　Phillips
Fibiger, Johannes
Finlay, Carlos
Fischer, Emil
Fischer, Ernest Otto
Fischer, Hans
Fisher, Irving
Flammarion, Camille
Fleming, Sir Alexander
Fleming, Sir John
　Ambrose
Flory, Paul John
Fokker, Anthony
Foucault, Jean Bernard
Fourdrinier, Henry
Fourier, Jean Baptiste
Fowler, Henry Watson
Franck, James
Franklin, Benjamin
Franklin, Sir John
Frémont, John Charles
Fresnel, Augustin
Freud, Sigmund
Friedman, Milton
Frisch, Ragnar
Frobisher, Martin
Froebel, Friedrich
Fromm, Eric
Fuchs, Leonhard
Fuchs, Johann
　Nepomuk von
Fulton, Robert
Funk, Casimir
Furnivall, Frederick
　James

Gabor, Denis
Gagarin, Yuri A.
Galen

SCIENTISTS AND EXPLORERS

Galilei, Galileo
Galois, Evariste
Galton, Sir Francis
Galvani, Luigi
Gama, Vasco da
Garand, John Cantius
Gasser, Herbert Spencer
Gatling, Richard J.
Gauss, Karl
Gay-Lussac, Joseph Louis
Geddes, Norman Bel
Geikie, Sir Archibald
Gesell, Arnold Lucius
Gesner, Konrad von
Giaever, Ivar
Gibbs, Josiah
Gilbert, Sir Humphrey
Gilbert, William
Gilboy, Bernard
Glaser, Donald
Glenn, John Herschel
Goddard, Robert Hutchings
Godwin-Austen, Henry Haversham
Goethals, George Washington
Goldenweiser, Alexander
Goodyear, Charles
Gorgas, William Crawford
Graham, Thomas
Granit, Ragnar
Grasse, François de (Comte)
Gray, Asa
Greely, Adolphus
Grenville, Sir Richard
Grignard, Victor
Gutenberg, Johann

Haber, Fritz
Haeckel, Ernst Heinrich

Hahn, Otto
Hahnemann, Samuel
Hakluyt, Richard
Haldane, John Scott
Hall, Charles Francis
Hall, Charles Martin
Halley, Edmund
Hammond, Laurens
Harden, Sir Arthur
Hargreaves, James
Hartline, Halden
Harvey, William
Haworth, Sir Norman
Heaviside, Oliver
Hedin, Sven
Heisenberg, Werner
Helmholtz, Hermann von
Henry, Joseph
Hering, Ewald
Hero
Herschel, Sir William
Hershey, Alfred Day
Herty, Charles Holmes
Hertz, Gustav Ludwig
Hertz, Heinrich
Herzberg, Gerhard
Hess, Victor Franz
Hess, Walter Rudolf
Hewish, Anthony
Heyerdahl, Thor
Heyrovsky, Jaroslav
Hicks, Sir John
Hill, Archibald
Hillary, Sir Edmund
Himshelwood, Sir Cyrus
Hipparchus
Hippocrates
Hitchcock, Edward
Hobbes, Thomas
Hodgkin, Sir Alan
Hoe, Richard March
Hoe, Robert
Hofstadter, Robert

Holland, John Philip
Honaius, Jodocus
Hooker, Sir Joseph
Hooton, Earnest
Hopkins, Sir Frederick
Hoskins, Roy Graham
Howe, Elias
Hubble, Edwin Powell
Hudson, Henry
Hudson, William Henry
Huggins, Sir William
Humboldt, Baron Alexander von
Hunter, John
Huntington, Ellsworth
Huxley, Sir Julian
Huxley, Thomas Henry
Huygens, Christian

Ives, James Merritt

Jacob, François
Jacquard, Joseph
Jeans, Sir James
Jenner, Edward
Jensen, Johannes
Jervis, John
Jiménez de Quesada, Gonzalo
Joliot-Curie, Frédéric
Joliot-Curie, Irene
Joliot, Louis
Jung, Carl Gustav

Kamerlingh, Onnes
Kane, Elisha
Kant, Immanuel
Karrer, Paul
Kastler, Alfred
Katz, Sir Bernard
Kemeny, John G.
Kendall, Edward
Kendrew, Sir John
Kenny, Elizabeth

SCIENTISTS AND EXPLORERS

Kepler, Johannes
Kettering, Charles Franklin
Keynes, John Maynard
Khan, Abu Taleb
Khorana, Har Gobind
Khwarizmi, al
Kindi, al
Kinsey, Alfred Charles
Kirchoff, Gustav
Kirwan, Richard
Koch, Robert
Koopmans, Tjalling
Kornberg, Arthur
Kossel, Albrecht
Krafft-Ebing, Richard von
Krebs, Sir Hans
Krogh, August
Kuhn, Richard
Kusch, Polykarp

La Farge, Oliver Hazard
Lagrange, Comte Joseph Louis
Lamark, Chevalier de
Lamb, Willis Eugene
Land, Edwin Herbert
Landau, Lev Davidovich
Landsteiner, Karl
Langmuir, Irving
Lankester, Sir Edwin
La Pérouse, Jean François de Galaup (Comte de)
Laplace, Pierre Simon de
Lartet, Edouard
La Salle, René de
La Salle, Robert Cavelier (Sieur de)
Laski, Harold
Lattimore, Owen
Lavoisier, Antoine Laurent
Lawrence, Ernest Orlando

Lawrence, Thomas Edward
Layard, Sir Austen
Leakey, Louis Seymour
Lederberg, Joshua
Lee, Tsung-Dao
Leeuwenhoek, Anton van
Leibnitz, Baron Gottfried von
Lenard, Philipp
Leonardo da Vinci
Lewis, Meriwether
Libby, Willard
Lilienthal, Otto
Linnaeus, Carolus (Carl von Linné)
Lippmann, Fritz Albert
Lippmann, Gabriel
Lipscomb, William
Lister, Baron Joseph
Livingstone, David
Locke, John
Lockyer, Sir Joseph
Lodge, Sir Oliver
Loeb, Jacques
Loewi, Otto

Mackenzie, Sir Alexander
Mackinder, Sir Halford
MacMillan, Donald Baxter
Magellan, Ferdinand
Magnus, Heinrich
Malinowski, Bronislaw
Malthus, Thomas Robert
Mansur, al
Marconi, Marchese Guglielmo
Marquette, Jacques
Mason, Charles
Maxim, Sir Hiram

Mayer, Maria Goeppert
McCormick, Cyrus Hall
McMillan, Edwin
Mead, Margaret
Medawar, Peter
Meitner, Lise
Melville, George
Mendel, Gregor
Menninger, Karl Augustus
Mergenthaler, Ottmar
Mesmer, Franz
Messier, Charles
Meyerhof, Otto
Michelson, Albert
Mill, John Stuart
Millikan, Robert Andrew
Montessori, Maria
Montgolfier, Joseph
Morgan, Thomas Hunt
Morley, Edward
Morse, Samuel F.B.
Mott, Sir Neville
Moulton, Forest
Muir, Joseph
Müller, Johann
Murray, Sir James

Nansen, Fridtjof
Napier, John
Nernst, Walther
Newcomb, Simon
Newton, Sir Isaac
Nicolle, Charles
Nobel, Alfred
Noguchi, Hideyo
Nordenskjöld, Baron Nils
Northrop, John Howard
Norwood, Richard

Ohm, George Simon
Omar Khayyam

SCIENTISTS AND EXPLORERS

Oppenheimer, J. Robert
Ostwald, Wilhelm
Otis, Elisha Graves

Palmer, Daniel
Park, Mungo
Parry, Sir William
Pascal, Blaise
Passy, Frédéric
Pasteur, Louis
Pauli, Wolfgang
Pauling, Carl
Pavlov, Ivan Petrovich
Peary, Robert Edwin
Pedrarias (Pedro Arias de Avila)
Picard, Jean
Piccard, Auguste
Pickering, Edward
Pike, Zebulon
Piozzi, Hester Lynch
Pitt-Rivers, Augustus
Pizarro, Francisco
Planck, Max
Poincaré, Jules Henri
Polo, Marco
Ponce de León, Juan
Porter, Sir George
Porter, Rodney
Powell, John Wesley
Priestley, Joseph
Prokhorov, Aleksandr
Przhevalsky, Nikolai
Ptolemy
Puckler-Muskau, Prince Hermann
Pullman, George
Purcell, Edward Mills
Pythagoras

Rabi, Isidor Isaac
Rae, John
Raleigh, Sir Walter
Raman, Sir Chandrasekhara

Ramsay, Sir William
Rasmussen, Knud
Rayleigh, John William Strutt (Baron)
Reed, Walter S.
Robinson, Sir Robert
Roentgen, Wilhelm
Russell, Bertrand Arthur (Earl)
Rutherford, Ernest

Sagan, Carl
Sakharov, Andrei
Salam, Abdus
Salk, Jonas
Sanger, Frederick
Santorini, Giovanni
Schiaparelli, Giovanni
Schick, Béla
Schoolcraft, Henry Rowe
Schwinger, Julian
Scott, Robert Falcon
Seaborg, Glenn
Secchi, Pietro Angelo
See, Thomas
Semënov, Nikolai
Seversky, Alexander
Shackleton, Sir Ernest Henry
Shapley, Harlow
Shepard, Alan Bartlett
Shockley, William
Siegbahn, Karl
Sikorsky, Igor Ivan
Simon, Louis
Smith, Jedediah
Smith, William
Smithson, James
Smyth, Henry
Snow, Baron Charles Percy
Socrates
Spemann, Hans

Spencer, Herbert
Sperry, Elmer Ambrose
Stanley, Sir Henry
Staudinger, Hermann
Stefansson, Vilhjalmur
Stein, William Howard
Steinmetz, Charles Proteus
Stephenson, George
Stern, Otto
Sternberg, George Miller
Stevens, John
Still, Andrew Taylor
Strabo
Sverdrup, Otto

Tatum, Edward Lawrie
Taussig, Frank William
Tereshkova, Valentina
Tesla, Nikola
Theiler, Max
Theophrastus
Thomson, Sir George Paget
Thomson, Sir Joseph
Ting, Samuel
Tiselius, Arne
Titchener, Edward
Todd, David
Tomonaga, Shinichiro
Townes, Charles Hard

Vallarta, Manuel
Vancouver, George
Vavilov, Nikolai I.
Verner, Karl Adolph
Verner, Pierre
Verrazano, Giovanni da
Vespucci, Amerigo
Virchow, Rudolf
Volta, Rudolf
Von Braun, Wernher

Wagner von Jauregg, Julius

SCIENTISTS AND EXPLORERS

Wainwright, Richard
Waksman, Selman
Wald, George
Wallace, Alfred
Walton, Ernest Thomas
Warbury, Otto
Wassermann, August von
Watson, James Dewey
Watson-Watt, Sir Robert
Watt, James
Wegener, Alfred L.
Weinberg, William Charles
Werner, Alfred

Westermarck, Edward
Westinghouse, George
Wheatstone, Sir Charles
Whitehead, Alfred North
Whitney, Eli
Whitney, Josiah
Wiener, Norbert
Wiley, Harvey
Wilkes, Charles
Wilkins, Sir George Hubert
Wilkins, Maurice
Wilkinson, Sir Geoffrey
Windaus, Adolf
Wissler, Clark

Wittig, Georg
Wollaston, William Hyde
Wright, Edward
Wright, Orville
Wright, Wilbur

Xenophon

Yalow, Rosalyn
Yang Chen Ning
Yukawa, Hideki

Zeppelin, Count Ferdinand von
Zinsser, Hans

SPORTS

aerobatics
aikido
air racing
alpine skiing
angling
archery
arm wrestling
asymmetrical bars
autocross
auto racing

badminton
ballooning
bandy
baseball
basketball
biathlon
bicycle racing
billiards
birdwatching
boating
bobsledding
boccie
bowl
bowling
boxing
bullfighting

canoeing
carom billiards
circuit racing
cockfighting
court handball
court tennis
crew
cricket
croquet
crossbow
cross country
crown green bowls
curling
cycling

darts
decathlon
disabled Olympics

discus
diving
dog racing
dog shows
dogsled racing
downhill racing
drag racing
dressage
duckpins

English billiards
equestrian events

falconry
faltboating
fencing
field hockey
figure skating
fishing
fives
flag football
flat green bowls
floor hockey
flying
football
fox hunting
frisbee
frog jumping
frontennis

Gaelic football
giant slalom
gliding
go karting
golf
greyhound racing
gymnastics

hammer throw
handball
hang gliding
harness racing
high jump
hiking
hockey

horizontal bar
horseback riding
horse racing
horseshoes
horse shows
horsevault
hunting
hurdles
hurling
hydroplaning

ice boating
ice dancing
ice skating

jai alai
javelin
jogging
judo

karate
karting
kayaking
kendo
kiting

lacrosse
lawn bowling
lawn tennis
log rolling
long-distance running
long jump
luge tobogganing

marathon
marbles
motocross
motorboating
motorcycle racing
motorcycling
mountaineering

netball

obstacle racing
orienteering

paddleball

SPORTS

paddleboard
paddle tennis
parachuting
parakiting
pelota
pentathlon
pistol shooting
platform tennis
pole vault
polo
pool
powerboating

quarter horse racing
quoits

racquets
rallying
rapid shooting
relay events
rifle shooting
rings
Risleyite
rodeo
roller derby
roller hockey
roller skating
roque
rounder
rowing
rugby
running

sailboarding
sailing
saucer
scuba diving
sculling
shinny
shooting
shot put
shuffleboard
skateboarding
skating
skeet
skibobbing
skiing
skijoring
ski jumping
skin diving
skittle
skydiving
slalom
sledding
snooker
snowmobiling
soaring
soccer
softball
speed boating
speed skating
spelunking
sprinting
squash racquet

squash tennis
steeplechase
stock car racing
surfing
swimming

table tennis
targetshooting
tennis
tenpins
tetherball
tobogganing
touch football
track and field
trampolining
trapshooting
triple jump
tug-of-war
tumbling

volleyball

water polo
water skiing
weight lifting
whitewater canoeing
wildwater canoeing
wrestling

yachting
yacht racing

STATES, THEIR ABBREVIATIONS AND CAPITALS
(including outlying areas)

Alabama AL (Montgomery)
Alaska AK (Juneau)
Arizona AZ (Phoenix)
Arkansas AR (Little Rock)

California CA (Sacramento)
Colorado CO (Denver)
Connecticut CT (Hartford)

Delaware DE (Dover)
District of Columbia DC
  (Washington)

Florida FL (Tallahassee)

Georgia GA (Atlanta)

Hawaii HI (Honolulu)

Idaho ID (Boise)
Illinois IL (Springfield)
Indiana IN (Indianapolis)
Iowa IA (Des Moines)

Kansas KS (Topeka)
Kentucky KY (Frankfort)

Louisiana LA (Baton Rouge)

Maine ME (Augusta)
Maryland MD (Annapolis)
Massachusetts MA (Boston)
Michigan MI (Lansing)
Minnesota MN (St. Paul)
Mississippi MS (Jackson)
Missouri MO (Jefferson City)
Montana MT (Helena)

Nebraska NE (Lincoln)
Nevada NV (Carson City)

New Hampshire NH (Concord)
New Jersey NJ (Trenton)
New Mexico NM (Santa Fe)
New York NY (Albany)
North Carolina NC (Raleigh)
North Dakota ND (Bismarck)

Ohio OH (Columbus)
Oklahoma OK (Oklahoma City)
Oregon OR (Salem)

Pennsylvania PA (Harrisburg)

Rhode Island RI (Providence)

South Carolina SC (Columbia)
South Dakota SD (Pierre)

Tennessee TN (Nashville)
Texas TX (Austin)

Utah UT (Salt Lake City)

Vermont VT (Montpelier)
Virginia VA (Richmond)

Washington WA (Olympia)
West Virginia WV (Charleston)
Wisconsin WI (Madison)
Wyoming WY (Cheyenne)

American Samoa (Pago Pago)
Guam (Agaña)
Northern Mariana Islands
  (Saipan)
Puerto Rico (San Juan)
Trust Territory of the Pacific
  Islands (Saipan)
Virgin Islands (Charlotte
  Amalie)

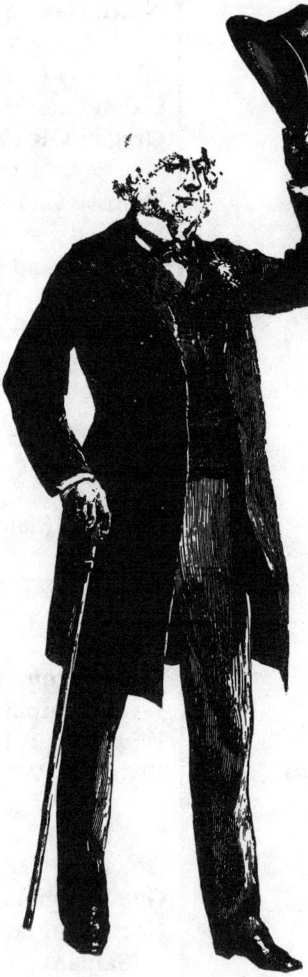

STATESMEN, DIPLOMATS, AND OTHER POLITICAL LEADERS
(Presidents of the U.S. are listed separately)

Acheson, Dean
Adams, Charles Francis
Adenauer, Konrad
Aga Khan
Alexander Nevsky
Allende, Salvador
Andrássy, Julius
Arafat, Yasser
Asoka
Asquith, Herbert
Ataturk (see Kemal)
Attila
Attlee, Clement
Augustus
Azikiwe, N.

Bacon, Francis
Baldwin, Stanley
Balfour, Arthur
Barbosa, Rui
Baruch, Bernard
Batista y Zaldivar, Fulgencio
Beaverbrook, William Aitken (Lord)
Begin, Menachem
Bello, Ahmadu
Ben Bella, Mohammed
Beneš, Eduard
Ben-Gurion, David
Benton, Thomas Hart
Bernadotte, Jean Baptiste
Bethmann-Hollweg, Theobald
Bevan, Aneurin
Bevin, Ernest
Bidault, Georges
Bismarck, Otto von
Blaine, James G.
Blum, Léon
Bodley, Thomas
Bohlen, Charles
Bolingbroke, Henry St. John (Viscount)

Bolívar, Simón
Bonaparte, Napoleon
Borden, Robert
Borgia, Cesare
Bourguiba, Habib Ben Ali
Brandt, Willy
Breckinridge, John C.
Brezhnev, Leonid
Briand, Aristide
Broz (Tito), Josip
Bryan, William Jennings
Bullitt, William
Bunche, Ralph
Burke, Edmund

Caballero, Francisco Largo
Caesar, Gaius Julius
Calhoun, John C.
Caligula
Calles, Plutarco
Cannon, Joseph Gurney
Carranza, Venustiano
Cartier, George
Castro, Fidel
Cavour, Camillo
Ceausescu, Nicolae
Chamberlain, Neville
Charlemagne (Charles I)
Chase, Salmon P.
Chateaubriand, René de
Chiang Kai-shek
Chou En-lai
Churchill, Winston
Ciano, Galeazzo
Clay, Henry
Clemenceau, Georges
Cleopatra
Clive, Robert
Cochise
Colbert, Jean Baptiste
Connally, Tom
Constantine

Cosgrave, William Thomas
Costello, John
Cripps, Stafford
Crockett, David
Cromwell, Oliver
Curzon, George Nathaniel

Daladier, Edouard
Dalai Lama
Danton, Georges
Davis, Jefferson
Dayan, Moshe
De Gaulle, Charles A.
De Groot, Hugo
De Valera, Eamon
Díaz, Porfirio
Diefenbaker, John
Diem, Ngo Dinh
Disraeli, Benjamin
Dollfuss, Engelbert
Dom Pedro II
Douglas, Frederick
Douglas, Stephen A.
Dubcek, Alexander
Dulles, John Foster
Du Plessis-Mornay, Philippe
Duvalier, François

Eden, Anthony
Eleanor of Aquitaine

Fadden, Arthur
Faisal
Farouk I
Forrestal, James Vincent
Franco, Francisco
Franklin, Benjamin
Fulbright, James William

Gadsden, James

STATESMEN, DIPLOMATS, AND OTHER POLITICAL LEADERS

Gallatin, Albert
Galt, Alexander
Gambetta, Léon
Gandhi, Mohandas (Mahatma)
Garibaldi, Giuseppe
Gasparri, Pietro
Genghis Khan
George, David Lloyd
Gerard, James
Geronimo
Giap, Vo Nguyen
Gladstone, William E.
Glass, Carter
Godunov, Boris
Goebbels, Joseph
Gomulka, Wladyslaw
Goulart, João
Grey, Edward
Gromyko, Andrei
Guevara, Ernesto
Guizot, François

Hadrian
Haig, Alexander
Haile Selassie
Halifax, Charles Montagu (Earl of)
Halifax, George Savile (Marquess of)
Hamilton, Alexander
Hammarskjöld, Dag
Hammurabi
Hampton, Wade
Hanna, Marcus
Hannibal
Harriman, William Averell
Hastings, Warren
Hatshepsut
Hay, John
Heath, Edward
Henry, Patrick
Herter, Christian

Hertzog, James Barry
Hindenburg, Paul von
Hirohito
Hitler, Adolf
Ho Chi Minh
Hoover, Herbert
Hopkins, Harry Lloyd
Horthy, Nicholas
Houphouët-Boigny, Félix
Houston, Sam
Hsüan-T'ung (Henry Puyi)
Hull, Cordell
Humphrey, Hubert H.
Husein ibn Ali

Ibn Saud
Ikeda, Hayato
Isabella I, Queen

Jaurès, Jèan Léon
Jefferson, Thomas
Juárez, Benito Pablo
Jusserand, Jules
Justinian I

Kanaris, Konstantinos
Kaunda, Kenneth
Kellogg, Frank Billings
Kemal Ataturk
Kennan, George F.
Kennedy, Joseph Patrick
Kenyatta, Jomo
Kerensky, Alexander
Khama, Seretse
Khomeini, Ruhollah (Ayatollah)
Khrushchev, Nikita
King, William Lyon Mackenzie
Kissinger, Henry Alfred
Koo, Wellington
Kossuth, Ferenc
Kosygin, Alexei
Kublai Khan

La Follette, Robert
La Guardia, Fiorello
Lansing, Robert
Laurier, Wilfrid
Laval, Pierre
Lenin, Vladimir Ilyich
Lie, Trygve
Liliuokalani
Litvinov, Maxim
Lloyd George, David
Lodge, Henry Cabot
Long, Huey
Lumumba, Patrice
Lycurgus

Macaulay, Thomas Babington
Macbeth
Macdonald, John Alexander
MacDonald, James Ramsay
Machiavelli, Niccolò
Mackenzie, Alexander
Mackenzie King, William Lyon
Macmillan, Harold
Macon, Nathaniel
Madariaga, Salvador de
Makino, Nobuaki
Malraux, André
Mann, Horace
Mannerheim, Carl Gustaf von
Mansur, al-
Mao Tse-tung
Marat, Jean Paul
Marcus Aurelius
Maria Theresa
Marshall, George C.
Marshall, John
Masaryk, Jan
Maximilian of Hapsburg
Mazarin, Jules
Mazzini, Giuseppe

226

STATESMEN, DIPLOMATS, AND OTHER POLITICAL LEADERS

Mboya, Tom
McAdoo, William G.
McCarthy, Joseph
Meighen, Arthur
Meir, Golda
Mellon, Andrew
Mendès-France, Pierre
Menelek II
Menzies, Robert Gordon
Metaxas, Joannes
Metternich Klemens von (Prince)
Mohammed Ali
Molotov, Vyacheslav
Mondlane, E.
Montezuma
More, Thomas
Morris, Gouverneur
Morris, Robert
Moshweshwe, King
Muñoz Marín, Luis
Murphy, Robert Daniel
Mussolini, Benito

Nasser, Gamal Abdel
Nehru, Jawaharlal
Nero
Nevsky, Alexander
Nkrumah, Kwame
Norris, George William
North, Frederick (Lord)
Novikov, Nikolai
Nyerere, Julius

Obregón, Alvaro
O'Connell, Daniel
Orlando, Vittorio
Osmeña, Sergio

Paderewski, Ignace Jan
Padmore, George
Papen, Franz von
Park Chung Hee
Parnell, Charles Stewart

Pearson, Lester
Peel, Sir Robert
Perkins, Frances
Perón, Juan Domingo
Pétain, Henri Philippe
Pilsudski, Józef
Pinckney, Charles
Pitt, William
Poincaré, Raymond
Pompidou, Georges
Pontiac
Potëmkin, Grigori
Powhatan
Ptolemy

Quezon y Molina, Manuel

Raleigh, Walter
Rasputin, Grigori
Rayburn, Sam
Reynaud, Paul
Rhee, Syngman
Rhodes, Cecil
Ribbentrop, Joachim von
Richelieu, Armand du Plessis (Cardinal)
Robespierre, Maximilien
Romulo, Carlos
Root, Elihu
Rosebery, Archibald Primrose (Earl of)
Rusk, Dean

Sadat, Anwar
Salazar, Antonio
Santa Anna, Antonio de
Sato, Eisaku
Sato, Naotake
Savonarola, Girolamo
Schuman, Robert
Schurman, Jacob
Schurz, Carl
Schuschnigg, Kurt von

Senghor, Léopold Sédar
Seward, William H.
Sforza, Carlo
Shah (Pahlavi, Mohammad Reza)
Shepilov, Dmitri
Sherman, John
Sherman, Roger
Sihanouk, Norodom
Smuts, Jan
Solon
Somoza, Anastasio and Luis
Souvanna Phouma,
Spaak, Paul-Henri
Stalin, Joseph
Stanton, Edwin
Stettinius, Edward
Stevenson, Adlai
Stewart, Robert (Viscount Castlereagh)
Stimson, Henry
Stuyvesant, Peter
Suharto
Sukarno, Achmed
Sulla, Lucius
Sumner, Charles
Sundiata
Sun Yat-sen

Tafawa, Balewa A.
Taft, Robert A.
Talleyrand-Périgord, Charles Duc de
Tamerlane (Timur)
Tecumseh
Thant, U
Thiers, Louis Adolphe
Tilden, Samuel
Tito (see Broz)
Tocqueville, Alexis de
Togliatti, Palmiro
Togo, Shigenori
Tojo, Hideki

STATESMEN, DIPLOMATS, AND OTHER POLITICAL LEADER

Touré, Sekou
Toussaint l'Ouverture, Pierre
Trotsky, Leon
Trujillo Molina, Rafael
Tshombé, Moise K.
Tubman, Harriet
Tubman, William
Tutankhamen
Tweed, William

U Thant

Vance, Cyrus
Vandenberg, Arthur H.
Vanier, Georges
Vargas, Getulio
Vargas, Sulilio
Venizelos, Eleutherios
Verwoerd, Hendrik
Victoria, (Queen)
Vorster, Balthazar Johannes

Wallace, Henry A.
Walpole, Robert
Webster, Daniel
Wenceslaus
Welles, Sumner
Wilhelmina
Wilson, Harold
Winant, John G.
Witte, Sergei

Yoshida, Shigeru

TRANSPORTATION—Land

ambulance
armored tank
automobile

baby carriage
barouche
barrow
bicycle
bier
bobsled
brougham
buckboard
buggy
bus

cable car
cabriolet
camel
camper
caravan
cariole
carriage
carryall
cart
caterpillar
chaise
chariot
coach
Conestoga wagon
convertible
conveyance
coupe
curricle
cutter
cycle

dogcart
dog sled
donkey
drag
dray
dromedary

electric train

elephant
elevator
equipage
escalator

four-in-hand
freight car

gig
go-cart
gondola

hack
hackney
hansom
hatchback
hayrack
hearse
hoist
horseback
horsecar

iceboat

jet
jinrikisha
jitney

kago

landau
landaulet
lift
limber
limousine
litter
llama
locomotive
lorry

minibike
monorail
moped
motorbike

motorbus
motorcade
motorcar
motorcycle
motor home
motor scooter
motor truck
mule

omnibus
oxen

packhorse
palanquin
perambulator
phaeton
pickup
pony
prairie schooner
pung
pushcart

rickshaw
rig
rockaway
rocket
roller coaster
roller skates

scooter
sedan
semitrailer
shay
skateboard
skates
skis
sledge
sleigh
snowmobile
snowshoes
stagecoach
stanhope
station wagon

TRANSPORTATION—Land

steam locomotive
steam train
streetcar
stroller
subway
sulky
surrey

tandem
tank
tank trailer
tarantass
taxicab
team
tilbury

toboggan
tractor
trail bike
trailer
train
tram
transport
trap
travois
tricycle
troika
trolley
truck
trundle
tumbrel

unicycle

van
vehicle
velocipede
victoria

wagon
wain
water buffalo
wheelbarrow

yak

zebu

TRANSPORTATION—Water

aircraft carrier
argosy
ark
armada

barge
bark
barkentine
bateau
battleship
bilander
boat
bottom
boyer
brig
brigantine
bucentaur
bumboat

caïque
canoe
caravel
catamaran
catboat
clipper
coaster
coble
cockleboat
cockleshell
collier
coracle
corvette
craft
cruiser
cruise ship

dahabeah
destroyer
dhow
dinghy
dory
dreadnaught
drogher
dugout

felucca
ferryboat

fleet
float
flotilla
freighter
frigate

galleass
galleon
galley
galliot
gig
gondola
gunboat

hooker
houseboat
hoy
hulk
hydrofoil

iceboat

jolly boat
junk

kayak
keelboat
ketch

launch
lifeboat
lighter
liner
longboat
lorcha
lugger

merchantman
motorboat

navy

ocean liner
outrigger

packet
paddle-wheel boat
pair-oar
pilot boat

pinky
pinnace
pirogue
pontoon
powerboat
proa
punt

raft
riverboat
rowboat

sailboat
sampan
schooner
scow
shallop
shrimp boat
side-wheeler
skiff
sloop
smack
steamboat
submarine
surfboard

tanker
tartan
tender
transport
trawler
trireme
tug
tugboat

umiak

vessel

water cab
waterski
whaler
wherry

xebec

yacht
yawl

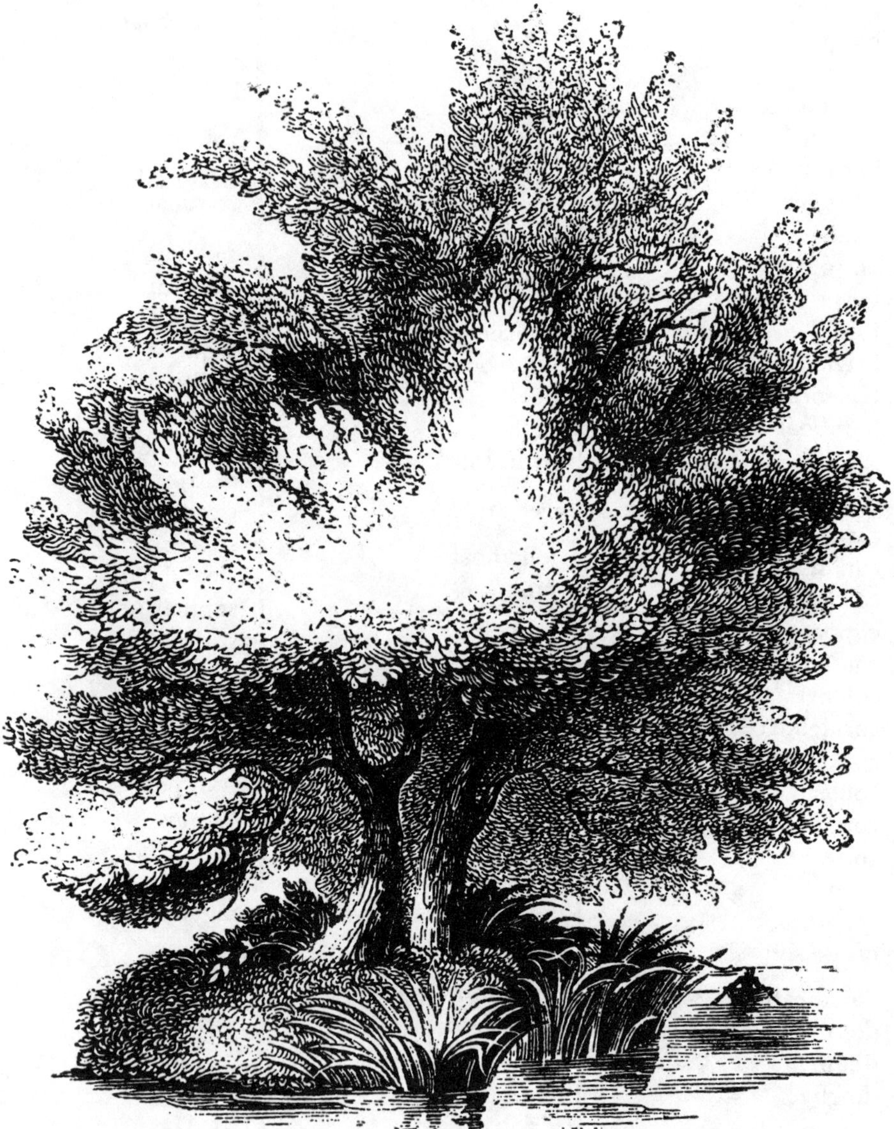

TREES AND SHRUBS

acacia
ailanthus
alder
allspice
althea
andromeda
angelica tree
apricot
aralia
arborvitae
arrowroot
arrowwood
ash
aspen
avocado
azalea

bald cypress
balm of Gilead
balsa
balsam
baobab
barberry
basswood
bayberry
bay
bearberry
beech
benjamin-bush
bilberry
birch
bitternut
bittersweet
blackberry
black gum
black haw
bladdernut
blueberry
bluebonnet
blue spruce
box elder
boxwood
boysenberry
bristly locust

buckeye
buckthorn
bunchberry
burning-bush
butternut
buttonball
buttonbush

camellia
camphor tree
candleberry
canoe birch
carob tree
cassia-bark tree
catalpa
cat brier
cedar
cedar of Lebanon
checkerberry
cherry
chestnut
chinaberry
chinquapin
chokeberry
chokecherry
coconut palm
coffee tree
cohosh
cork oak
cornel
cottonwood
crab apple
cranberry
crape myrtle
cryptomeria
cucumber tree
cypress

dewberry
dogwood
Douglas fir
downy hawthorn
dwarf alder
dwarf birch

dwarf cherry
dwarf oak

ebony
eglantine
Egyptian thorn
elderberry
elm
eucalyptus
euonymus

fetterbush
filbert
fir
flowering ash
forsythia
fringe tree

gallberry
gardenia
genista
ginkgo
goldenrain tree
gooseberry
grapefruit tree
great laurel
greenbrier

hackberry
hardhack
haw
hawthorn
hazel
heather
hemlock
hickory
Himalayan cypress
hobblebush
holly
honey locust
honeysuckle
hornbeam
horse chestnut
huckleberry

TREES AND SHRUBS

hydrangea

ironwood

jacaranda
jasmine
Judas tree
Juneberry
juniper

Kentucky coffee tree
kumquat

larch
lauan
laurel
leatherwood
lilac
linden
liquidambar
live oak
loblolly
locust
Lombardy poplar
longleaf pine

magnolia
mahogany
mango
maple
mesquite
mimosa
mockernut
mock orange
Monterey pine
mountain ash
mountain cranberry
mountain laurel
mulberry
muskwood
myrtle

nanny plum
Norway maple
Norway pine

oak
oleaster
olive
opossum wood
Osage orange

pachistima
pachysandra
pagoda tree
palmetto
paloverde
paper birch
parasol pine
paulownia
pawpaw
pear
pea tree
pecan
pepper tree
persimmon
pine
pin oak
pinon
pistachio
planer tree
plum
poinciana
poison ivy
ponderosa pine
poplar
potentilla
prickly ash
privet
pyracantha

quince

raspberry
redbud
red cedar
red maple
red oak
red gum
redwood

rhododendron
rosemary
rose of Sharon
rough-barked poplar
royal palm

sago palm
sassafras
savin
sequoia
serviceberry
shagbark
sheepberry
silver bell
slippery elm
smilax
snowball
soapwort
sorrel tree
sour gum
sourwood
southernwood
spirea
spruce
stag bush
strawberry bush
sugarberry
sugar maple
sumac
sweet bay
sweetbrier
sweet gum
sycamore
syringa

tamarack
tamarisk
tan oak
teaberry
teak
thimbleberry
thorn
titi
tree of heaven

TREES AND SHRUBS

tulip tree
tupelo

umbrella tree

viburnum

wahoo

walnut
wax myrtle
white birch
white oak
white pine
willow
wintergreen
wisteria

witch hazel
wolfberry

yellow birch
yellow poplar
yew

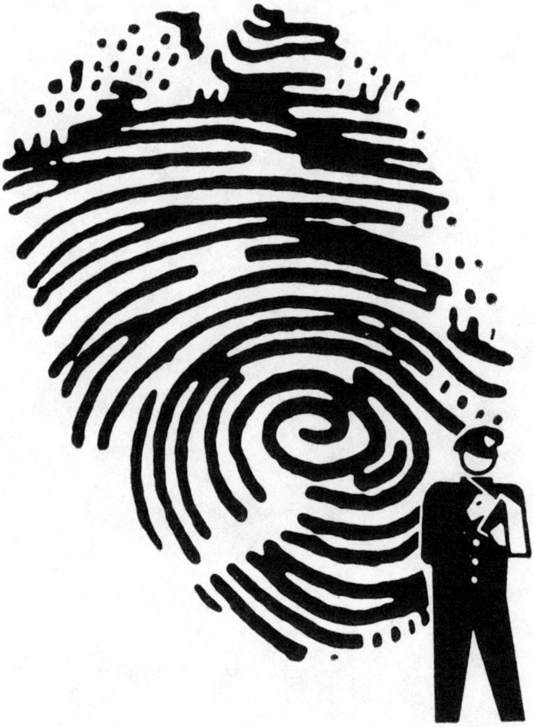

VIOLENCE

abhor
abhorrent
abuse
aggravate
aggression
agitation
agitator
agonize
altercation
anger
annihilate
anxiety
argument
arson
assail
assassinate
assault
atrocity
attack
auto-da-fe
avenge

barbarous
batter
battery
battle
beat
behead
belligerent
billingsgate
blackmail
blast
bloodshed
bloodthirsty
blow
blow one's top
blow over
blow up
bludgeon
bluster
boil over
bomb
bombard
boot

brand
brawl
break out
bruise
brutality
brutalize
brute force
burst
bust
buster
butchery

calumny
cannibalism
capital punishment
carnage
castrate
casualty
cataclysm
cataclysmic
cataplexy
catastrophe
cat-o'-nine-tails
clash
clobber
club
coercion
coercive
combat
compulsion
concentration camp
condemned
conflict
confute
conquer
convulsion
corporal punishment
corrupt
crazy
cremate
crime against humanity
criminal
criminology
cripple

crucifixion
crucify
cruelty
crush
cudgel
curse
cutthroat
cyclone

daimon
damage
danger
death
death penalty
debacle
decapitate
decimate
decollate
defame
defoliate
degrade
deleterious
delinquency
demolish
demon
denigrate
despair
desperado
destroy
destructive
detest
detonation
devastate
devil to pay
diabolic
dictator
disable
disaster
discharge
discordant
disfigure
disparage
dispute
distortion

237

VIOLENCE

disturb
donnybrook
doomed
dragon
draw and quarter
drub
duel
duress

earthquake
effervescence
electrocution
eliminate
encroach
epilepsy
eradicate
eruption
euripus
euthanasia
evict
evil
exacerbation
exasperation
excoriate
excruciate
execrate
execution
explosion .
extermination
extinction
extinguish
extirpate

fanatical
fascism
fear
felo-de-se
felony
ferment
ferocious
fervor
feticide
fetters
feud

fiendish
fierceness
fight
filicide
fire-eater
firing squad
fit
flagellate
flaming
flare
flash
flog
fly off
force
fracas
frantic
fratricide
frenzy
frightful
fume
furious
fury

gallows
gangster
garrote
gas chamber
genocide
goad
gore
guerrilla
guillotine
gun down
gunman

hacking
handcuffs
handgun
hanging
hangman
hara-kiri
harsh
hate
havoc

headlong
headsman
headstrong
hecatomb
hellcat
hellion
holocaust
homicide
hostage
hostility
hurled
hurricane
hysterics

immolation
immoral
impairment
impetuosity
implode
incendiary
incitement
infanticide
inflame
infraction
infringement
infuriate
injure
inpetuous
inquisition
intense
invalidation
invasion
irritate

jarring
jingoism
juggernaut

killer

lambast
lash
lethal
let off steam

238

VIOLENCE

licentious
lightning
liquidate
loathing
lynch

macabre
madcap
madden
madness
maelstrom
maim
malicious
malign
mangle
manslaughter
manslayer
martyr
masochism
massacre
mass murder
master
matricide
maul
mayhem
melee
menace
might
misanthrope
misuse
mortify
mug
murder
mutilate

obloquy
offensive
outburst
outrage

pain
paroxysm
parricide
passion

patricide
perdition
phobia
plunder
pogrom
police state
pound
prison
provoke
punishment
psychotic

quarrel
quarter
quell

rabble-rouser
rabid
rabies
racism
rack
rage
raise cain
raise the devil
raise the roof
rampage
rape
rapine
ravage
ravening
ravish
rebel
rebellious
recidivism
regicide
repudiation
repugnant
retaliate
retribution
revenge
revolt
ride roughshod
riot

roar
rough
rough-and-tumble
roughed-up
roughhouse
row
rowdy
rumpus
run amuck
run riot
run wild
rush

sabotage
sacrifice
sadism
samurai
sanguinary
satanic
savage
savagery
scathing
scorn
scourge
sear
seethe
seppuku
severity
shackle
shatter
shock
skirmish
slap
slash
slaughter
slave
slay
slice
smash
smite
sniper
sororicide
spasm
spread havoc

VIOLENCE

squall	throttle	vicious
stimulate	thug	victim
sting	thuggee	victimize
stir up	thunderstorm	vilification
storm	tirade	vilify
straitjacket	tooth and nail	violate
strangler	tornado	violence
strike	torrent	violent
strong-arm	torture	virago
subdue	touch off	vituperation
subjugate	tough	volcano
suicide	tragedy	volley
suppress	treason	
suttee	trespass	warfare
switchblade	triggerman	weapon
	troublous	whip
tackle	tumultuous	whirlpool
tantrum	turbulent	wicked
tear	turmoil	wild
temper		wild beast
tempest	uncontrollable	wound
tempestuous	ungovernable	wreak
termagant	unrestrained	wreck
terrorist		writhe
thrash	vampire	
threaten	vanquish	Xanthippe
throe	vehement	xenophobia

WEATHER

acid rain
adiabatic
advection
aerothermodynamics
air mass
airstream
altocumulus
altostratus
anabatic
anemometer
aneroid barometer
anthropogenic particles
anticyclone
atmosphere
aurora australis
aurora borealis

backing
barograph
barometer
barometric
Beaufort Scale
blizzard
bora
Buys Ballot's Law

calvus
capillatus
castellanus
ceilometer
Celsius
centigrade
chinook
circulation
cirrocumulus
cirrostratus
cirrus
climate
climatologist
clinometer
cloudburst
cloud meter
clouds
cloud seeding

coalescence process
cold front
condensation
conduction
confluence
congestus
contrail
convection
convergence
coriolis effect
cumulonimbus
cumulus
cyclogenesis
cyclone
cyclonic

depression
dew point
diurnal variation
doldrums
downdraught
drizzle
dropsondes
drought
dry haze
dust storm

eastbound
easterly
east-northeast
east-southeast
eastward
emission
environment
equinoctial storm
equinox
evaporation
exosphere
extratropical

Fahrenheit
fibratus
filling
floccus

foehn
fog
forecast
forecaster
fractostratus
fractus
front
frontogenesis
frost
funnel

gale
geostrophic
gradient
graupel
gust

Hadley cell
hail
hailstone
harmattan
haze
hemisphere
horse latitudes
humidity
hurricane
hydrograph
hydrometer
hygrometer

·imbalance
incus
instability
intermittent rain
inversion
ionosphere
isobar
isodrosotherm
isotach
isothere
isotherm
isothermal zone
isothermbrose
isothermobath

241

WEATHER

jet stream

katabatic wind

latitude
lenticularis
lightning
longitude

maritime
mean temperature
mediocris
mercurial barometer
mesosphere
meteorology
millibar
mistral
moisture
monsoon

nebulosus
nimbostratus
nimbus
noctilucent
nocturnal wind
northbound
northeasterly
northeastward
northerly
north-northeast
north-northwest
northwesterly
northwestward

occluded front
overcast
ozone

pileus
pluviometer
Polar Cell
polar front
polar lights
pollution
precipitation

pressure
prognosticate
psychrometer

radar
radiation
radiosonde
rainbow
raindrop
rainfall
rain gauge
rainmaker
rain showers
rainstorm
recurvature
relative humidity
ridge

Saint Elmo's fire
sandstorm
satellite
saturation
scud
shallow fog
silver iodide
simoom
sirocco
sky obscured
sleet
slush
smog
snowfall
solstice
southbound
southeasterly
southeastward
southerly
south-southeast
south-southwest
southwesterly
southwestward

spissatus
squall
stationary front

stratiformis
stratocumulus
stratosphere
stratus
sunspot
synoptic chart

temperature
thermal wind
thermocouple
thermograph
thermometer
thunderhead
thunderstorm
tornado
trade winds
tropopause
troposphere
trough
turbulence
typhoon

uncinus
updraft

vane
vapor
veer
velocity
virga
visibility

warm front
waterspout
water vapor
water witching
waterworks
weatherman
weather vane
westbound
westerly
west-northwest
westward
whirlwind
wind

SPELLING DEMONS 4500 Easily Misspelled Words

abandon
abbey
abbreviate
abdicate
abduction
aberrant
abetting
abeyance
abhorrent
ablution
abnegate
abnegation
abnormality
abolitionist
abominable
aborigine
abortion
abortive
abrasion
abscond
absence
absenteeism
absinthe
absolutely
absorbent
absorption
abstinence
abstractly
abstruse
absurdity
abundance
abysmal
abyss
academician
accede
accelerator
accentuate
acceptance
access
accessory
accidentally
acclaim
acclamation
acclimate

accolade
accommodate
accompany
accomplice
accordance
accordion
accountability
accouterment
accreditation
accruing
accumulation
accuracy
accusation
accustom
acetate
acetone
acetylene
achieve
achromatic
acidhead
acidity
acknowledge
acme
acoustic
acquaintance
acquiesce
acquire
acquisition
acquittal
acre
acreage
acrid
acrimonious
acrobat
acronym
acrostic
activate
actor
actuality
actuary
acuity
acumen
adage
adamant

adaptability
addenda
addicted
additional
addressee
adduce
adept
adequately
adherence
adhesion
adieu
adjacent
adjournment
adjudicate
adjunct
adjustable
adjutant
administrator
admirable
admiration
admissible
admittance
admonition
adolescence
adoption
adorable
adornment
adroit
adulation
adulterate
advantageous
adventuresome
adversaries
advertisement
advisable
advisement
adviser
advisory
advocacy
aerial
aerobics
aeronautic
aerosol
aesthetic

DEMONS

affable
affectionate
affidavit
affiliate
affinity
affirmation
affliction
affluence
affront
afghan
Afro
aftereffect
afterward
agglomeration
aggrandizement
aggravate
aggregate
aggressor
aggrieve
aghast
agility
agitator
agreeability
agriculture
agronomy
airborne
air-condition
air-cooled
air express
airfield
air force
air hole
airiness
air lane
airlift
airline
airmail
air piracy
air pocket
airport
air raid
air rifle
airsick
airstrip

airtight
akimbo
alabaster
alacrity
albeit
albino
albumen
alchemy
al dente
alfresco
algae
alias
alibi
alienate
alignment
alimony
alkaline
allegation
allegedly
allegiance
allergy
alleviate
alleys
alliance
alligator
alliterative
allocation
allotment
allowance
all right
alluvial
almond
alpaca
alphabetize
already
alteration
alternative
although
altimeter
altruistic
alum
aluminum
alumnae
alumni

alumnus
amateur
ambassador
ambergris
ambidextrous
ambiguity
ambivalence
ambulance
amenable
amendment
amenity
amethyst
amiability
amicability
ammonia
ammunition
amnesty
amoeba
amorous
amorphous
ampere
amphibious
amphitheater
amplification
amulet
anachronism
analogies
analogous
analysis
analyst
analyze
anarchy
anathema
ancestor
anchorage
anchorman
ancient
ancillary
andiron
anecdote
anemometer
anemone
anglophile
anglophobe

DEMONS

anguish
animosity
animus
annex
annihilate
anniversary
annotate
announcement
annoyance
annually
annuity
annulled
anodize
anodyne
anoint
anomaly
anonymity
anonymous
antagonism
antarctic
antebellum
antedate
antediluvian
antenna
anterior
anthology
anthracite
anthrax
anthropoid
anthropology
anthropomorphic
antibussing
anticipate
anticlimactic
antigen
antipathy
antiquary
antiquity
antithesis
antonym
anxiety
apathetic
aperture

aphorism
apiary
apologetically
apostasy
apothecaries
apotheosis
appall
apparatus
apparition
appeasement
appellate
appendage
appetizer
applause
applicability
appointee
apposition
appraise
appreciate
apprehensible
apprentice
apprise
approbation
appropriate
approximate
appurtenance
apropos
aquarium
aqueduct
aquiline
arabesque
arable
arbitrary
arboretum
archaeology
archaic
archenemy
archetype
archiepiscopal
archipelago
architect
archives
arctic
arduous

area code
argosy
argument
argyle
aristocracy
armistice
aromatic
arraignment
arrant
arrogance
arrogant
arroyo
arsenic
artesian
articulate
artifact
artifice
artillery
artisan
asbestos
ascendancy
ascertain
ascetic
asininity
askance
askew
asperity
asphalt
aspiration
assail
assassin
assassination
assault
assemblage
assert
assess
assiduity
assign
assimilate
assistance
associate
assuage
assume
assurance

DEMONS

asterisk	availability	bandage
asteroid	avalanche	bandanna
astigmatism	avaricious	bandeau
astound	aversion	bandit
astral	aviary	bandolier
astrodome	aviator	banister
astrology	avocation	bankbook
astronaut	avoidance	bank draft
astronomer	avuncular	bank note
astute	awesome	bank rate
asylum	awry	bankroll
asymmetric	axiomatic	bankrupt
athlete	axle	banned
athwart	azure	banquet
atmospheric		bantam
atomizer	babushka	barbarian
atrium	baby-sitter	barbecue
atrocious	baccalaureate	barbiturate
atrocity	baccarat	bargain
attaché case	bacchanal	barkeeper
attainable	bachelor	barmaid
attar	bacilli	barnacle
attendant	backlash	barometer
attenuate	back seat	barricade
attorney	backslide	barrier
attribution	back talk	barroom
attrition	backwoods	basal
attune	bacteria	basalt
audacious	badger	base pay
audacity	baffle	basically
audible	baggage	bas-relief
audience	bailiff	bassinet
auditor	bailiwick	bathe
auspicious	balcony	bathhouse
austerity	balderdash	baton
authenticity	balk	battalion
author	ballast	battery
autobahn	ball bearing	battle-ax
autobiographical	ballistic	battle-scarred
autocracy	ballot	bauble
automation	ballyhoo	bayonet
autonomous	balminess	bayou
autumnal	bamboozle	bearable
auxiliary	banal	beater

DEMONS

beatitude
beauteous
beautician
Bedouin
bedraggled
bedridden
beeswax
beggar
behemoth
beige
belatedly
bel canto
belfry
belie
believe
belladonna
belles lettres
bellicose
belligerence
bellyache
beneficence
beneficiary
benefited
benevolence
bequeath
bereavement
berserk
beryl
besiege
besmirch
bestial
betrayal
betrothal
bettor
betwixt
beveling
biannual
bias
bibliography
bibliophile
bicentennial
biennial
bigamy
bigotry

bijou
bikini
bilateral
bilingual
bill of lading
binocular
biodegradable
biographer
bipartisan
bird dog
bird's-eye
biscuit
bismuth
bison
bisque
bitumen
bituminous
bivouac
blasé
bleach
bleep
blender
blitz
blitzkrieg
bloodcurdling
blouse
bludgeon
blue-eyed
blusterous
board foot
bocaccio
bogeyman
boisterous
bolero
bombardier
bona fide
bonanza
bonfire
bonus
bookie
boomerang
boondoggle
bootee
bootleg

borax
boreal
borough
botanist
boudoir
bouillon
boulevard
boundaries
bounden
bounteous
bouquet
bourbon
bourgeoisie
boutique
boutonniere
boycott
bracket
braggadocio
braggart
Braille
brainstorm
brain trust
brainwashing
braise
brassiere
bravura
brazier
breach
breadth
breathe
breathtaking
breeches
breezeway
brewery
bric-a-brac
briefcase
brigand
brigantine
brighten
brilliance
brilliantine
briquette
brisket
bristle

DEMONS

broach
broad-minded
brochure
brooch
brother-in-law
brougham
brown bagging
Brownie point
browse
brunette
brusque
brutal
buccaneer
budget
buffalo
bugle
bulge
bulletin
bullion
bull's-eye
bungalow
bungle
buoy
bureau
bureaucracy
burgeon
burglaries
burial
burlesque
bursitis
bushel
businessman
bustling
busyness
butcher
buxom
bygone
bylaw
bypass
by-product

cabana
cabaret
cabbage

cabinet
cablegram
cable TV
caffeine
caisson
cajolery
calamitous
calculable
calculate
calculator
calibrate
caliph
calisthenics
calligrapher
calmly
calories
calumny
Calvary
calypso
camaraderie
cambric
cameos
camisole
camouflage
campground
canapé
canceled
cancellation
candelabra
candidacy
candor
canister
cankerous
cannibalism
canopies
cantankerous
canyon
capabilities
capacitor
caparison
capitalize
capitulate
caprice
capricious

capsize
capsule
captain
caption
captivate
captor
capture
caravan
carcass
cardiac
cardigan
cardinal
careen
career
caress
cargoes
caribou
caricature
carillon
carmine
carnivorous
carol
carom
carousal
carriage
carrion
carrousel
cartel
cartographer
cartridge
cascade
cashew
cashmere
casino
casserole
castanet
caste
castigate
castle
casualty
cataclysm
catalog
catalyst
catamaran

DEMONS

catamount
catastrophe
catastrophic
categorize
caterpillar
catharsis
cathartic
cathode
cat-o'-nine-tails
cat's-paw
caucus
caudal
cauliflower
cauterize
cautious
cavalcade
cavalier
cavalry
caviar
cavil
cedar
cede
ceiling
celebrate
celebrity
celestial
cellophane
celluloid
cemetery
censorial
census
centaur
centenary
centennial
centipede
centrifugal
centrifuge
ceramic
ceremonious
ceremony
certification
chafe
chaff
chafing dish

chalet
challenge
challis
chameleon
chamois
champagne
chancellery
chancellor
chandelier
channel
chaos
chaotic
chaparral
chapeau
chaperon
characterization
charade
charitable
chartreuse
chasm
chassis
chaste
chattel
chauffeur
chauvinism
cheesecloth
chemise
chenille
cheroot
chicanery
chimera
chimpanzee
chinchilla
chintz
chivalrous
chlorinate
chlorine
chlorophyll
christen
chromatic
chromium
chronicle
chronology
chronometer

chrysalis
chrysanthemum
chute
chutzpah
cicada
cinnamon
cipher
circuit
circuitous
circularization
circumcision
circumference
circumlocution
circumnavigate
circumscription
circumspection
circumstantial
circumstantiate
citation
cite
citronella
civilization
clairvoyance
chamber
clandestine
classicism
clause
cleavage
clemency
cliché
clientele
climactic
clone
clout
coalescence
coast guard
cochineal
cockatoo
coconut
coddle
codex
codicil
coerce
coercion

DEMONS

coexistence
coffer
cogitate
cognac
cognizant
coherent
cohesion
coincidence
colander
coliseum
collaborator
collate
colleague
collectible
collector
collegian
collegiate
collision
colloquial
collusion
cologne
colonel
colonnade
color-blind
colossal
Colosseum
colossus
combatant
comedian
comedienne
comma
commander
commandos
commemoration
commencement
commend
commensurate
commentator
commercialization
commiserate
commissar
commission
commitment
committee

commodious
commodore
communicable
communicant
communicate
communiqué
commutation
comparable
comparison
compassion
compatible
compensatory
competence
competitive
competitor
compilation
complacency
complement
complementary
completely
completion
complexion
compliancy
complication
complicity
compliment
component
composition
comprehension
compression
comptroller
compulsion
compulsory
compunction
computation
concealment
concede
conceited
conceivable
concentration
concentric
concept
conceptual
concession

concessionaire
concierge
conciliation
concoction
concomitant
concurrence
condemned
condescension
condiment
conditioner
condominium
conductor
conduit
confectionery
confederacy
confetti
confidence
confidential
conflagration
confluence
confrontation
confusion
congeal
congeniality
congestion
conglomerate
congratulatory
conifer
conjugal
conjunction
connoisseur
connubial
conqueror
conscience
conscientious
conscious
consecutive
consensus
consequential
considerable
consignment
consistency
consommé
conspicuous

DEMONS

conspirator
constable
constabulary
constancy
consternation
constituency
construction
construing
consular
consulate
consultant
consummate
consumption
contemporaneous
contemptible
contemptuous
contentious
contiguous
continence
contingency
continuity
contortionist
contractor
contradictory
contraption
contrariness
contretemps
contributor
contrivance
controller
controversial
conundrum
convenience
conventionality
convergence
conversant
conversationalist
conversion
convertible
conviviality
convolution
cooperative
coordinate
copier

copious
coquette
cordiality
cordially
cordovan
corduroy
corer
corespondent
corkscrew
cornucopia
corollary
corona
coronet
corpulence
corral
correction
correlate
correspondence
corridor
corroborate
corrosion
corrugate
corruption
corsage
corset
cortege
cosmetologist
cosmology
cosmonaut
cosmopolitan
cossack
costume
coterie
cotillion
cougar
council
countenance
counterfeiter
coupe
coupling
coupon clipper
courageous
courier
courteous

courtesan
courtesy
court-martial
covetous
coward
coyly
coyote
crackle
cradle
cravat
credence
credible
creditable
credulous
crematory
creole
crescent
crevice
cribbage
criminally
criminology
criteria
criticism
criticize
critique
crochet
crocodile
crocus
croquet
croquette
cross-examine
cross-stitch
crotchety
crouton
cruel
cruise
cruller
crumple
crustaceous
cryptic
crystallize
cuckoo
cudgeled
cuisine

DEMONS

culinary	davit	definable
culminate	dawdle	definitive
culpable	dazzling	defogger
cultivator	deadlock	defoliate
cummerbund	deaf-mute	defroster
cumulative	debacle	degeneracy
cumulus	debarkation	degradation
cuneiform	debatable	degree
cupola	debauchery	deign
curator	debilitate	delectable
curfew	debit	delegate
curiosity	debonair	deleterious
curlicue	debris	delicacies
curriculum	debtor	delicatessen
curry	debut	delicious
cursory	decadence	delineation
custom	decanter	delinquency
cuticle	decapitate	delirious
cutlass	decathlon	deliverance
cut-rate	decease	deluge
cybernetics	decedent	deluxe
cyclamate	deceive	demagogue
cyclone	decency	demilitarize
cyclops	decent	demise
cylinder	deceptive	demitasse
cynical	decibel	demobilize
cynicism	deciduous	demographic
cypress	decimate	demonstrator
cyst	decipher	denial
czar	decision	denigrate
	declamation	denominator
dabble	declarative	denouement
dachshund	declension	deodorant
daguerreotype	décolleté	dependable
dahlia	decorator	dependent
dailies	decorum	deportation
dais	dedicate	depository
dalliance	deductible	depravation
damask	defamation	depression
dandruff	defector	deprivation
dangle	defense	deputize
dastardly	deference	derangement
daughter-in-law	defiance	derelict
dauphin	deficient	derivative

DEMONS

derogatory	directory	distinct
descend	dirigible	distinguish
descendant	disaffection	distortion
desensitize	disagreeable	distract
deservedly	disappearance	distraught
desiccation	disappointment	distress
designer	disassociate	distributor
desirability	disavowal	disturbance
desperate	disburse	diurnal
destitution	discernible	divergence
destructible	disciplinary	diverse
desultory	discipline	divisibility
detachment	disconcert	docility
detergent	discontinue	docket
deterioration	discouragement	doctrinaire
deterrent	discourteous	documentary
detestable	discreditable	doggerel
devastation	discriminate	doggie bag
development	discuss	dogmatic
diabetes	disease	doilies
diabolical	disembarkation	doldrums
diagnostician	dishevel	doleful
dialogue	disillusion	dolphin
diaper	disinfectant	domesticity
dichotomy	disobedient	domicile
dictatorial	disperse	domineering
dictionary	disposable	dorsal
didactic	dispossess	dossier
diesel	disproportionate	dotage
difference	disqualification	doublet
differentiate	disreputable	doubloon
difficulty	dissatisfied	doubtless
diffidence	dissension	dowdy
dignitary	dissent	dowel
digression	dissertation	dowry
dilapidate	disservice	draftsmen
dilemma	dissimilar	dragoon
dilettante	dissipate	draught
diligence	dissolute	dreadnought
diminutive	dissonance	drearily
dingbat	distance	dribbling
dinghy	distension	drollery
dinosaur	distillate	dromedary
diphthong	distillery	drought

DEMONS

dubious
ductile
dulcet
dullard
dumpling
dungaree
dungeon
duplicator
duplicity
duress
dynamic
dynamite
dynasty

eagle
earliest
earnest
earring
easel
easement
ebony
ebullient
eccentricity
echelon
echoes
éclair
eclectic
eclipse
ecologist
economical
economize
ecstasy
ecstatic
edelweiss
edginess
edible
edict
edifice
editorial
educable
effacement
effectual
effeminate
effervescent

effete
efficacious
efficient
effigy
efflorescent
effrontery
effulgence
egoist
egotism
egregious
egress
eider
eighth
ejaculation
ejection
elaborate
elasticity
elation
electioneer
elector
electricity
electrode
electrolysis
electrolyte
electromagnet
elegant
elegy
element
elevator
eligibility
elliptic
elocution
elongate
eloquent
elucidate
elves
emanate
emancipate
emasculate
embargoes
embarrass
embassy
embellish
embezzle

embodiment
embroidery
embryonic
emergency
emeritus
emigrant
emigration
eminence
eminent
emissary
emollient
emperor
emphasis
emphasize
empirical
employable
emulate
enameling
enamor
enchantment
enchantress
encompass
encourage
encroachment
encyclical
encyclopedia
endeavor
endemic
endurable
energize
enervate
enforceable
enfranchisement
engine
engineer
engrave
engross
engulf
enhance
enigma
enlighten
enlist
enliven
ennui

254

DEMONS

enormity
enrage
enrich
enrolled
en route
ensconce
enslavement
ensue
entailment
entangle
enterprise
enthrall
enthusiastic
enticement
entitle
entourage
entrepreneur
entwine
enveloped
environment
envisage
epaulet
ephemeral
epic
epicurean
epigram
epigraph
epilogue
epitaph
epithet
epitome
epoch
epoxy
equaled
equally
equanimity
equestrian
equinox
equitable
equivalence
eradicator
erasable
erratic
erroneous

erudite
escalator
eschew
escrow
esoteric
especially
espionage
espouse
espresso
esprit
estimable
estrangement
et cetera
etching
ethereal
ethnic
etymological
euphemism
euphonious
eventually
eviscerate
evocative
exacerbate
exaggerate
exceed
excel
excelsior
excerpt
exclamatory
excretion
exculpate
excusable
executioner
executive
executor
executrix
exegesis
exemplification
exhale
exhausted
exhibitor
exhilarate
exigency
existence

exorbitant
exotic
expatriate
expectancy
expediency
expeditionary
expelled
expendable
expense
experience
explanatory
expletive
explicable
explicit
exploitation
expurgate
extemporaneous
exterminate
externally
extinction
extinguishable
extirpate
extol
extortion
extraction
extracurricular
extraneous
extraordinary
extrasensory
extravaganza
extricable
extrovert
exuberance
eyrie

fable
fabulous
facade
facet
facetious
facsimile
fallacious
fallible
familiar

DEMONS

fanaticism
fantasy
farewell
fascination
fascism
fashionable
fastback
fastener
fastidious
father-in-law
fathom
fatigue
fatuous
faucet
faulty
faux pas
feasibility
February
fecundity
feeble
feign
felonious
feminine
fenestration
ferment
ferocious
ferret
ferrous
fervor
fescue
festoon
fete
fey
fiancé
fiancée
fiasco
fictitious
fidgety
fiduciary
fiendish
fiesta
fiftieth
figurative
filbert

filial
filigree
fillet
financial
financier
finicky
fiscal
fissure
fizzle
flabbergast
flaccid
flaky
flagellate
flagrancy
flambé
flamboyant
flammable
flannel
flaunt
fledgling
flimsy
flippant
flotilla
flotsam
flouncing
fluorescent
fluoridation
forbearance
forbidden
forcible
forebode
forecast
forecastle
foreclose
forefather
forefinger
forefront
foregone
foreground
forehead
foreign
foreman
foremost
forenoon

forensic
forerunner
foresee
foresight
forethought
forfeit
forfeiture
formidable
formula
forthright
fortieth
fortuitous
fragile
frankincense
fratricide
fraudulent
freak-out
freckle
freighter
frequency
freshener
fricassee
frieze
frigate
frigid
frivolous
frontier
fruition
fueling
fulfillment
full-bodied
full-length
fumigate
fundamentalism
funnel
furrier
fuselage
fusion

gable
gadget
galaxy
gallantry
galleon

DEMONS

galley	giraffe	gratuitous
gambrel	gist	gratuity
garage	gizzard	gravitation
garbage	glacial	gregarious
gargoyle	glacier	grenadine
garnet	gladiolus	greyhound
garnish	glamour	griddle
garnishee	glaze	grievance
garrison	glazier	grimace
garrulous	gleeful	grinder
gaseous	glisten	gripe
gastronomy	gloaming	gristle
gauge	globally	grotesque
gazebo	globular	grudge
gazette	glossary	Guernsey
gazetteer	gluttony	guillotine
gelatinous	glycerin	guinea
gendarme	gnarled	gullibility
generalissimo	gnash	gymnasium
generator	gnat	gypsy
generosity	gnaw	
genius	gnome	habeas corpus
gentleman	goal	haberdashery
geodetic	gobbledygook	habitable
geographical	gondolier	habitual
geological	gooey	hacienda
geometry	gopher	hackneyed
geranium	gorgeous	haggle
germane	gormandize	halcyon
gerrymander	gospel	halfhearted
gesticulate	gossamer	half-mast
geyser	goulash	half-moon
ghastliness	gourd	half-truth
gherkin	gourmet	halfway
ghetto	government	halitosis
ghoul	governor	hallucination
gibberish	gracious	halve
giblet	grammar	hammock
gigantic	Grammy	handiwork
giggle	grandeur	handkerchief
gigolo	grandiose	handyman
gimmick	grateful	harangue
gingham	grater	harass
ginkgo	gratification	harbor

DEMONS

hard hat
hardiness
harlequin
hashish
hassle
hastiness
hatchback
haughty
haul
haversack
havoc
hay fever
hazardous
heavenly
hedgehog
hegemony
hegira
heifer
height
heinous
heiress
heirloom
helicopter
heliotrope
hemisphere
hemlock
hepatica
herbage
herbivorous
hereditary
heretofore
herewith
heritage
hermitage
heroes
hesitate
heterogeneous
heterosex
hexagonal
heyday
hiatus
hiccup
hickory
hideous

hierarchy
hieroglyphic
highwayman
hilarious
hindrance
hindsight
hippodrome
hippopotamus
hirsute
histrionic
hoax
hobgoblin
hocus-pocus
hoeing
hoggish
holiday
hollandaise
holocaust
homely
homeopathy
homesite
homicide
homogeneous
homogenize
homologous
homonym
honeycomb
honeydew
honorable
honorarium
hoodlum
hoodoo
horizon
horny
horoscope
horrible
horror
horticulture
hosiery
hospitable
hospitality
hostelry
huarache
hullabaloo

humanitarian
humiliate
hundredth
hungrily
hurrah
hurricane
hybrid
hydrangea
hydraulic
hydrochloric
hydrodynamics
hydrolysis
hyperbola
hypercritical
hypertension
hyphen
hypnotize
hypocrisy
hypocrite
hypotenuse
hypothesis
hypothetical
hysteria

iambic
ibex
ibis
iceberg
icicle
iciness
idealist
identification
idiocy
idiosyncrasy
idiotic
idly
idyllic
igloo
ignominious
ignoramus
ignorance
iguana
illegality
illegibility

DEMONS

illegitimacy	impetuosity	incipient
illiteracy	impetus	incision
illogical	implacable	inclement
illumination	implement	incognito
illusion	implicate	incoherence
illustrative	importance	incombustible
illustrious	importunity	incommunicable
imaginary	impostor	incomparable
imbecility	impotency	incompatibility
imitator	impregnable	incompetence
immaculate	impresario	incomprehensible
immaterial	improbability	inconceivable
immature	impromptu	incongruous
immeasurable	impropriety	inconsequential
immediately	improvement	inconsistency
immensity	improvisation	inconsolable
immersion	impudence	inconspicuous
immigration	impugn	incontestable
imminence	imputable	incontrovertible
immobilization	inaccessible	inconvenience
immoderate	inaccuracy	incorrigible
immorality	inadequate	incorruptible
immortality	inadmissible	incredible
immovable	inadvertent	increment
immutability	inalienable	incriminate
impalpable	inanimate	inculcate
impart	inanity	incurable
impartiality	inapplicable	indebtedness
impasse	inappreciative	indecency
impassioned	inappropriate	indefatigable
impassive	inarticulate	indelible
impatience	inartistic	indelicacy
impeachment	inaudible	indemnification
impeccable	inaugural	indictment
impediment	inauspicious	indigenous
impenetrable	incalculable	indigent
imperative	incandescent	indigestible
imperceptible	incapacity	indignant
imperialist	incarcerate	indiscernible
imperious	incense	indiscriminate
impermeable	incessant	indispensable
impersonator	incestuous	indisputable
impertinence	incidence	indistinctly
impervious	incinerator	indomitable

DEMONS

indubitable
indulgence
industrialize
inebriate
inedible
ineffectual
ineligibility
ineptitude
inevitable
inexplicable
inexpressible
infallible
infancy
infantile
infatuate
infectious
inferential
inferior
inferred
infidelity
infinite
infinitesimal
infinity
inflammable
inflate
inflexible
infliction
influence
infrared
infringement
infuriate
infusion
ingenious
ingenue
ingenuous
ingratitude
inhabitant
inherent
inheritance
inhibition
inimitable
iniquity
initial
injudicious

injunction
injurious
innocence
innocuous
innovation
innuendo
inopportune
inordinate
inquiry
inquisitor
insatiable
inscrutable
insecticide
insidious
insignia
insinuation
insistence
insofar
insolence
insolvent
insouciance
instability
installation
instantaneous
instigate
instinct
institutional
instruction
insufferable
insufficient
insurrection
intangible
integrity
intellectual
intelligence
intensity
intention
intercede
interchangeable
interim
interlocutory
interment
interminable
intermittent

internment
interpret
interpreter
interracial
interrogate
interruption
intersperse
intestinal
intimacy
intimidate
intolerant
intractable
intrepidity
intricacy
intrigue
intrinsic
introductory
intrusion
intuitive
invariable
inveterate
inviolable
invisible
involuntarily
invulnerable
iota
irascible
iridescence
irrational
irreconcilable
irrefutable
irrelevant
irrepressible
irresponsible
irrigation
isthmus
italicize
itinerant

jamboree
jangle
javelin
jet lag
jockey

DEMONS

jodhpur	label	lightning
jollity	laborious	limb
jonquil	labyrinth	limeade
journalist	lacerate	limerick
journey	lackadaisical	limit
jubilee	lacquer	limousine
judgment	ladle	linen
judiciary	lagoon	lingerie
juggernaut	lament	linguist
juicer	lamprey	liniment
jukebox	language	linoleum
julep	languid	lioness
julienne	languorous	liqueur
junction	lapel	liquidate
jurisprudence	larcenous	liquor
juror	lariat	literacy
justification	laryngitis	literally
juxtaposition	lascivious	literary
	lassitude	literature
kaleidoscope	latticework	litmus
kangaroo	launder	livelihood
kayak	lazily	living will
kennel	leaven	llama
kerosene	lectern	loathsome
kettle	ledger	lobbying
khaki	leech	locale
kiln	legalize	locomotive
kilometer	legend	lodging
kilowatt	legitimacy	logistics
kimono	leisure	longevity
kindergarten	lemonade	longitudinal
kindling	lengthy	loquacious
kindred	leniency	louver
kinetic	lethargic	lozenge
kiosk	lettuce	lucid
knapsack	leverage	ludicrous
knave	levity	lugubrious
kneel	liability	luminous
knowledgeable	liaison	lunatic
knuckle	libelous	luncheon
kohlrabi	liberator	lurch
kooky	librarian	luscious
kowtow	license	luxurious
kudos	licorice	lyceum

DEMONS

lying	manifold	matricide
lynch	Manila	matriculate
	manipulation	matrimonial
macabre	mannequin	matronly
macaroni	mannerism	mattress
macaroon	mansion	maturity
machination	manslaughter	maudlin
macho	mantilla	mauve
machinery	manual	maverick
mackerel	manure	maxim
maddening	manuscript	mayhem
maelstrom	maple	mayonnaise
magazine	maraschino	meager
magician	marathon	measurable
magistrate	marble	mechanism
magnanimous	margin	medallion
magnate	marigold	mediate
magnetic	marijuana	medicate
magnificence	marionette	medicine
magnitude	maritime	medieval
maharaja	marmalade	mediocre
mahogany	maroon	melancholia
mailgram	marquee	melee
mainsail	marquetry	mellifluous
maintenance	marquis	melodrama
majesty	marriageable	melon
maladroit	marshall	memento
malapropism	marshmallow	memoir
malefactor	marsupial	memorandum
malevolent	martial	memorial
malfeasance	martinet	memorize
malicious	marvelous	menace
malign	masculinity	menagerie
malodorous	masquerade	mendacious
mammal	massacre	mendicant
manageable	masseur	menial
managerial	masseuse	mental
mandarin	masticate	mentor
mandible	mastiff	mercantile
maneuver	mastodon	mercenary
Manhattan	matador	merchandise
maniacal	mathematician	mercurial
manicure	matinee	merger
manifest	matriarch	meridian

262

DEMONS

meringue	miscellaneous	monosyllable
meritorious	mischievous	monotonous
mermaid	misconception	monsieur
mesmerize	misconstrue	monstrosity
mesquite	miscue	moorage
message	misdemeanor	morale
metallurgy	miserable	morass
metamorphism	misnomer	mordant
metaphysics	misogynist	morphine
meteorite	mispronounce	mortality
methodical	misspell	mortgage
meticulous	mistaken	mortuary
metric	mistiness	mosaic
metropolitan	mistletoe	mosquito
mezzanine	mistrial	motif
miasma	misusage	motivate
micrograph	mitigate	mountaineer
microwave	moat	mounting
midget	mobilize	mousse
midriff	moccasin	moustache
migratory	mode	mouthwash
milady	modeling	movable
mildew	moderator	mucilage
militant	modernity	muddiness
militaristic	modicum	muddle
militia	module	muffler
millennium	mohair	mulatto
millet	moiré	mulberry
milligram	moist	mullion
millimeter	molasses	multifarious
millionaire	molecule	multilateral
mimeograph	mollification	multimedia
mimosa	mollusk	multimillionaire
mineralogy	momentarily	multinational
mingle	monarch	multiplicity
miniature	monasticism	multitudinous
minimum	monitor	mummery
minnow	monochrome	municipality
miraculous	monocle	mural
mirage	monogamous	murmuring
mirror	monogram	muscatel
misanthropic	monolith	muscle
misapprehension	monologue	muse
miscegenation	monopolistic	musketry

DEMONS

mutilation
mutton
muzzle
myriad
mysterious
mysticism
mystique

natal
naïve
napkin
narcissus
narrative
nascent
nasturtium
naughtily
navigable
navigator
nebula
necessary
necrology
nectar
ne'er-do-well
nefarious
negligee
negligence
negotiation
neighbor
neither
nemesis
neolithic
neophyte
nephew
nepotism
nestle
neutrality
nevertheless
nicety
niche
nickel
nicotine
niggardly
nihilism
nimble

nincompoop
ninetieth
ninety
ninth
nitroglycerin
nobility
nocturnal
no-fault
nomadic
nom de plume
nomenclature
nominee
nonchalance
noncombatant
nondescript
nonentity
nonpartisan
nonsensical
normally
nostalgia
nostril
notarize
notary
noteworthiness
noticeable
notoriety
notorious
nourish
nouveau riche
novelette
noxious
nozzle
nuance
nuclear
nuisance
nullification
numbness
numerator
numerology
numismatic
nursery
nutrient
nutritious
nymph

oasis
obbligato
obdurate
obedience
obeisance
obelisk
obese
obey
obituary
obligatory
oblige
oblique
obliteration
oblivious
obnoxious
obscene
obsequious
observatory
obsession
obsolescence
obsolete
obstacle
obstinate
obstreperous
obstructionist
obtrusive
occasion
occidental
occlusion
occupancy
occur
occurred
oceanographer
octagonal
octopus
oculist
oddity
ode
odious
odoriferous
odyssey
offensive
officer
officially

DEMONS

officious
often
ofttimes
ointment
oligarchy
olympiad
ombudsman
omelet
ominous
omission
omitted
omnibus
omnipotence
omnivorous
onerous
onus
opalescent
opaque
operative
opine
opinion
opponent
opportunist
opposite
oppressive
opt
optimism
optional
opulence
oracle
orchid
ordeal
ordinance
ordinarily
ordnance
organism
organization
orgy
oriental
orifice
origami
originally
originator
oriole

ornamentation
orphanage
orthodox
oscillate
osculate
osmosis
ostensively
ostentatious
ostracism
ostracize
ostrich
ottoman
ought
outdoors
outmaneuver
out-of-the-way
outrageous
outrigger
outright
outweigh
overbalance
overcapitalization
overcharge
overdrawn
overkill
overnight
overseas
oversized
oversleep
overweight
owlish
oxalic acid
oxide
oxtail
oxygen

pacific
pacifier
paddle
paddock
padlock
padre
pageant
pajamas

palace
palatable
palatial
palaver
palazzo
palisade
palliate
palmetto
palmistry
palomino
palpitate
paltry
pamphleteer
panchromatic
pandemonium
panegyric
paneled
panic
panicked
panorama
pantaloon
pantomime
pantry
papaya
papier-mâché
papoose
paprika
papyrus
parachute
paraffin
parallel
paraphernalia
parasite
parasol
parcel
parentage
parenthesis
pareu
parfait
parliament
parochial
parquetry
parricide
parsimonious

DEMONS

partial	pejorative	personality
participate	pell-mell	personnel
participle	penalize	perspicacity
particle	penchant	perspicuity
particularly	pendulous	persuade
partisan	pendulum	pertinence
passageway	penetrate	perversive
passenger	peninsula	pervious
passerby	penitentiary	pessimistic
passionate	pennant	pesticide
pastel	penologist	pestilence
pasteurization	pension	petrify
pastime	pentagonal	petulance
pastrami	penurious	pewter
pastry	pepsin	phalanx
paternity	percale	phantom
pathetic	perceivable	pharaoh
pathological	perceptible	pharmaceutical
pathos	percolator	pheasant
patience	percussive	phenomenon
patient	peremptory	philanderer
patriarch	perennial	philanthropy
patrician	perfidious	philatelic
patricide	perforation	philology
patriotic	performance	phlegmatic
patronize	perfumery	phoenix
paunchiness	perfunctory	phonetic
paucity	perilous	phosphorescent
pauper	periodic	photoelectric
pavilion	peripheral	photogenic
pawnbroker	perishable	photography
peccadillo	perjurer	photostat
pectoral	permanence	phraseology
peculiar	permeate	physic
pecuniary	permissible	physicist
pedagogical	permitted	physiography
pedaling	pernicious	piazza
pedantic	perpetrator	pica
pedestrian	perpetually	picayune
pedicure	perpetuity	piccalilli
pedigree	perplexed	pickerel
pediment	perseverance	pickle
peerage	persistence	picnic
peevish	personage	picnicking

DEMONS

pictorial
picturesque
pidgin
piggyback
pigmy
pillage
pimple
pinafore
pineapple
pinnacle
pinochle
pioneer
piquant
piracy
piranha
pistachio
piteous
pitiful
pittance
pitter-patter
pizza
pizzeria
placable
plagiarism
plaintiff
plaintive
plait
planetarium
plantation
plateau
platinum
platonic
platoon
plaudit
plausible
playwright
plaza
pleading
pleasantry
pleasurable
pleat
plebeian
plebiscite
pledge
plenipotentiary
plenteous
plentiful
plethora
pliable
pliers
plumage
plumber
plummet
plural
plutocrat
plywood
pneumatic
poacher
podium
poetry
pogrom
poignant
poise
polarization
polemic
policyholder
polish
politburo
pollinate
pollution
poltergeist
poltroon
polyandry
polychromatic
polygamy
polygraph
polyphonic
polytechnic
polyunsaturated
pomegranate
pompadour
pompous
ponderous
pontoon
populace
popularity
porcelain
porcupine
porous
porridge
portable
portentous
portfolio
portraiture
positive
posse
possessor
posterior
posterity
postern
posthumous
postmistress
postmortem
postnasal
postponement
postulate
potable
potash
potassium
potency
potentate
potential
potpourri
pottage
poultice
pragmatic
prairie
praline
prattle
preamble
precarious
precaution
precede
precedence
precinct
precious
precipice
precipitate
precipitation
precipitous
precise
preclusion

DEMONS

precocious
preconceive
predatory
predecessor
predestination
predetermine
predicament
predicate
predict
predilection
predispose
predominance
preeminence
preempt
preface
prefatory
prefect
preference
pregnancy
preliminary
premeditation
premise
premium
premonition
prenatal
preparatory
preparedness
preponderance
preposterous
prerequisite
prerogative
presage
prescient
prescribe
presentiment
preservation
preside
presidency
presidential
pressure
prestidigitation
prestige
prestigious
presumable

presumptuous
pretense
preternatural
pretext
pretzel
prevail
prevalence
prevaricate
prevention
previous
prey
primacy
primate
primer
primeval
primitive
primogeniture
primordial
principality
prior
prism
prisoner
pristine
privacy
privilege
probability
probation
probity
problematical
proboscis
procedural
proceeding
processional
proclaim
proclamation
proclivity
procrastination
procreation
procrustean
proctor
procurable
procurement
prodigious
prodigy

profanity
professional
proffer
proficiency
profile
profitable
profiteer
profligacy
profligate
profound
profundity
profuse
progenitor
progeny
progress
prohibit
projectile
projector
proletariat
proliferate
prolific
prolong
promenade
prominence
promiscuity
promontory
promotion
prompt
promulgation
pronounce
pronunciation
propaganda
propel
propellant
propeller
propensity
property
prophylaxis
propinquity
propitiate
proponent
proposal
propound
proprietary

DEMONS

proprietor
propriety
propulsion
prosaic
proscenium
proscribe
proscription
prosecute
prosecution
prospect
prospectus
prosperity
prostitution
prostrate
prostration
protagonist
protectorate
protégé
protest
protestation
protocol
prototype
protract
protractile
protrude
protrusion
protuberance
protuberant
provenance
provender
provident
provider
province
provincial
provisional
proviso
provocative
provoke
prowess
proximity
proxy
prudence
prudential
prudish

prurience
prurient
pseudonym
psychiatrist
psychic
psychology
psychopath
puberty
publication
publicist
publisher
pueblo
puerile
pugilism
pugnacious
puissance
pulchritude
pulsate
pulverize
pumice
pummel
pumpernickel
pumpkin
puncheon
punctilious
punctual
punctuate
punctuation
puncture
pundit
pungency
punitive
punster
punter
puny
puppetry
purchase
purely
purification
purifier
purify
purity
purloin
purport

purpose
purser
pursuant
pursue
pursuit
purveyance
purveyor
purview
pusillanimity
pustulant
pustular
putative
putrefaction
putrefy
putrescence
putrid
puzzle
pygmy
pylon
pyorrhea
pyramid
pyre
pyromania
pyrrhic
python

quadrant
quadruped
quadruple
quagmire
qualm
quandary
quarrel
quarreling
queasiness
querulous
questionnaire
quiddity
quiescence
quintessence
quintuplet
quixotic
quoit
quorum

DEMONS

rabbi
rabid
raccoon
raciness
racketeer
raconteur
radar
radial
radial tire
radiance
radiant
radicalism
radii
radius
raffle
ragamuffin
raglan
ragout
raillery
raiment
raisin
rambling
rambunctious
ramekin
ramification
rampant
rampart
ramshackle
rancid
rancor
random
rankle
ransack
ransom
rapacious
rapidity
rapier
rapport
rap session
rapt
rapture
rarebit
rarefaction
rarity

rascal
raspberry
ratchet
ratfink
ratification
ratify
ratio
ration
rational
rationale
rationalize
rattan
raucous
ravage
ravel
raven
ravenous
ravine
rayon
razor
reactionary
reactor
readily
realia
realize
realm
realtor
reasonable
reassurance
rebellion
rebuff
rebuke
recalcitrant
recapitulate
recapture
recede
receipt
receive
recent
receptacle
reception
recipe
recipient
reciprocal

recital
reclamation
recline
recluse
recognize
recollect
recommend
recompense
reconcile
reconnaissance
reconnoiter
recreation
recrimination
recruit
rectangle
rectification
rectify
rectilinear
rectitude
recurred
recurrence
recycle
redeem
redemption
redolence
redoubtable
redound
redress
reduce
redundant
reel
refer
referee
reference
referendum
referred
refinement
reflection
reflexive
reforestation
refractory
refrain
refrigerate
refrigerator

DEMONS

refuge
refugee
refulgent
refurbish
refusal
refuse
refutable
regal
regale
regalia
regardless
regatta
regency
regenerate
regicide
regime
regimen
regional
register
registrar
regress
regrettable
regularity
regurgitate
rehabilitate
rehearsal
reimburse
reinforce
reiterate
rejection
rejoice
rejoinder
rejuvenate
relate
relaxation
relegate
relent
relevance
relevant
reliable
reliance
relic
relief
relieve

relinquish
relish
reluctant
rely
remainder
remand
remarkable
remedial
remembrance
reminder
reminisce
remittance
remittent
remnant
remonstrance
remote
remunerate
renaissance
render
rendezvous
rendition
renegade
renege
rennet
renounce
renovate
renown
rental
renunciation
repair
reparation
repartee
repatriate
repeal
repeat
repel
repellent
repentance
repercussion
repertoire
repertory
repetition
replenishment
replete

replica
repository
repossess
repoussé
reprehensible
reprieve
reprimand
reprisal
reproach
reprobate
reptilian
repudiate
repugnance
repulsion
reputable
repute
request
require
requisition
requital
requite
rescind
rescue
resemblance
reservoir
reside
residence
residential
residue
resign
resilient
resin
resistance
resolution
resolve
resonance
resourceful
respectable
respite
resplendent
respond
respondent
restaurateur
restitution

DEMONS

restive	rifle	ruckus
restoration	rightful	rudiment
restrict	rigid	rueful
resultant	rigorous	ruffian
resume	riotous	ruinous
résumé	ripoff	rumble
resumption	riposte	ruminant
resurgence	risibility	rummage
resurrect	riskiness	rumor
retaliate	risqué	rumpus
retentive	rival	rupture
reticent	rivet	rural
retirement	rivulet	russet
retort	robot	rustic
retract	robust	rustle
retreat	rococo	rutabaga
retribution	rodent	ruthless
retrievable	rodeo	
retroactive	rogue	sabbatical
retrocession	romaine	saber
retrogression	romanticism	sable
retrospect	rookery	sabotage
reusable	rookie	saboteur
reveal	rooster	sabra
revel	rosin	sacrilegious
revenge	roster	saddle
revenue	rostrum	sadism
reverberate	rotary	saffron
reverie	rotate	saga
reversal	rotisserie	sagacious
reversible	rotogravure	sagacity
revert	rotund	sagamore
revile	rouge	sagebrush
revision	rough	sahib
revolutionary	roughage	salaam
revulsion	roulade	salability
rheostat	roulette	salable
rhetoric	roundelay	salacious
rhubarb	roustabout	salad
rhyme	routine	salamander
ribald	rowdy	salami
ricochet	rubicund	salaried
ridicule	rubric	salience
riffle	rucksack	salmagundi

DEMONS

salmon	sauté	scrivener
salon	sauterne	scrumptious
saloon	savagery	scrutiny
saltine	savant	scuffle
salubrious	savory	scullery
salutation	scaffolding	sculptor
salutatorian	scald	scurrilous
salvage	scallion	scuttlebutt
samovar	scallop	scythe
sample	scandalous	seaborne
samurai	scapegoat	seafarer
sanatorium	scapula	seaman
sandal	scarab	seamstress
sandwich	scarcely	séance
sangfroid	scarlet	seasonal
sanguine	scathing	secede
sanitary	scatter	secession
sanity	scavenger	seclusion
sapphire	scenario	second
sarcasm	scenery	secondary
sarcophagus	scent	secrecy
sardine	scepter	secretary
sardonic	schedule	secrete
sardonyx	schematic	secretive
sargasso	schism	sectionally
sarong	scholastic	sector
sarsaparilla	schooner	security blanket
sartorial	schmuck	sedative
sassafras	scientific	sedentary
satchel	scimitar	sediment
sateen	scintillate	seditious
satellite	scion	seduce
satiate	scissors	sedulous
satirical	scornful	seedling
saturate	scorpion	seepage
saturnine	scoundrel	seer
satyr	scourge	seersucker
saucepan	scouring pad	segregate
saucer	scratch	seize
sauerbraten	screech	seldom
sauerkraut	scribble	self-addressed
sauna	scrimmage	self-discipline
saunter	scrip	self-employed
sausage	script	self-esteem

DEMONS

self-expression
self-indulgence
self-preservation
self-respect
self-sacrifice
self-starter
self-sufficient
seltzer
selvage
semantic
semaphore
semester
semicolon
seminar
senescent
senile
seniority
sensation
sensory
sensuous
sententious
sentiment
sentry
sepal
separate
sepia
septuagenarian
sequel
sequester
sequin
serape
serendipity
serge
sergeant
serialize
serious
serpentine
serrate
servitude
sesame
sesquicentennial
sesquipedalian
setaceous
settee

severance
sewage
sexagenarian
shaman
shamble
shamus
sharpener
sheaf
shears
shellac
shelves
shepherd
sheriff
shield
shirtdress
shoddily
shoulder
shovel
shrapnel
shrewd
shriek
shrink
shrinkage
shrubbery
shuffle
shyster
sibilant
sibling
sibyl
sickle
sidereal
siege
siesta
sieve
sifter
signature
significance
signify
silage
silesia
silhouette
silo
simian
similar

simile
simple
simplicity
simulate
simultaneous
sincere
sincerity
sinecure
sinewy
singeing
singular
sinister
sinuous
siphon
siren
sirloin
sirocco
site
situated
sixtieth
sizable
sizzling
skein
skeptic
skeptical
skepticism
skewer
skinny-dip
skirmish
skittish
skulk
skunk
slacken
slanderous
slattern
sleaziness
sleepy
sleuth
slither
sloe-eyed
slogan
slope
slothful
slouch

DEMONS

slovenliness
sludge
sluggish
sluice
smashed
smoky
smolder
smorgasbord
smother
smudge
smuggle
snafu
sneer
sneeze
snicker
sniveled
snobbish
snorkel
soar
sobriety
sobriquet
sociability
society
sodality
sodden
softener
sojourn
solace
solder
soldier
solecism
solemn
solemnity
solenoid
solicitor
solicitous
solidarity
soliloquy
solitaire
solitary
solstice
soluble
solvable
solvent

sombrero
somersault
somnambulism
somnolent
sonnet
sonority
soothe
soothsayer
sophisticated
sophistry
sophomore
soporific
sorcerer
sorghum
sorority
sorrel
soubrette
soufflé
soulful
sourdough
souvenir
sovereignty
spacious
spaghetti
spangle
spaniel
spasmodic
spastic
spatial
spatula
specie
specification
specimen
specious
spectacle
spectroscope
spectrum
speculate
speedily
speleology
sphagnum
spherical
sphinx
spigot

spinal
spin-off
spinto
spittoon
splurge
spoilage
spondee
sponge
spongy
sponsor
spontaneity
spontaneous
sporadic
sportive
sprawl
spree
sprightly
sprinkle
sprocket
spumoni
spurious
sputnik
squabble
squadron
squalid
squall
squalor
squawk
squeak
squeamish
squeegee
squirrel
stability
stabilizer
stable
stadium
stagnant
stalactite
stalagmite
stalemate
stallion
stamina
stampede
stanchion

DEMONS

staple
starch
startle
startling
statistician
statuary
statuesque
statuette
stature
status
statute
statutory
steadfast
stealth
steeplechase
steerage
stenciled
stenographer
stenographic
stentorian
steppe
stereo
stereophonic
stereopticon
stereotype
sterilizer
stevedore
steward
stiffen
stifle
stigma
stiletto
stimulant
stimuli
stimulus
stingy
stipend
stipple
stipulate
stirred
stirrup
stockbroker
stodgy
stoic

stolid
stomachache
stoppage
storable
storage
stowage
straggle
straightedge
strainer
strangulate
stratagem
strategic
strategy
stratosphere
strengthen
strenuous
stricture
stringent
strophe
structural
struggling
studios
studious
stultify
stupefy
stupidity
stupor
sturgeon
stylish
stylus
stymie
suave
subconscious
subcutaneous
subjunctive
sublimate
submergible
submersible
submission
subordination
subpoena
subservient
subsidiary
subsidize

subsistence
substantial
subterfuge
subterranean
subtle
subtlety
subversion
succeed
success
successor
succinct
succotash
succulent
succumb
suede
suet
sufficient
suffocate
suffragette
suffuse
suggestive
suicidal
suitable
suitor
summary
summit
summons
sumptuous
sundae
superb
supercilious
superficial
superfluous
superiority
superstitious
supervisor
supple
supplementary
supplier
support hose
suppression
supremacy
surcease
surfeit

DEMONS

surmise
surprise
surrender
surreptitious
surrogate
surround
surveillance
surveyor
survivor
susceptible
suspicious
sustenance
svelte
swab
swastika
sweater
swindle
sycophant
syllabic
syllable
syllabus
syllogism
sylph
sylvan
symbolic
symbolize
symmetrical
sympathetic
sympathy
symposium
synchronize
syndicate
synod
synonym
synonymous
synopsis
synthesis
systematic

table
tablespoonful
tabloid
taboo
tacit

taciturn
tackle
tactful
tactician
tactics
tactile
talc
talisman
tamarack
tangible
tangle
tannic
tantalize
tantamount
tapestry
tariff
tarlatan
tarpaulin
tarragon
tartaric
tassel
tattoo
taunt
tawdry
taxidermy
technical
technician
technique
tedious
tedium
telegraphy
telepathy
television
temerity
temperance
temperate
tempestuous
template
temporarily
temporize
tempt
tenacious
tenacity
tenancy

tendency
tendril
tenement
tenon
tensile
tension
tentacle
tentative
tenuity
tenuous
tenure
tepid
tequila
tercentenary
termagant
terminal
terminology
termite
terrace
terra-cotta
terrain
terrapin
terrarium
terrazzo
terrestrial
terrific
terrify
terrorism
testify
test-tube
tetanus
textile
texture
theatrical
thenceforth
theoretical
theory
thermometer
thermos
thesis
thicket
thieves
thorough
threnody

277

DEMONS

threshold
through
thwart
thyme
tier
timbale
timidity
timorous
tinsel
tintype
tirade
tissue
titanic
tithe
titillate
titular
tobacco
toboggan
tocsin
toga
toggle
tolerable
tolerance
tolerant
tomorrow
tongue
tonnage
toothpaste
topaz
topiary
topic
topical
topography
toque
toreador
torment
torpedo
torpid
torpor
torque
torrential
torrid
torso
tortuous

torture
totaled
totalitarian
totem
touché
tourmaline
tournament
tourney
tourniquet
towage
towel
tower
tract
tractor
tradition
traduce
traffic
tragedienne
tragedy
trait
traitor
trajectory
trample
trampoline
tranquil
tranquillity
transcendent
transcontinental
transcript
transference
transferred
transfix
transgression
transgressor
transient
transistor
transit
translation
transliterate
translucent
transmit
transmittal
transom

transparent
transpire
transportation
transpose
trapeze
trauma
travail
traveled
traverse
travesty
treacherous
treacle
treadle
treason
treasurer
treasury
treatise
trellis
tremble
tremendous
tremor
tremulous
trenchancy
trenchant
trepidation
trespass
triad
triangular
tribal
tributary
tribute
trickery
trickle
trident
triennial
trifle
trigger
trillium
trilogy
trinket
tripartite
triplet
triplex
triplicate

DEMONS

tripod	typhoon	upbringing
triptych	typical	upheaval
trisect	typify	upholster
triumphal	typist	uproarious
triumvirate	typography	upswept
trivet	tyrannical	up-to-date
trivial	tyro	urban
troglodyte		urbane
trope	ubiquitous	urchin
trophy	ubiquity	urgency
tropic	ulterior	urgent
troublesome	ultimate	useless
trousers	ultraviolet	usurer
trousseau	ululation	usurp
trowel	umbilical	usury
truant	umbrage	utensil
truculent	umbrella	utilitarian
truffle	unanimity	utilize
truism	unanimous	utterance
truncate	uncalled-for	
truncheon	unconscionable	vacancy
tryst	unconscious	vaccination
tubular	unction	vaccine
tuition	unctuous	vacillate
tulip	underprivileged	vacuous
tulle	undoubtedly	vacuum
tumble	undulation	vagrancy
tumult	unequivocal	vague
tungsten	unerring	vainglorious
tunic	unfamiliar	valedictorian
tunnel	unification	valentine
turbojet	unilateral	validate
turbulence	uninhibited	validity
turgid	unintelligible	valise
turmoil	unionize	valorous
turpentine	unique	valuable
turpitude	universality	vampire
turret	university	vandalism
tussle	unkempt	vanquish
tutelage	unmitigated	vaporize
tutelary	unparalleled	variance
tutor	unusual	variation
twilight	unwonted	variety
tycoon	upbraid	various

DEMONS

vegetable
vehement
vehicle
vehicular
velocipede
velocity
vendetta
venerate
ventilation
ventriloquism
venue
veracious
verbatim
verbiage
verdigris
verification
vermicelli
vermicide
vernacular
versatile
version
versus
vertex
vertical
vertiginous
vessel
vestibule
vestige
veteran
vexatious
viable
viaduct
viand
vibrant
vibrator
vicarious
vice versa
vicinity
vicious
vicissitude
victimize
victorious
victual
video

vigilance
vigilante
vignette
vigorous
vilify
village
villain
vinaigrette
vindicate
vineyard
vintage
violate
violence
virago
vireo
virgin
virile
visage
visceral
viscosity
viscount
visibility
visionary
visor
visualize
vitality
vitiate
vitreous
vitrify
vitriol
vituperation
vivacious
vocabulary
vocational
vociferous
volatile
volcanic
volition
volley
voltage
voluble
voluminous
voluntarily
volunteer

voluptuous
vomit
voodoo
voracious
vortex
vulcanize
vulgarity
vulnerable
vulture
vying

wafer
waffle
wager
waitress
wallet
wallow
wampum
wanderlust
wanton
warden
warily
warmonger
warrior
wassail
wastage
wastrel
waterborne
waterlogged
water-repellent
water-resistant
wattage
wealthy
weapon
wearisome
weaver
wedding
weigh
weight
weird
well-advised
well-beloved
well-handled
well-heeled

DEMONS

well-off	whodunit	wreak
well-spoken	whoever	wreath
wellspring	wholehearted	wreckage
well-timed	wholly	wrench
well-to-do	whoop	wrestler
well-wisher	wickedness	wrestling
well-worn	wicket	wretched
welter	widower	wrinkling
werewolf	wield	writhe
wharf	windjammer	wrought
wharves	windowsill	wry
whatsoever	winnow	
wheelwright	winsome	yachtsman
whence	wisely	yardage
whereas	wistful	yaw
wherefore	witchcraft	yawl
wherewithal	wither	yeomanry
wherry	witticism	yeshiva
whey	wizened	yodel
whimsical	woebegone	yoga
whine	wondrous	ytterbium
whipstitch	woodbine	yttrium
whirlwind	woolly	
whisk broom	worrisome	zealous
whiskey	worsted	zephyr
whistle	wraith	zigzagging
whittle	wrangle	zither
whoa	wrathful	zoology

SOUND-ALIKE WORDS WITH CLUES TO MEANINGS

NOTE: Most of the words paired together here are homonyms. They are pronounced exactly the same, though they have different meanings and are spelled differently. Some other pairs look (or sound) alike enough to be confusing, but are not true homonyms.

accept (receive)
except (exclude)

access (admittance)
excess (surplus)

ad (advertisement)
add (to sum up)

adapt (to adjust)
adopt (to accept)

affect (influence)
effect (result)

aid (help)
aide (assistant)

aisle (passageway)
isle (island)
I'll (I will)

already (previously)
all ready
  (completely ready)

altar (church)
alter (change)

ante- (before)
anti- (against)

arc (curved line)
ark (ship)

area (field)
aria (melody)

ascent (rise)
assent (agree)

assay (to test)
essay (composition)

aural (heard)
oral (spoken)

aye (yes)
eye (see)

bail (security)
bale (bundle)

bare (naked)
bear (carry, animal)

baron (noble)
barren (sterile)

bazaar (market)
bizarre (strange)

beach (shore)
beech (tree)

beau (suitor)
bow (knot)

beer (drink)
bier (funeral)

berry (fruit)
bury (to conceal)

berth (bed)
birth (born)

boar (swine)
bore (drill, dull)

bolder (braver)
boulder (stone)

bough (tree)
bow (bend)

burro (donkey)
burrow (dig)

cache (hiding place)
cash (money)

calendar (time)
calender (press)

callous (hardened)
callus (hard skin area)

cannon (gun)
canon (law)

canvas (cloth)
canvass (solicit)

capital (city)
capitol (building)

carat (weight)
carrot (vegetable)

casque (helmet)
cask (box)

cellar (basement)
seller (salesman)

censer (incense burner)
censor (critic)

cereal (food)
serial (following)

cession (giving up)
session (meeting)

choral (singing)
coral (skeletons)

chord (music)
cord (rope)

clique (group)
click (noise)

coarse (rough)
course (route)

complacent (pleased)
complaisant (obliging)

consul (diplomat)
counsel (advice)

council (assembly)

councilor (assembly
  member)
counselor (adviser)

creak (noise)
creek (stream)

283

SOUND-ALIKE WORDS WITH CLUES TO MEANINGS

cue (hint)
queue (line)

currant (berry)
current (today, electricity)

cymbal (music)
symbol (sign)

desert (dry area)
dessert (sweet)

devise (to plan)
device (a scheme)

discreet (prudent)
discrete (distinct)

doe (deer)
dough (bread)

dual (two)
duel (fight)

dyeing (color)
dying (death)

earn (gain)
urn (vase)

elicit (draw out)
illicit (unlawful)

elusive (baffling)
illusive (deceptive)

emerge (rise out of)
immerge (plunge into)

envelop (surround)
envelope (stationery)

ewe (sheep)
yew (tree)

exercise (physical)
exorcise (expel)

faint (weak)
feint (pretend)

fair (just)
fare (payment)

fairy (pixie)
ferry (boat)

faker (swindler)
fakir (Hindu monk)

faun (rural deity)
fawn (deer, flatter)

faze (worry)
phase (stage)

fir (tree)
fur (hair)

flair (ability)
flare (torch)

flea (insect)
flee (run)

flew (p.t. fly)
flu (influenza)
flue (chimney)

flour (food)
flower (plant)

forego (precede)
forgo (omit)

foreword (introduction)
forward (advance)

fort (strong place)
forte (ability)

forth (ahead)
fourth (number four)

foul (unfair)
fowl (bird)

gait (walk)
gate (door)

gamble (bet)
gambol (play)

gibe (taunt)
jibe (agree)

gild (cover with gold)
guild (organization)

gnu (animal)
knew (p.t. know)
new (not old)

gorilla (ape)
guerrilla (warfare)

grate (grillwork)
great (large)

grill (broil)
grille (lattice)

grip (grasp)
grippe (flu)

grisly (horror)
grizzly (gray, bear)

guessed (an opinion)
guest (visitor)

hail (ice, salute)
hale (healthy)

hair (fur)
hare (rabbit)

hallow (holy)
hollow (empty)

handsome (looks)
hansom (cab)

hangar (garage)
hanger (for clothes)

hay (grass)
hey (exclamation)

heal (mend)
heel (foot)

hear (listen)
here (this place)

heard (listened)
herd (group)

heroin (drug)
heroine (hero)

SOUND-ALIKE WORDS WITH CLUES TO MEANINGS

hew (chop)
hue (color)

higher (taller)
hire (employ)

hoard (amass)
horde (crowd)

hoarse (harsh)
horse (animal)

holey (ragged)
holy (sanctified)

humerus (bone)
humorous (funny)

idle (inactive)
idyll (poem)
idol (false god)

impassable (not allowing passage)
impassible (emotion)

jam (jelly)
jamb (door part)

jinks (frolic)
jinx (bad luck)

colonel (officer)
kernel (seed)

key (lock)
quay (wharf)

knead (massage)
need (require)

knit (fabric)
nit (insect)

lay (put down, non-professional)
lei (flowers)

leak (crack)
leek (vegetable)

lentil (bean)
lintel (upper bar of doorway)

levee (dike)
levy (tax)

liar (untruthful)
lyre (music)

links (joints)
lynx (animal)

maize (corn)
maze (puzzle)

manner (mode)
manor (estate)

mantel (shelf)
mantle (coat)

material (fabric, essential)
materiel (military supplies)

medal (award)
meddle (interfere)

miner (mine worker)
minor (under age)

morning (forenoon)
mourning (grieving)

knave (fool)
nave (church)

naval (Navy)
navel (belly)

nay (no)
neigh (horse noise)

oar (boat)
ore (mineral)

palate (mouth)
palette (for paint)

parish (church)
perish (die)

parlay (bet)
parley (talk)

pedal (bicycle)
peddle (to sell)

peak (top)
pique (provoke)

peer (look, equal)
pier (dock)

pidgin (language)
pigeon (bird)

pistil (flower)
pistol (gun)

plum (fruit)
plumb (weight)

pole (post)
poll (vote)

premier (first in rank)
premiere (first time)

principal (school, main)
principle (ideal)

profit (gain)
prophet (predicts future)

quarts (measure)
quartz (stone)

quire (24 sheets)
choir (singers)

rabbet (groove)
rabbit (animal)

raise (elevate)
raze (cut down)

reek (strong odor)
wreak (inflict)

reign (rule)
rein (lead, curb)

285

SOUND-ALIKE WORDS WITH CLUES TO MEANINGS

roe (fish eggs)
row (column)

roomer (lodger)
rumor (gossip)

root (tree)
route (highway)

rote (memory)
wrote (p.t. write)

rye (grain)
wry (distorted)

scull (oar)
skull (head)

seam (sew)
seem (appear)

sear (burn)
seer (prophet)

sense (judgment)
cents (money)

serf (peasant)
surf (ocean)

serge (fabric)
surge (wave)

shear (cut)
sheer (thin)

sheath (knife covering)
sheathe (cover, protect)

sheik (Arab chief)
chic (stylish)

slay (kill)
sleigh (sled)

sleight (skill)
slight (little)

stake (post)
steak (meat)

stationary (unmoving)
stationery (letter paper)

stile (fence)
style (fashion)

straight (direct)
strait (narrow passage)

taper (reduce)
tapir (animal)

taught (instructed)
taut (tense)

tenant (lessee)
tenet (opinion)

timber (wood)
timbre (tonal quality)

topee (sun hat)
toupee (wig)

troop (group)
troupe (group of actors)

turban (headdress)
turbine (engine)

vain (proud)
vane (weather)
vein (blood)

valance (drapery)
valence (chemistry)

vial (glass tube)
vile (bad)
viol (music)

waist (midriff)
waste (misuse)

waiver (surrender of rights)
waver (move to and fro)

warrantee (person insured)
warranty (guarantee)

weather (climate)
whether (if)

wrung (squeezed)
rung (p.t. ring, step)

yoke (harness)
yolk (egg)